12557426

SO-DPL-891

HENRY JAMES
and the
DARKEST ABYSS
OF ROMANCE

HENRY JAMES
and the
DARKEST ABYSS
OF ROMANCE

William R. Goetz

Louisiana State University Press
Baton Rouge and London

Designer: Christopher Wilcox
Typeface: Times Roman
Typesetter: Moran Colorgraphic
Printer: Thomson Shore, Inc.
Binder: John Dekker & Sons, Inc.

Library of Congress Cataloging in Publication Data

Goetz, William R.
    Henry James and the darkest abyss of romance.

    Includes index.
    1. James, Henry, 1843–1916—Technique.   2. Point of view (Literature)
3. First person narrative.   4. Self in literature.   I. Title.
PS2127.T4G64   1986   813'.4   85-19715
ISBN 0-8071-1259-3

Chapter 4 was first published, in slightly different form, as "Criticism and Autobiography in James's Prefaces" in *American Literature*, LI (1979), 333–48. The author is grateful for permission to reprint.

for
JOELLE
and
CHRISTOPHER

CONTENTS

PREFACE
and
ACKNOWLEDGMENTS

T HIS STUDY originated in the observation of what seems to be a paradox: namely, that the work of Henry James, though famous for its dramatic and objective qualities and for a reticence of the author that is one source of the ambiguity of much modern literature, is in fact deeply concerned with the question of the presence of the author in his works. It comes as no surprise that James, as a highly self-conscious artist, was always aware of his stance as author toward his work. What may prove more interesting, however, is the recognition that the author's presence in his work is not for James something to be concealed, or overcome, by the manipulation of formal narrative solutions, but instead is a positive value that precedes and gives a meaning to the choice of a particular narrative technique. The study that follows is therefore on the borderline between the formal and the referential. I am interested in the formal or technical question of the ways in which James will admit the signs of the author's self into his writing, but I study these formal concerns against the background of James's notion of the identity of the self, or what he calls "the signs by which I know myself." If the formal question is most obviously relevant to James's practice in his novels and other fiction, the second question, that of the self, leads immediately to much of James's nonfictional writing, notably his criticism of other authors, his Prefaces to his own works, and his autobiography. One of my objectives is in fact to offer a way of defining the relation between James's fictional and nonfictional production by showing how all of it emanates from the same set of notions concerning the author's self and the possible modes of his self-expression in writing.

These questions have been widely neglected in critical studies of James, which over the years have been preponderantly thematic and formalist in their scope. Ironically, but also appropriately, the formalism of most Jamesian studies has been implicitly based on a theory of literature that derives its authority from James's own writing, both critical and fictional, and that takes the absolute autonomy of the literary work, its total severance from its creator, as an article of faith. The view of James's work as impersonal and objective has thus been a self-perpetuating one. The partial supplanting of New Critical formalism by a Gallic inspired structuralism in recent years has done nothing serious to change these assumptions and in fact has probably solidified them.

There have of course been some notable exceptions and two in particular that I gladly cite as inspirations for the present study. Laurence Holland's *The Expense of Vision* is certainly the best full-length study of James to come to terms with James's involvement in his literary work; in fact the "intimacy" of James with his fictional characters and situations, and the particular embarrassments and triumphs that this intimacy entails, are the themes of Holland's work. And in a series of articles, Charles Feidelson has developed a theory about the relations of James's autobiography to his fiction, centered on the notion of James as the "man of imagination," that has proved extremely valuable for the approach I am taking.[1]

The first and most salient of James's stated rules for the presentation of the author in his texts is his famous rejection of the "I" form of narration in fiction, or more precisely in the novel. The reasoning behind this rejection forms one of the main topics of my introductory chapter, where I shall try to show that what may appear to be a rather idiosyncratic preference on James's part cannot be explained as a purely formal or aesthetic judgment

---

1. Laurence Holland, *The Expense of Vision: Essays on the Craft of Henry James* (Princeton, 1964); Charles Feidelson, "James and the 'Man of Imagination,' " in Frank Brady, John Palmer, and Martin Price (eds.), *Literary Theory and Structure* (New Haven, 1973), 331–52.

but is ultimately a philosophic one, expressing an almost ontological hesitation as to the relation of the existential self to the written ''I.'' From one perspective, this relation might be approached through the category of autobiography. James is certainly interested in how all of an author's writing, fictional as well as nonfictional, becomes part of an autobiography, either because the object one writes about is always, ultimately, oneself, or because one's literary work is a written *act* that takes its place as an integral part of one's life. Yet I do not wish to imply that autobiography is a fixed category for James, a mode of writing that is always available and unproblematic, or that autobiography as an established genre has a priority for James, and can be defined in a descriptive or indeed normative way. In fact, James is far from wishing to define a genre of autobiography or to suggest that the author's self-expression is confined to just one kind of work. His thinking about the use of the ''I'' does lead him, as we shall see, to suggest a division of genres, defined by the different modes of the author's self-reference and of his relation to his fictional characters, but the genres James identifies are primarily of pragmatic value for him, and none of them coincides with any traditional definition of autobiography. Self-reference, then, and the problematic relation of a nonfictional author to works which, according to library classification, may be either fictional or nonfictional, are the focal points of this study, more than autobiography in a generic sense is. Obviously, however, James's own autobiography is a prime exhibit for my argument, and it forms the subject of Chapters 2 and 3 below.

In introducing the theme of the author's presence in James's work, however, I shall not be trying to uncover traces of autobiographical content in James's work or to compare his life with his fiction. Nor will I be trying to sketch a psychological portrait or perform a psychoanalysis of Henry James. Other critics, most notably of course Leon Edel in his biography, have demonstrated the relevance of James's life to his work. James's own thinking about the autobiographical dimension of fiction, however, is quite a different issue from the possibly unconscious use he made of the material of his own life in his fiction. When James asserts that the author is present in every page he writes, he does not mean that the author is describing himself empirically but that he is present ideally, through the quality of his imagination and through his consciousness of what it is to be a writer. The chapters that follow, then, do not seek to rival the biographer's approach to James any more than they seek to rival the formalist's approach to his fiction. Rather, they are concerned with the path that leads from the author as empirical subject to the author as a presence in the written text. The whole of James's work, ranging from the fiction to the criticism, the self-criticism, and the autobiography, constitutes both a complete exemplification of this problem and an elaborate series of reflections on it.

My indebtedness in this work extends first to the teachers with whom I studied James and other novelists during my graduate studies at Yale: Peter Demetz, Peter Brooks, J. Hillis Miller, and the late Paul de Man. I am also grateful to several colleagues and friends at the University of Texas at Austin who read portions of various drafts of the manuscript and offered valuable and charitable criticism as well as encouragement: Evan Carton, Wayne Lesser, William Nemir, Walter Reed, Ramón Saldívar, and Thomas Whitbread. Two anonymous readers for Louisiana State University Press offered much useful criticism that has allowed me to tighten my argument and make the finished product better than it would otherwise have been.

Work on the book was supported by two Summer Research Grants from the University Research Institute of the University of Texas at Austin.

Finally, alongside the official dedication, I would like to thank my parents for their loving support and counsel during, as well as before, the writing of this book.

ABBREVIATIONS

AN	*The Art of the Novel*, ed. R. P. Blackmur (New York, 1934).
FN	*The Future of the Novel*, ed. Leon Edel (New York, 1956).
MY	*The Middle Years* (New York, 1917).
NB	*The Notebooks of Henry James*, ed. F. O. Matthiessen and Kenneth Murdock (New York, 1947).
NN	*Notes on Novelists* (1914; rpr. New York, 1969).
NSB	*Notes of a Son and Brother* (New York, 1914).
PP	*Partial Portraits* (Ann Arbor, 1970).
SBO	*A Small Boy and Others* (New York, 1913).

HENRY JAMES
and the
DARKEST ABYSS
OF ROMANCE

1

THE PRESENCE
OF THE AUTHOR

HENRY JAMES'S achievement as a theorist and practitioner of the novel is often regarded as forming one stage in the modern movement toward impersonality, the disappearance of the author from his work, of the self-reflexivity of literature or *écriture*. In this scheme, James is seen as the link between Gustave Flaubert and James Joyce, or even Samuel Beckett, the New Novelists, and other postmodernists, in the progressive cultivation of novelistic technique for its own sake. Surely there is much to be said for this view of James as a father of modernism, an antiromantic theorist who argued that novel writing was a craft like any other that could be learned through a mastery of certain techniques. His major critical testament, the prefaces he wrote for the New York Edition of his novels and tales, pleads again and again for an "objective" approach to the problems of representation, and against a merely subjective or personal intervention in the form of "the mere muffled majesty of irresponsible 'authorship' " (*AN*, 328). Not only did James in his critical theory protest against a naïve intrusion of the author or the author's voice into his fictional works, but he also managed to a remarkable degree to keep autobiographical content out of the novels he wrote. He never wrote the kind of fictionalized autobiography produced by the major novelists of the generation that followed him: D. H. Lawrence, Virginia Woolf, James Joyce, Marcel Proust, and Thomas

Mann. James's stress on the complex indirectness of his "reflector" method of narration, on his dramatic showing of subject matter as opposed to authorial telling, on the necessity for craft, calculation, even deception in the novelist's choice of the mode for telling his story—all these preoccupations point to the diminished importance of the author's autobiography for his literary works. "Literature is an objective, a projected result," James wrote in "The Lesson of Balzac" (1905); "it is life that is the unconscious, the agitated, the struggling, floundering cause" (*FN*, 101).

Yet the conception of James as the impersonal master, interested only in the objective institution of the novel and narrative modes, is one-sided. There is in all his work an equally important concern not only with the rendering of subjectivity in fiction (which is obvious) but with the presence of the author in his fiction. James's work, taken as a whole, can be read as the product of a struggle between two tendencies, one toward impersonality and one toward self-expression.

Although James never advocates a conscious imprinting of the author's personality onto his fictional work, he recognizes that there is an important sense in which the author cannot keep himself out of his work. His essay of 1888 on Guy de Maupassant, an author for whom he felt much affinity at the time, illustrates the complexity of his position on this question. He suggests that Maupassant was naïve in implementing his "objective and impersonal" narrative manner if he believed that it kept his fiction free from the coloring of his personality. The author's projection of himself into his characters is "the limitation, the difficulty of the novelist, to whatever clan or camp he may belong." Yet this does not mean that Maupassant was wrong to strive to exclude himself from his works, even if he should have known his goal was impossible: "Let us hasten to add that in the case of describing a character it is doubtless more difficult to convey the impression of something that is not one's self (the constant effort, however delusive at bottom, of the novelist) than in the case of describing some object more immediately visible. The operation is more delicate, but that circumstance only increases the beauty of the problem" (*FN*, 205). James seems to be saying that, no matter how much distance he seeks to put between himself and one of his characters, the author will still infuse himself in all the parts of his work. James's position is reminiscent of Flaubert's classic statement on authorial impersonality, with its carefully balanced terms: "The artist should be in his work like God in his creation, invisible and all-powerful; he should be felt everywhere and seen nowhere." [1] Ironically, James turned this maxim against its author. In his 1902 essay on Flaubert, James, finding fault with the choice of Emma Bovary and Frédéric Moreau as protagonists and "central intelligences" in the novels of Flaubert, concludes that such a choice can only be seen as evidence of "a defect of his mind" (*FN*, 139).

If in the essay on Maupassant James treats the author's presence in his fiction as a problem, elsewhere he treats it as an essential asset. Perhaps the best-known passage appears in the Preface to *The Portrait of a Lady*. Here James asserts that the final value of a work of art depends upon "the amount of felt life concerned in producing it," and he continues: "The question comes back thus, obviously, to the kind and the degree of the artist's prime sensibility, which is the soil out of which his subject springs. The quality and capacity of that soil, its ability to 'grow' with due freshness and straightness any vision of life, represents, strongly or weakly, the projected morality." On the next page, where he introduces the "house of fiction," James elucidates his image. "The spreading field, the human scene, is the 'choice of subject'; the pierced aperture, either broad or balconied or slit-like or low-browed, is the 'literary form'; but they are, singly or together, as nothing without the posted presence of the watcher—without, in other words, the consciousness of the artist. Tell me what the artist is, and I will tell you of what he has *been* conscious" (*AN*, 46). This is an extraordinary statement, coming as it does in the midst of a series of essays seemingly so concerned with literary form for its own sake. James's thesis, however, is clearly that questions of form and method, along with the choice of subject matter, all derive from the prior question of the author's subjectivity; in fact the final, ideal inseparability of subject and treatment (a theme running through the Prefaces) depends precisely on their common grounding in the author's consciousness. If, according to Flaubert and his French disciples (as James describes it in his essay on Turgenev), morality and art were "two perfectly separate things" (*PP*, 302), for James the priority of the author's

1. Gustave Flaubert to Mlle. Leroyer de Chantepie, February 19, 1857, in Flaubert, *Correspondance* (9 vols.; Paris, 1926–33), IV, 164, my translation.

consciousness fuses them together. As he wrote, long before the Prefaces, in "The Art of Fiction" (1884): "There is one point at which the moral sense and the artistic sense lie very near together; that is in the light of the very obvious truth that the deepest quality of a work of art will always be the quality of the mind of the producer. In proportion as that intelligence is fine will the novel, the picture, the statue partake of the substance of truth and beauty. . . . No good novel will ever proceed from a superficial mind" (*FN*, 25).

Whatever he may intend, then, the author necessarily writes himself into his fictional works. But as the passages just quoted clearly show, this necessary presence does not mean that literary works can be read simply as fictionalized versions of an autobiography, that is, as the transposition onto a fictional plane of experiences from the author's life. As we shall see, James went to lengths to avoid this kind of self-revelation, against which he had an immediate personal aversion as well as strong theoretical objections. Instead, we have seen James emphasize that it is the quality of the author's mind—of his artistic sensibility and imagination—and not the content of his life that must be reflected in his work.

Yet it is still possible to see this process of reflection as tantamount to a kind of autobiography, especially in the case of an author like James. For James, the writing of fiction is a part—in fact the most important part—of the life. By this I do not mean merely that James spent much of his life at his writing desk (though this fact is relevant) but that he admitted "no arbitrary, no senseless separations" between the writing of fiction and the other gestures of his experience. These words come from the last pages of the prefaces, where James proudly asserts his continued responsibility for his literary works: "Our literary deeds enjoy this marked advantage over many of our acts, that, though they go forth into the world and stray even in the desert, they don't to the same extent lose themselves; their attachment and reference to us, however strained, needn't necessarily lapse—while of the tie that binds us to *them* we may make almost anything we like" (*AN*, 347–48). James's fiction is James's life in written form. Being written, it is more permanent and more reliable testimony to his life than are his other acts. Thus, the status of the fiction for James's autobiography, though crucial, is quite different from the status of "fictionalized autobiography," and it is more than the reflection I have just suggested. In the case of fictionalized autobiography, the fictional works would be truthful only according to a correspondence theory of truth; they would have value to the degree that they accurately reflect the conditions of the author's life or (more subtly) to the extent that they represent the author's attempt symbolically to alter or supplement his life. But since the works of fiction are in themselves primary manifestations of James's existence, they need not correspond to any extraliterary reality, whether material or psychological; their main value is not mimetic but performative: they are literary *deeds*.

This is precisely the way James treats works of fiction written by other novelists. It is not surprising that so much of his own writing, outside of his fiction, was dedicated to inquiries into other artists' minds and the ways in which their consciousness could be discovered through their work. For James, biography and criticism were mutually supporting, indeed almost indistinguishable, disciplines; his early biography of Nathaniel Hawthorne (1879) and his volume *Partial Portraits* (1888) testify to this fact, as do the later *Notes on Novelists* (1914) and even the somewhat anomalous biography *William Wetmore Story and His Friends* (1903). In all these studies James is continually moving through the quality of the works to the quality of the mind, indeed of the whole man or woman, that produced them. Moreover, the principle that any work must be suffused by the author's own sensibility applies to these critical-biographical essays no less than to the works they discuss. Whenever James judges the work of a Balzac, a Hawthorne, or a Trollope, he is measuring and testing it against his own sensibility, if only implicitly. Biographical criticism thus presupposes a degree of personal involvement on the part of the critic.

If in the works just named the presence of the critic-biographer remains subordinate to the subject at hand, this is no longer the case in another group of works whose autobiographical intent is more explicit. Some of these works are private and not intended for publication—for instance, James's lifelong, voluminous correspondence, where the virtual presence of an intimate audience encourages but also limits self-revelation. Perhaps a more pure example is the *Notebooks*, where, in the absence of any audience, James projects himself as his own interlocutor (''oh mon bon!'') and communes with himself on the glories and travails of the artistic vocation. Other, more public works are no less intensely self-referential. In *The American Scene*, the sensibility of the "restless analyst" himself is at least as strongly felt as is the American scene, the ostensible subject.

It is in the two major works of the end of his career—the Prefaces to the New York Edition (published between 1907 and 1909) and the three volumes of the autobiography, *A Small Boy and Others* (1913), *Notes of a Son and Brother* (1914), and the fragmentary *Middle Years* (1917)—that James made his most explicit autobiographical statements. If James's fiction is already an implicit narrative of his life as an artist, then the Prefaces, which take the form of a chronological review of the fiction, compose a kind of autobiography of the literary works, rendering their referential value for James explicit. They are intended of course as a *Gradus ad Parnassum* of the novelist's art, but they also tell "the history of the growth of one's imagination" (*AN*, 47), as they trace the works back to their "germs" in the author's mind. The Prefaces thus pave the way for James's formal autobiography, which he began a few years after their completion. If the Prefaces are the autobiography of James as the author of a certain corpus of texts, the three volumes of memoirs are the autobiography of the artist as a young man, before he became an author. These volumes, too, are explicitly a history of James's imagination, but now James treats his imagination as it interacted directly with the world, not as it was rendered concrete in his literary works. The Prefaces and the autobiography thus form a diptych, together claiming to furnish a complete history of the development of James's imagination.

There is thus a fundamental continuity between James's fiction, which already contains an autobiography *in potentia*, and the explicitly autobiographical works that capped his career in the twentieth century. This continuity is revealed in James's relation as author to his fictional characters. Most of James's novels are biographical in the broad sense in which this is true of the classic nineteenth-century novel: his works are most often the "portrait" of a lady or a man. But his penchant for psychological complication, his "inward turn," ensured that the story would be not so much one of what happens to his character as one of how that character experiences what is happening to her or him. James asserts "the unreality of the sharp distinction, where the interest of observation is at stake, between doing and feeling" (*AN*, 65). Moreover, the cultivation of his sensitive "reflectors" or "central intelligences" is a way not only to develop a greater biographical intensity and fidelity but to promote the *auto*biographical involvement of the author with his character. "My report of people's experience—my report as a 'story-teller'—" writes James, "is essentially my appreciation of it, and there is no 'interest' for me in what my hero, my heroine or any one else does save through that admirable process. . . . I then see their 'doing,' that of the persons just mentioned, as, immensely, their feeling, their feeling as their doing, since I can have none of the conveyed sense and taste of their situation without becoming intimate with them" (*AN*, 65–66). Biographical penetration leads to authorial involvement, and nothing is more characteristic in this passage than James's resorting to an unabashed, unqualified "I" to describe his close relationship with his fictional heroes. Laurence Holland, who has discussed this aspect of James's work better than anyone else, claims that James invented the novel of "intimacy," an intimacy based primarily on this relation between author and character but extending to the reader as well.[2] James's preference for this kind of intimacy with his characters helps explain his affinity for George Eliot and his lack of affinity for writers like William Thackeray and Anthony Trollope, whom he accused of remaining too aloof and ironic toward their fictional creatures.

With this kind of involvement, it is inevitable that the quality of the fictional protagonist's mind tends more and more to be assimilated to the mind of the author. The chronological development of James's art is in part precisely such a refinement of the reflector method as to allow the characters' minds increasingly to approximate the magisterial intelligence and sensitivity of that of their creator. Or more accurately, since the novels themselves are the place where James's growth in intelligence and self-consciousness occurs, the technique of the reflector contributes to, as much as it mirrors, James's understanding of his own grasp of the world; the novelistic technique and the content of James's consciousness are correlative. In the Prefaces, the chronological process is sometimes distorted by James's fondness for seeing evidence of his most sophisticated method even in early novels, like *Roderick Hudson*, *The American*, and (from a decade later) *The Prin-*

2. Laurence Holland, Preface to *The Expense of Vision: Essays on the Craft of Henry James* (Princeton, 1964), x.

cess Casamassima. (The Prefaces to these novels contain many of the central statements on the reflector technique.) But this very distortion of the historical record in the Prefaces confirms the teleology of the process involved: it is natural that the Prefaces, written even later than the novels of the "major phase," should place a new emphasis on the problem of point of view and, specifically, on the assimilation of the hero's consciousness to the author's.

The way in which this process tends from the biographical to the autobiographical can be seen at one of the most climactic moments in the whole series of essays, occurring in the Preface to *The Ambassadors.* In recalling this novel, which he names "quite the best, 'all around,' of my productions" (*AN*, 309), James notes that its greatest interest for him lay in the challenge of rendering the rich quality of Strether's consciousness, a consciousness, he implies, more acute than that of any of his previous reflectors. "My poor friend should have accumulated character, certainly; or rather would be quite naturally and handsomely possessed of it, in the sense that he would have, and would always have felt he had, imagination galore, and that this yet wouldn't have wrecked him. It was immeasurable, the opportunity to 'do' a man of imagination, for if *there* mightn't be a chance to 'bite,' where in the world might it be?" (*AN*, 310). Although James does not put it thus, this opportunity is surely that of representing his own imagination in the mode of fiction. For even if the superficial similarity between Strether's age and circumstances and James's may be coincidental, what is essential is that Strether, the "man of imagination," is the very image of James as a creative artist. Through the Prefaces, James has been giving a genetic account of the writing of his novels as constituting "the history of the growth of one's imagination." His imagination itself emerges as the hero of these pages, so that when Strether's history too turns out to be that of a man of imagination, there is a curious doubling of the narratives of the artist and his fictional character.

Yet the convergence of the two is not complete. Strether is not yet wholly, or even predominantly, a man of imgination, nor indeed did James want him to become one:

This personage of course, so enriched, wouldn't give me, for his type, imag-

> ination in *predominance* or as his prime faculty, nor should I, in view of other
> matters, have found that convenient. So particular a luxury—some occasion,
> that is, for study of the high gift in *supreme* command of a case or of a ca-
> reer—would still doubtless come on the day I should be ready to pay for it;
> and till then might, as from far back, remain hung up well in view and just
> out of reach. The comparative case meanwhile would serve—it was only on
> the minor scale that I had treated myself even to comparative cases. (*AN*, 310)

This statement tends to deflate, retrospectively, the intelligence of those
"super-subtle fry" James had taken such pride in creating. Even Strether,
the culmination of a long line of intelligent, reflective centers, is said to be
only a "comparative case" of imaginative intelligence. The passage, however, leaves open the question of why James should not have found it convenient to treat a case of the imagination in "*supreme* command," and
whether he would ever in fact attempt to do so.

The best answer to these questions has been supplied by Charles Feidelson, who has argued that the only example of a complete man of imagination James could have had in mind was himself.[3] The Preface to *The Ambassadors*, even if it remains a study of literary forms, points beyond itself
to a later moment, which lies beyond fictional production altogether, in the
realm of autobiography. At the same time it shows how James's autobiographical urge developed strictly from the fictional technique he cultivated
in his novels. When this preface was written in 1907, James had as yet no
concrete plans to write the autobiography, the instigation for which came
only with the death of his brother William in 1910. Yet when he did begin
to write in 1911, it was as if he were picking up the thread of the Prefaces
exactly where he had left it. In particular, a climactic passage near the end
of the second volume of the autobiography, *Notes of a Son and Brother*,
echoes the passage from the Preface to *The Ambassadors*. Approaching the
end of his narrative, James begins to talk of his autobiography as the response to "a long-sought occasion, now gratefully recognized, for making
trial of the recording and figuring act on behalf of some case of the imaginative faculty under cultivation." He goes on:

---

3. Charles Feidelson, "James and the 'Man of Imagination,' " in Frank Brady, John Palmer, and Martin Price (eds.), *Literary Theory and Structure* (New Haven, 1973), 331–52.

The personal history, as it were, of an imagination, a lively one of course, in a given and favourable case, had always struck me as a task that a teller of tales might rejoice in. . . . The idea of some pretext for such an attempt had again and again, naturally, haunted me; the man of imagination, and of an "awfully good" one at that, showed, as the creature of that force or the sport of that fate or the wielder of that arm, for the hero of a thousand possible fields—if one could but first "catch" him, after the fashion of the hare in the famous receipt. . . . Meanwhile, it no less appeared, there were other subjects to go on with, and even if one had to wait for him he would still perhaps come. It happened for me that he *was* belatedly to come, but that he was to turn up then in a shape almost too familiar at first for recognition, the shape of one of those residual substitutes that engage doubting eyes the day after the fair. He had been with me all the while, and only too obscurely and intimately—I had not found him in the market as an exhibited or *offered* value. I had in a word to draw him forth from within rather than meet him in the world before me, the more convenient sphere of the objective, and to make him objective, had to turn nothing less than myself inside out. What was *I* thus, within and essentially, what had I ever been and could I ever be but a man of imagination at the active pitch? (*NSB*, 369–71)

The insistence on the long period of waiting and gestation that preceded the novelist's discovery of his ultimate theme shows the autobiography to be in a sense the culmination of James's entire career. It shows the continuity, too, between his fictional representation of a consciousness like Strether's and his final representation of himself in the mode of nonfictive autobiography. Whereas Strether was still a "comparative case," James himself presumably furnished something closer to that absolute case of an imagination in "*supreme* command" that had always been his ideal. Yet there was good reason for James's hesitation before acknowledging himself as a possible theme for artistic representation. To represent himself from within meant to perform the seemingly painful and unnatural act of "turning [himself] inside out" like a glove. He would have to be careful, as he goes on to say, "that objectivity, the prize to be won, shouldn't just be frightened away by the odd terms of the affair" (371). The term *objectivity* helps explain why an act of self-narration that might seem natural to other authors is described here as so problematic and even tortured. Accustomed to being the objective historian of his fictional heroes' consciousness, James could scarcely conceive of turning his imagination in upon itself, of assuming what he called in the Prefaces "the double privilege of subject and object" (*AN*, 321).

The transition from the fictional work, which culminated (in this regard) in *The Ambassadors*, to the formal autobiography was logical, then, but not without its difficulties. Writing about fictional characters in the third person was easier for James than writing about himself in the first person. It seems, indeed, that it was not only the transition from fiction to nonfiction that was important for James but also the change in the personal pronoun. The use of the "I" was fraught with difficulties for James. If he did not, like his friend Henry Adams, resort to an oblique third-person narration in his own autobiography, he did take other precautions. Moreover, he did practically banish the "I" narrator in his practice and theory of the novel. This question of the pronoun, far from being a merely technical one, helps explain James's complex attitude towards autobiographical writing, and his conception of the relations between autobiography in the modes of fiction and nonfiction. We can therefore approach these questions by examining the two major statements James made against the use of the first person in the novel.

The first of these appears, appropriately, in the Preface to *The Ambassadors*. The author tells us he had originally considered casting Strether's story in the first person, but quickly changed his mind: "Had I meanwhile made him at once hero and historian, endowed him with the romantic privilege of the 'first person'—the darkest abyss of romance, this, inveterately, when enjoyed on the grand scale—variety, and many other queer matters as well, might have been smuggled in by a back door. Suffice it, to be brief, that the first person, in the long piece, is a form foredoomed to looseness, and that looseness, never much my affair, had never been so little so as on this particular occasion" (*AN*, 320). By the use of other characters, including *ficelles*, to whom Strether's story could plausibly be told (thus supplying the reader with the necessary information), James hoped to avoid "the large ease of 'autobiography,' " just as he could by the same means avoid the alternative need for an omniscient narrator to intervene with his "inserted block of merely referential narrative" (*AN*, 321). By removing *both* possible authorial figures (Strether and the omniscient narrator), James could achieve dramatic intensity and objectivity by providing internal motivation for the work's expository material, making it appear to flow out of the action itself. He concludes: "Strether . . . encaged and provided for as 'The Ambassadors' encages and provides, has to keep in view proprieties much stiffer and more salutary than any our straight and credulous gape are likely to bring home to him, has exhibitional conditions to meet, in a word, that forbid the terrible *fluidity* of self-revelation" (*AN*, 321).

James's second important statement against the first-person narrative, addressed to H. G. Wells early in 1911, recorded his response to Wells's recently published work, *The New Machiavelli*. In the equivocal style that characterizes many of his comments on his literary friends' work, James moves gradually from an acute if somewhat general praise (calling Wells "the most interesting and masterful prose-painter of [his] English generation") to a severe critique of his literary method, or rather his lack of method. Most particularly, James deplores his friend's use of the first person:

> I make remonstrance—for I do remonstrate—bear upon the bad service you have done your cause by riding so hard again that accurst autobiographic form which puts a premium on the loose, the improvised, the cheap and the easy. Save in the fantastic and the romantic (Copperfield, Jane Eyre, that charming thing of Stevenson's with the bad title—'Kidnapped'?) it has no authority, no persuasive or convincing force—its grasp of reality and truth isn't strong and disinterested. R. Crusoe, e.g., isn't a novel at all. There is, to my vision, no authentic, and no really interesting and no *beautiful*, report of things on the novelist's, the painter's part unless a particular detachment has operated, unless the great stewpot or crucible of the imagination, of the observant and recording and interpreting mind in short, has intervened and played its part— and this detachment, this chemical transmutation for the aesthetic, the representational, end is terribly wanting in autobiography brought, as the horrible phrase is, up to date.[4]

Taken together, these two statements reveal a series of closely related terms that are clearly laden with value for James: terms like *tightness*, *authority*, *detachment*, and *disinterest*. The only way to do justice to James's observations is to trace these key terms in other crucial passages of his critical writings so that his more or less systematic use of such terms becomes ap-

---

4. Henry James to H. G. Wells, March 3, 1911, in Percy Lubbock (ed.), *Letters of Henry James* (2 vols.; New York, 1920), II, 181–82.

parent and leads to the matrix of critical distinctions that he thought essential. Only then will we be able to see that the question of first-person narration, far from being a narrowly formal or technical one, is immediately related in James's mind to the central issues of fictional representation.

Tightness or "the precious element of closeness" (*AN*, 164) is for James a quality of fiction that should be complementary to its mimetic value. Fiction should represent life but it must also have its own self-contained and self-justifying form. The ideal of such an objective, complete form James often found in drama, of which he wrote: "We are shut up wholly to cross-relations, relations all within the action itself; no part of which is related to anything but some other part—save of course by the relation of the whole to life" (*AN*, 114). The literary work has, as it were, a pure inside in which it is possible to remain "shut up" before the work is compared to real life. This self-contained quality of the work is for James its objectivity. Drama in particular achieves its ideal of objectivity by treating everything scenically and refusing to "go behind" what can be shown on the stage (*AN*, 110–11).[5] In fiction, the reflector character acquires merit as a narrative instrument only by virtue of the objectivity he provides. "The person capable of feeling in the given case more than another of what is to be felt for it, and so serving in the highest degree to *record* dramatically and objectively, is the only sort of person on whom we can count not to betray, to cheapen or, as we say, give away, the value and the beauty of the thing" (*AN*, 67). Here, for once, it appears that the reflector is nothing more than what his name indicates, an apparatus for reflecting the objective reality surrounding him.

Yet the reflecting character's drama is not merely objective, it is also personal or subjective; what the reflector records is *his* adventure. Elsewhere James even uses the term *inward drama* (*AN*, 205), and in discussing *What Maisie Knew*, he writes, "The action of the drama is simply the girl's 'subjective' adventure—that of her quite definitely winged intelligence" (*AN*, 157). Even if James's distrust of the term is indicated by the quotation marks (we will see them again), it is clear that the drama can accommodate a dimension of subjectivity. There is no contradiction between drama and sub-

5. On James's theory of the dramatic novel, see Joseph Wiesenfarth, *Henry James and the Dramatic Analogy* (New York, 1963), 1–43.

jectivity for James because the subjectivity of the drama is *contained* within the larger objectivity of the written work. Strether is "encaged and provided for" by the third-person narrative in which he finds himself. The same is true by definition for all James's reflecting characters who do not narrate their own stories and whose minds are thus contained as objects within the fiction of the novel. Maisie's or Strether's subjectivity is contained within the text, not prolonged or continued outside of it, as would have been the case if they had been granted the dangerous "double privilege of subject and object."

By insisting that the voice and the consciousness of Strether be encaged within the text, James implies that the alternative, allowing Strether to speak in the first person, would be a disturbing and unwarranted incursion of the author into the work. This implication is bound to surprise us, who have categories like the implied author and the authorial persona that make us dutifully separate the first-person voice appearing within the fiction from the voice of the actual author; but when James calls the first-person form autobiographical, it appears he is referring not simply to the autobiography of a fictional character but to that of the actual author. Thus, for him, the first-person form constitutes an unacceptable confusion of fact and fiction. The value he assigns to the "I" offers an important clue to how James conceives the relation of fiction to nonfiction. In the *Notebooks*, where James worked out for himself the "germs" of his stories, the "I" can be seen shifting back and forth between these realms. When he is describing the narrative stance for a story to be told in the first person, James, surprisingly, often identifies himself with the fictional narrator, at least in pronoun. "I must tell the story as an eye-witness; I am on the ship and partly an actor in the drama," he writes in his sketch for "The Patagonia" (*NB*, 88); and later, of "The Coxon Fund": "I must do it from my own point of view—that of an imagined observer, participator, chronicler. I must picture it, summarize it, impressionize it, in a word—compress and confine it by making it the picture of what I see" (*NB*, 160). In such passages, James's own "I" glides imperceptibly into the "I" of the created narrator; there is no clear demarcation between the two.

It would be possible, perhaps, to read these passages as though they had only a formal or grammatical significance and did not imply a real identification between James and his fictional narrators. If, for instance, we wanted to insist on the objectivist or impersonal view of James, we might find support in a structuralist theory of language that would explain the Jamesian "I" as a shifter, that is, a word whose referent changes with the situation of the utterance in question. The concept of the shifter, first named by Roman Jakobson, has been made widely current through the work of the structural linguist Emile Benveniste. In a pair of articles, Benveniste has argued that the system of first- and second-person pronouns in French (or any language that distinguishes similarly among persons), unlike the system of third-person pronouns, has an existence that depends entirely on the "instance de discours," that is, the situation of the speaker performing the utterance.[6] The first-person pronoun, then, is necessarily subjective in nature, as opposed to the objective third person. Yet this subjectivity is, in a sense, an illusion. It does not refer back to the concrete existence of the speaker in his preverbal reality but is founded on his position as speaker or on language itself: "It is in and through language that man constitutes himself as a *subject*, because language alone establishes the concept of 'ego' in reality, in *its* reality which is that of being."[7] Benveniste is validating Rimbaud's poetic statement, "Je est un autre," from a linguistic standpoint. His radical conclusion is that our innermost sense of subjectivity is a kind of mirage produced by grammatical usage, specifically by the fact that each of us is free to assume the "I" in our common language.

Alongside the critique of subjectivity that arises from Benveniste's structural linguistics, a poststructuralist critique of literary language based more on rhetoric than grammar and associated in America with the names of Jacques Derrida, Paul de Man, and J. Hillis Miller, has launched an even more formidable attack on traditional notions of the subject's control over his own language and the possibility of referentiality in language. An illustrative argument, particularly relevant for our purposes, can be found in an

6. The articles are "La Nature des pronoms" and "De la subjectivité dans la langue," in Emile Benveniste, *Problèmes de linguistique générale* (Paris, 1966), 251–66. Both are translated in Benveniste, *Problems in General Linguistics*, trans. Mary Elizabeth Meek (Coral Gables, Fla., 1971), 217–30.

7. Benveniste, "Subjectivity in Language," in his *Problems in General Linguistics*, 224, translation slightly modified.

essay ostensibly devoted to autobiography, in which de Man argues that autobiography cannot be identified as a genre. Such identification, he says, is based on the assumption that referentiality is a property of a certain class of texts that sets them apart from fictional texts. Instead of being a ground of generic distinction, de Man suggests, referentiality may be only an *effect* of the choice of a figure of speech used in a particular text. Autobiography dissolves as a genre, then, and becomes nothing more than the sign for a moment of misunderstanding in the interpretation of the intention of the work: "Autobiography, then, is not a genre or mode, but a figure of reading or of understanding that occurs, to some degree, in all texts. The autobiographical moment happens as an alignment between the two subjects involved in the process of reading in which they determine each other by mutual reflexive substitution."[8]

De Man's conclusions, like Benveniste's, may be inevitable in the context of poststructuralist assumptions concerning textuality, the self, and the intentionality that links the two. It is, however, by no means certain that these conclusions are compatible with Henry James's thinking about his relation to his fictional and autobiographical texts or that they explain his use of the first-person pronoun. For James, the use of the "I" always has reference to a real existential self, and this holds true for works classified as fiction as much as for works of nonfiction. One of his most interesting statements on the identity of the individual can be found in a late, little-known essay James wrote in response to an inquiry, entitled "Is There a Life After Death?" James gives only a tentative response to the question in his title; what is of interest for us is the way in which he refers the problem of an afterlife back to the problem of the kind of consciousness we enjoy while alive. The only kind of afterlife he can conceive would be the continuing existence of the individual consciousness, which would have earned the right to survive death by having been fully conscious while on earth. The paradox, as he puts it, is that the afterlife must be personal even though it is certainly dissociated from bodily identity. The passage most relevant for our purposes is one in which James asks what it means to have a personal ex-

8. Paul de Man, "Autobiography as De-facement," *Modern Language Notes*, XCIV (1979), 919–30.

perience or consciousness here on earth. The answer to this question, he surmises, is also the key to the question of an afterlife:

> I practically know what I am talking about when I say, "I," hypothetically, for my full experience of another term of being, just as I know it when I say "I" for my experience of this one; but I shouldn't in the least do so were I not *able* to say "I"—had I to reckon, that is, with a failure of the signs by which I know myself. In presence of the great question [of immortality] I cling to these signs more than ever, and to conceive of the actual achievement of immortality by others who may have had like knowledge I have to impute to such others a clinging to similar signs.[9]

The passage implies that consciousness is always immediately self-consciousness; to have an experience is to be aware of it as *my* experience. The sense of "having" experiences is what produces self-consciousness in the first place. But James suggests that the process of self-consciousness also necessarily passes through a linguistic moment when the self recognizes its own ability to use the "I" form for self-reference. This verbal form is itself an *act* that posits, and through positing guarantees, the identity of the object to which it refers. This act is not a theoretical but a practical one ("I *practically* know what I am talking about when I say, 'I' "), which is of the nature of a major premise, or hypothesis, that allows a belief in the self at all. James's first sentence is itself an example of the practical act of positing because it begins with that very assumption of the "I" that the entire passage is trying to account for. The "I" is the most important of the "signs by which I know myself." Since others use the "I" too, James imputes to them the same "signs" of identity that he registers in himself.

The inference to be drawn from James's essay is that for him the "I" could never have a purely linguistic significance, because the linguistic form always supports, and is supported by, an existential reality. For the same reason, the choice of the "I" can never be a sheerly formal or technical decision even in the writing of narrative fiction. The most striking conclusion of James's thinking, in fact, is that the use of the "I" partially obliterates the distinction between fictional and nonfictional discourse. The first person, wherever it is used, must refer to the reality of its author. It is for this reason

9. F. O. Matthiessen, *The James Family* (New York, 1947), 607.

that the first-person form in fiction automatically violates the objectivity of the work, if that objectivity is defined as the work's autonomous existence apart from the source of its creation.

This conclusion obviously runs counter to the attitude of most recent, especially formalist-inspired criticism, which would treat the "I" of the fictional narrator as belonging to the same level of fiction as all of the other characters. For one modern analogue to James's position, however, we can turn to a critic whose views on this question have been widely considered iconoclastic. In her *Logic of Literature* (*Logik der Dichtung*), Käte Hamburger has argued that the fictional status of first-person narrative is different from that of third-person narrative.[10] In fact she grants the term *fiction* only to the third-person variety, reserving the term "feigned reality statement" (*fungierte Wirklichkeitsaussage*) for first-person address. The first person, according to Hamburger, anchors a text in the empirical existence of its author; hence any text in which the author uses an "I"—whether as an omniscient narrator or as a character involved in the story—is as close to genuine autobiography as it is to genuine (*i.e.*, third-person) fiction. However much this view has been challenged by other critics, it is similar to James's theory of the use of the first person as it describes a possible overlap between fiction and nonfiction.

We can now summarize James's position on the first-person narrator in fiction by setting it against the traditional ways of describing this device, especially according to the polarity of subject and object. One of these ways is to maintain that the first person is the most subjective form of narration because the entire narrative is filtered through a limited point of view belonging to a single character. A second possible argument, however, is that the first-person form is the most objective one because the author himself is excluded and the source of the storytelling is brought into the fictional realm itself, which thereby becomes self-contained. James accepts neither position, nor does he maintain a dialectical synthesis of the two. Instead, he holds

10. Käte Hamburger, *The Logic of Literature*, trans. Marilynn J. Rose (2nd ed.; Bloomington, Ind., 1973), esp. 142–75, 311–41. For a similar view, see David Goldknopf, *The Life of the Novel* (Chicago, 1972), 32–33.

that first-person narrative is indeed subjective, not because of the narrator's presence but because the *author*'s subjectivity is implicated too.[11]

This belief helps explain why, in the Preface to *The Ambassadors*, James treated the first-person narrator as virtually equivalent to the omniscient narrator, conflating two forms that would normally seem quite different. The omniscient narrator, practicing "the mere muffled majesty of irresponsible 'authorship' " (*AN*, 328), is also in effect a first-person narrator since he can refer to himself explicitly as the producer of the fiction, one who exists on its border or outside of it. Thus, for James, both of these narrative situations amount to comparable violations against the objectivity of the fiction. The objections he raises against the omniscient narrator thus reveal something of his grounds for rejecting first-person narration as well.

Probably James's most serious indictment of the self-conscious authorial or omniscient narrator first appeared in his essay on Trollope (1883). (He recapitulated much of the same argument in "The Art of Fiction," written the following year.) The particular trait of Trollope's authorial narration that disturbs him is the narrator's habit of knocking the floor out from under his fictional creation by exposing its fictionality. Trollope "took a suicidal satisfaction" in reminding the reader that the story he was telling was only make-believe. The result of this habit, as it affects a passage of *The Warden*, is this: "The whole passage, as we meet it, is a sudden disillusionment; we are transported from the mellow atmosphere of an assimilated Barchester to the air of ponderous allegory" (*FN*, 247). In this intentional disillusionment, we recognize the situation of romantic irony; even the term *allegory* (though James could not intend this reference) matches the usage of the romantic theorists of irony and the novel.[12] But James had no tolerance for such an ironic or allegorical undermining of the novel's fictional illusion. He concludes: "It is impossible to imagine what a novelist takes himself to

11. For interpretation of first-person narration according to the poles of subjectivity and objectivity, see, for example, Bertil Romberg, *Studies in the Narrative Technique of the First-Person Novel* (Stockholm, 1962); Franz Stanzel, *Narrative Situations in the Novel*, trans. James P. Pusack (Bloomington, Ind., 1971), esp. 59–70, 162–69.

12. For a discussion of the theory of irony and the novel, see Paul de Man, "The Rhetoric of Temporality," in Charles Singleton (ed.), *Interpretation: Theory and Practice* (Baltimore, 1969), 173–209.

be unless he regard himself as an historian and his narrative as history. It is only as an historian that he has the smallest *locus standi*. As a narrator of fictitious events he is nowhere; to insert into his attempt a backbone of logic, he must relate events that are assumed to be real'' (*FN*, 248).

What is interesting here is not only James's argument that the novel's realism is destroyed by the authorial intrusion but his concurrent argument that the author destroys *himself* by his intrusion. Paradoxically, the author's assertion of his own reality and of his absolute authority over his fictional world does not solidify his position but undermines it. Even when he tries to detach himself from his created world by betraying the latter's unreality, even when he finds the proper Archimedean distance from that world necessary to lift it from its bearings, he finds ironically that he himself is left standing in thin air. This is the ''suicidal'' danger James discovers in the logic of romantic irony.

There are thus both good and bad ways for the author to be ''nowhere'' in relation to his work. In the good, Flaubertian version, he is ''nowhere visible'' in the fiction; it stands outside him, objective. In the bad version, as soon as he asserts his presence in the fiction, he finds that he is ''nowhere'' at all, either inside or outside of the work; he has been hoist with his own petard. Moreover, this entire argument is designed to apply just as much to the first-person narrator as to the Trollopean omniscient narrator. The ''abyss of romance'' with which James flirted while writing *The Ambassadors* is another name for the place, or nonplace, to which Trollope consigned himself. The final moral to which James points is the extreme, almost impossibly tenuous status of the novel's fictional world. On the one hand, he affirms the absolute unreality of this world; it is a fiction so pure that the slightest contagious germ of reality can contaminate and destroy it. This total detachment from reality depends upon and defines the fiction's objectivity, its existence as a totally constituted, self-contained object. On the other hand, this unreality of the novelistic world must never be named in the work itself; the fiction must remain, as it were, quite unconscious of its own fictional status. What James says in the Preface to his volume of ghost stories might be extended to all of his fictional works: they are meant to represent ''an annexed yet independent world'' (*AN*, 171), a world that must be like ours (in order to have mimetic value) but also must be completely equal to and independent from ours, a true heterocosm.

James's insistence on narrative values like "tightness" and "dramatic objectivity" leads, then, to the privileging of one narrative situation over the other possible ones. If we assume a standard triadic scheme of narrative situations such as that offered by Franz Stanzel (or by James's follower Percy Lubbock), where all narratives are seen as authorial (omniscient), first-person, or focalized ("point of view" in the strict sense), we can easily see how James's preference for the dramatic leads him to give priority to the focalized method.[13] In fact, as we have already seen, such a triad tends to resolve itself for James's purposes into a dyad, where the only pertinent opposition is between showing and telling, or mimesis and diegesis.[14] The distinction between authorial and first-person narration loses its significance for James because he views both as diegetic modes, where the voice of the mediating narrator continually makes itself felt and thereby diminishes the effect of the mimetic illusion. For this reason, James usually deprecates not only authorial intrusions that call attention to the narrative situation (as we saw in his criticism of Trollope) but also framing devices that complicate the mediation through which the story is presented to the reader.

In his essay of 1897 on George Sand, James is primarily interested in the light her work sheds on "the relation between experience and art at large" (*NN*, 161). James, who has been reading her correspondence at the same time as her fiction, has grave reservations about Sand's use of her amorous affairs with Alfred de Musset, Prosper Mérimée, and others as material for her novels.[15] Beyond the moral issues, he also finds disturbing formal and aesthetic consequences, arguing that the reader's strong sense of the author's presence in her work detracts from the story's dramatic vividness. Noticing that her novels appear "rather pale and faint, as if the image projected—not intense, not absolutely concrete—failed to reach completely the mind's eye," he attributes this deficiency to "a sort of diffusion of the whole

13. See Stanzel, *Narrative Situations in the Novel*; Percy Lubbock, *The Craft of Fiction* (1921; rpr. New York, 1957).

14. For the use of *mimesis* and *diegesis* to define the dramatic and narrative poles of storytelling, see Gérard Genette, *Narrative Discourse*, trans. Jane E. Lewin (Ithaca, 1980), 162–70.

15. See Holland, *The Expense of Vision*, 132–34.

thing by the voice and speech of the author'' (*NN*, 183). In consequence, her work "affects the reader . . . not as a first but as a second echo or edition of the immediate real, or in other words of the subject. The tale may in this particular be taken as typical of the author's manner; beautifully told, but told, as if on a last remove from the facts, by some one repeating what he has had from another and thereby inevitably becoming more general and superficial, missing and forgetting the 'hard' parts and slurring them over and making them up. Of everything but feelings the presentation is dim" (*NN*, 184). It is as if each narrative possessed only a fixed amount of representational value, which must be divided up between its mimetic and diegetic phases. Hence, by a "sacred fount" kind of logic, when too much energy is invested in the mediating voice that tells the story, the dramatic immediacy of the story itself is reduced to a mere shadow or echo of what it might have been.[16]

A similar logic is at work in the pages James devoted to Joseph Conrad's *Chance* in his essay "The New Novel" (1914). Whereas in Sand's work James found the autobiographical voice too conspicuous, in *Chance* he is disturbed by Conrad's predilection for framing through multiple first-person narrators. Conrad indeed multiplies these "producers" of his fiction so much, James complains, "as to make them almost more numerous and quite emphatically more material than the creatures and the production itself in whom and which we by the general law of fiction expect such agents to lose themselves. We take for granted by the general law of fiction a primary author, take him so much for granted that we forget him in proportion as he works upon us, and that he works upon us most in fact by making us forget him" (*FN*, 280–81). It is precisely this beneficent, Flaubertian forgetting of the author that Conrad's method denies us. Marlow's cumbersome presence risks a "flight of the subjective" in which objectivity falls by the wayside. The reader's attention can no longer focus on the story, the true object; rather, it is Conrad's own "eccentricities of recital" that have become the protagonist of the drama. With the story itself thus diminished (just as it was in George Sand), "*Chance* is an example of objectivity, most precious of aims,

16. James's point has been expressed by Gérard Genette in *Narrative Discourse*, 166. For a similar statement, see Dorrit Cohn, *Transparent Minds* (Princeton, 1978), 25.

not only menaced but definitely compromised; whereby we are in presence of something really of the strangest, a general and diffused lapse of authenticity.'' If most readers have nevertheless approved of the book, it can only be because Conrad has given them a ''bribe of some authenticity other in kind'' to compensate for his failure to give them his primary story. This bribe consists of the author himself: ''What Mr. Conrad's left hand gives back then is simply Mr. Conrad himself. . . . His genius is what is left over from the other, the compromised and compromising quantities'' (*FN*, 281–82).

What is finally most striking in James's criticism of George Sand, Conrad, and Trollope too, is that he sees such divergent narrative techniques as leading to essentially the same catastrophe. Whether it is Trollope's ironic omniscient narrator, George Sand's transparently autobiographical one, or even Conrad's chain of dramatized first-person narrators, the result is always the destruction of the dramatic illusion, a diverting of the reader's attention to the position of the author, and hence a dangerous exposure of the latter. Although the key quality of authenticity certainly depends upon the reader's implicit sense of that primary author whose presence he can take for granted, an explicit revelation of the author can degenerate into ''the mere muffled majesty of irresponsible 'authorship.' '' The authorship of Trollope, like that of George Sand and of Conrad, is irresponsible; it fails of its chance to be genuine authority.

In his book *Beginnings*, Edward Said has offered a definition of *authority* that is close to the notion James was using. *Authority* for Said includes ''the power of an individual to initiate, institute, establish—in short, to begin,'' and it also implies ''that the individual wielding this power controls its issue and what is derived therefrom.'' But Said also suggests that the notion of authority can scarcely exist without the idea of its own ''molestation,'' that is, the recognition that all authority is a ''sham.'' In particular, he identifies the late nineteenth century as the moment of the breakdown of authority, the time when the literary author—and he includes James—recognized his own fictionality and consequently doubted his own power to ''authorize a fiction.'' [17] If this self-doubt did touch James, however, the only way he manifests it is in a reinforced effort to deny and overcome it by reasserting the

17. Edward Said, *Beginnings: Intention and Method* (New York, 1975), 83, 84, 152.

author's necessary control over his fiction. Perhaps it might be said that James's very insistence on this question—in the vigorous tone of his critique of Trollope, for example—is a symptom of the unease he felt. In any case, the spectacle of James fighting a rear-guard action against the more self-conscious Trollope is an odd one, and it shows the lengths to which James was willing to go to defend the objectivity of the literary fiction as well as the authority of its creator.

The obverse of objective, for James, is romantic. Both the Preface to *The Ambassadors* and the letter to H. G. Wells used *romance* and its derivatives to define the condition of first-person narrative in the novel. It remains to be seen why James makes this rapprochement, that is, how his theory of "I" narration intersects with his theory of romance. For this, we need to go to the passage where James gives his best known definition of *romance*, in the Preface to *The American*.

His attempt in this passage to differentiate between two basic modes of fiction can be seen in the context of a long-standing opposition made in the English-speaking world between novel and romance, occasioned by the fact that English uses both these terms to designate long works of narrative fiction.[18] If the eighteenth century had witnessed the triumph of the novel, the late eighteenth and the nineteenth centuries saw various attempts to restore romance to its rights. The most notable of these attempts, relative to James, was that of Nathaniel Hawthorne. In the Preface to *The American*, James's position is somewhat like Hawthorne's in the Preface to *The House of the Seven Gables*: the term *romance* had been denigrated for so long that his defense of it must take the form of an apology. Yet James does defend it, even to the point of shifting the terms of the customary opposition. Instead of opposing novel to romance, he classifies the romance as one legitimate type of the novel and now contrasts romance and realism as the novel's two chief modes. Although he does not use the label *realism*, he explicitly con-

18. For two discussions of James's concept of romance within the tradition, see Elsa Nettels, *James and Conrad* (Athens, Ga., 1977), 80–107; Richard Chase, *The American Novel and Its Tradition* (New York, 1957), 21–28. For a general discussion of novel and romance, see Ralph Freedman, "The Possibility of a Theory of the Novel," in Peter Demetz, Thomas Greene, and Lowry Nelson, Jr. (eds.), *The Disciplines of Criticism* (New Haven, 1968), 57–77.

trasts "the air of romance" to the "element of reality" (*AN*, 30). James even goes far toward equating the authenticity of these two poles of fiction as novels. Each of the poles, he argues, stands for a "deflexion" from the most central tendency of the novel. In "men of the largest responding imagination before the human scene" (he names Honoré de Balzac and, rather less expectedly, Walter Scott and Emile Zola) he suggests that "the deflexion toward either quarter has never taken place" (*AN*, 31), implying that the ideal toward which the novel should strive is a synthesis of these opposites. Yet, for all this apparent impartiality, James still implies that romance conceals within itself the risk of straying away from the heart of the "human scene" and therefore from the essence of narrative fiction.

Indeed, James introduces his main distinction between realism and romance as a distinction not between two literary modes but between two types of experience. The *real* stands for "the things we cannot possibly not know, sooner or later," while the *romantic* means "the things that can reach us only through the beautiful circuit and subterfuge of our thought and our desire" (*AN*, 31–32). James elaborates on the romantic: "The only *general* attribute of projected romance that I can see, the only one that fits all its cases, is the fact of the kind of experience with which it deals—experience liberated, so to speak; experience disengaged, disembroiled, disencumbered, exempt from the conditions that we usually know to attach to it and, if we wish so to put the matter, drag upon it, and operating in a medium which relieves it, in a particular interest, of the inconvenience of a *related*, a measurable state, a state subject to all our vulgar communities" (*AN*, 33).

Like many theories of romance, James's relies on the distinction between a pleasure principle (the "subterfuge of . . . our desire") and a reality principle; it also alludes to the criterion of verisimilitude. What makes the statement peculiarly Jamesian, however, is the insistence on the medium of romance and on its lack of a related state, its exemption from "our vulgar communities." James is describing not just a kind of experience but also a literary form adequate to render it. What romance lacks is precisely relations, the intersubjective relations that alone can impose a check or a control on the individual experience that has become disengaged. The need for relations, however, brings us immediately back to the dangers of the first-person form of narration, for this is the form that lacks the control of relations, because it assigns the roles of both subject and object, of interpreter and actor, to the same person. Romance thus becomes virtually synonymous with first-person narration, while realism is presumably to be found only in a third-person narration that contains the individual subject in a medium that ensures objectivity. This formal realism is an adequate literary mode insofar as it reflects the essential relatedness of the human condition; first-person romance is deficient insofar as it fails to reflect it.

James's insistence on relations explains why, ultimately, he cannot grant romance a status equal to that of realism for the novel. He acknowledges that romance can be of the greatest value, but only if its operation is concealed; it is the narrative mode that dares not tell its name:

> The greatest intensity may be so arrived at evidently [in romance]—when the sacrifice of community, of the "related" sides of situations, has not been too rash. It must to this end not too flagrantly betray itself; we must even be kept if possible, for our illusion, from suspecting any sacrifice at all. The balloon of experience is in fact of course tied to the earth, and under that necessity we swing, thanks to a rope of considerable length, in the more or less commodious car of the imagination; but it is by the rope we know where we are, and from the moment that cable is cut we are at large and unrelated: we only swing apart from the globe. . . . The art of the romancer is, "for the fun of it," insidiously to cut the cable, to cut it without our detecting him. (*AN*, 33–34)

The reference to the imagination again invites a comparison with the statements on first-person narrative with which we began. In this passage it is important to notice that the imagination is not exclusively associated with romance; it has a part to play in any kind of literary experience, including realism. The difference is one of degree. In realism the imagination is still anchored to the ground, to the relations of experience, while in romance it is liberated, completely on its own. We are reminded that, with Strether, James risked only a "comparative case" of the man of imagination; this presumably allowed *The Ambassadors* to keep its grounding in realism. In the image of "the balloon of experience," then, James is saying the same thing he would say in the later Preface: the author of a novel cannot afford the danger inherent in an imagination disembroiled, cut off, or unrelated to experience; he cannot risk the possibility that the subjectivity of the fictional character will overrun the entire text.

Thus the opposition between realism and romance, which seemed at first purely descriptive, finally becomes normative. (In fact James was already using the terms evaluatively in the letter to H. G. Wells when he wrote that *Robinson Crusoe* "isn't a novel at all" but belongs rather with "the fantastic and the romantic.") Romance can be allowed in the novel only if it disguises itself as realism, whereupon, however, it can enhance the whole and produce "the greatest intensity." The difference between realism and romance began as a difference between two kinds of experience in life, but it ends by dictating, at least implicitly, a corresponding difference between modes of narrative. The need for a medium of experience translates into a formal need for the consciousness of the fictional character to be imbedded in the relations afforded by an objective, third-person voice. Hence James's critique of romance as suffering from a lack of relatedness reinforces his earlier requirement that the novel embody an objective fiction; objectivity has to do essentially with the subject's being fixed and determined by its relations.

Thus some of the central tenets of James's theory of fiction militate against the direct form of self-revelation inherent in first-person narration. The use of the "I" by the narrator violates the self-enclosed, objective nature of the fiction and threatens to founder it in the abyss of a subjective romance. Since James's logic applies these dangers not only to a first-person narrator but to a dramatized authorial narrator as well, James must prefer, within a typology of narrative situations, an impersonal, focalized third-person narrator, who hides his own subjectivity behind that of the characters.

The real virtue of focalized narrative for James is that it does not exclude subjectivity but assigns it its proper place. By formally separating the narrative voice from the character, James is allowing the latter's subjectivity to express itself fully, but also objectively, that is, within the formal confines of the text. And only in this indirect manner can the author's own subjectivity find expression in his fictions. *Impersonal* narration in James does not mean that the author has renounced the expression of his sensibility, which we saw James claim at the outset. It only means he is taking the precaution, for the sake of the authenticity of his fiction, of concealing himself behind his characters. In the Preface to *The Golden Bowl*, James notes "the still marked inveteracy of a certain indirect and oblique view of my presented action.'' But he adds, paradoxically, that for him this method might just as well be called ''the very straightest and closest possible'' mode of narration (*AN*, 327). Narration based on point of view is the most direct because it allows the observing or reflecting character to come as close as possible to the privilege of self-narration without crossing the dangerous boundary of the first person. Moreover, since (as we have seen) James as author strives towards an intimacy with his fictive protagonist, the latter's approach to autobiographical narrative would also mean that the author is achieving the maximum desirable degree of self-revelation. Thus the indirect, focalized mode of narration promises two layers of genuine, if concealed, autobiography—that of the fictional character first, but also, through him, that of the author.

There is much critical opinion that James's focalized, third-person narrative amounts to a veiled first-person narrative. Wayne Booth, who has sought to deflate distinctions based solely on grammatical person, argues that ''the most important unacknowledged narrators in modern fiction are the third-person 'centers of consciousness' through whom authors have filtered their narratives.'' He explains, ''We should remind ourselves that any sustained inside view, of whatever depth, temporarily turns the character whose mind is shown into a narrator.''[19] Similarly, Laurence Holland has written that the function of James's narrators or observers, whether technically in the first or the third person, is ''essentially the same.''[20]

Booth's and Holland's remarks may help explain the effect that James's focalized point of view has on the reader. After reading the story of Lambert Strether, Isabel Archer, or Fleda Vetch, we feel we have been granted an intimate glimpse into the workings of their consciousness, a glimpse that could be achieved only through a virtual overlapping of our perspective with theirs. Yet in an important sense this thesis runs flatly counter to what we have seen to be James's stated belief that there *is* an essential difference between first- and third-person narrators. Ideally, we should be aware that the source of the intimacy we feel with a Jamesian observer is precisely the oblique method of narration, which has perhaps given us insights that even

19. Wayne Booth, *The Rhetoric of Fiction* (Chicago, 1961), 153, 164.
20. Holland, *The Expense of Vision*, 173–76.

the most direct kind of self-narration, even the most fluid interior monologue for instance, could not offer. Dorrit Cohn has recently shown how certain narrative techniques stressing objectivity—the distance between the author and the ostensible narrator—manage to achieve the greatest intimacy or subjectivity in their report on characters. "Precisely those authors who, in their major works, most decisively abandon first-person narration (Flaubert, Zola, James), instituting instead the norms of the dramatic novel, objective narration, and unobtrusive narrators, were the ones who re-introduced the subjectivity of private experience into the novel: this time not in terms of direct self-narration, but by imperceptibly integrating mental reactions into the neutral-objective report of actions, scenes, and spoken words." [21] Elsewhere Cohn shows how the objective, focalized method of Flaubert and James allows them to go further in exploring a character's consciousness than a direct monologue by the character would allow because they are able to probe depths of the fictional mind that would not be accessible to the character's own verbal report. Semiconscious or unconscious thoughts, for example, which by definition could not become the theme of the character's self-analysis, are readily available to a third-person, focalized narrator. Thus one can at least plausibly maintain the paradox that it is only through his third-person narrative that James is able to create the illusion of first-person intimacy.

But this does not yet explain how the author himself can achieve self-revelation through the oblique, third-person form. For the author, everything depends on finding the right balance so that his subjectivity is expressed in the work in such a way as to maintain his authority but not so crudely or overtly as to risk the "terrible fluidity" of a self-revelation. In third-person, focalized narration, the authorial voice virtually identifies itself with the voice of the fictive protagonist and shares in his subjective adventures even while remaining technically distinct, thus impersonal, authoritative, and responsible for the entire work. James's interest in keeping the narrative voice distinct from that of the characters explains his aversion not only to first-person narration but also to the so-called *style indirect libre*. [22]

21. Cohn, *Transparent Minds*, 115, and see 56–57, 129–140, 167.

22. Of the many studies of the *style indirect libre*, a recent and reliable one is Roy Pascal, *The Dual Voice* (Manchester, 1977). Dorrit Cohn twice uses the term *free indirect style* in reference to James. *Transparent Minds*, 108, 129–30.

The latter would seem to be close to James's technique, since it too occurs within a focalized, third-person narrative, and it was used liberally by both Flaubert and Zola, authors whom James not only read but studied. Yet James for the most part eschews the free indirect style, presumably because it implies by definition a mingling of the voice of the narrator with that of the character. James prefers to introduce what Dorrit Cohn calls the mental reactions of his characters not by mimicking their language, as the free indirect style does, but by analyzing their thought.[23] The Jamesian analysis of mental processes, in its often abstract or figurative style, is conducted wholly in the language of the narrator, who thus stands midway between author and character, keeping his anonymous identity separate from both.

James believes that this method alone can afford intimacy without fluidity, authority without irresponsible authorship. It is in a focalized novel like *The Golden Bowl* that he achieves this tenuous goal most fully: "It's not that the muffled majesty of authorship doesn't here *ostensibly* reign; but I catch myself again shaking it off and disavowing the presence of it while I get down into the arena and do my best to live and breathe and rub shoulders and converse with the persons engaged in the struggle that provides for the others in the circling tiers the entertainment of the great game" (*AN*, 328). This statement proposes the paradox that only by renouncing the overt privileges of the omniscient narrator can James commit himself to his fiction and achieve true authority for it. In the dangerous gladiatorial sport he describes, James surreptitiously introduces himself (again, the autobiographical "I") into the fictive combat, but without irresponsibly breaking the fictional illusion as Trollope would. Thus the focalized mode, which is too often taken to mean the disappearance of the author, is actually the contrary. As Laurence Holland writes, "James's detachment and objectivity . . . are not the index of severance from his world but of engagement with it."[24] Yet, as Holland points out, this engagement of the author is only vicarious, and this vicariousness keeps his self-revelation from being direct and hence dangerous.

23. For a discussion of this technique, see Ian Watt, "The First Paragraph of *The Ambassadors*: An Explication," in Henry James, *The Ambassadors*, ed. S. P. Rosenbaum (New York, 1964), 465–84.

24. Holland, *The Expense of Vision*, 118.

James's discovery of the reflector method, then, is his major solution to the problem of how to avoid the "I" in works of fiction. But it must be recalled that James rules out first-person or autobiographical narration only in what he called, in the letter to H. G. Wells, "the long piece," or the full-length novel. This means that in addition to the distinction between first- and third-person narration, James distinguishes between long and short works of fiction. Moreover, he also distinguishes between works of fiction and works of nonfiction such as autobiography in the normal sense. In the latter, as in short stories or novellas (as opposed to novels), James implies, the use of the "I" may be warranted. For the moment, I shall make only a couple of anticipatory remarks as to why James should have permitted the first person in these genres while censuring it in the novel.

The use of the "I" in actual autobiography is clearly exempt from the main objection James raised against the same use in the novel, that there is a possible confusion between the real self of the author and the self of the fictive narrator. In autobiography, this distinction does not exist, unless one makes the peculiarly modernist assumption that the act of writing, by itself, can produce only a fictional version of the author—an assumption James does not make.[25] A different distinction that does pertain to autobiography, that between the experiential and the narrating selves, does not raise the same problems. As we shall see in the next chapter, however, the presumed right one has to use the "I" in writing about oneself evokes a complicated response from James and leads him to overlay autobiography with a form of memoirs that would relieve him of some of the burden he feels when writing with immediate reference to himself.

In his short stories, James uses first-person narration about as frequently as third-person. Among the well-known literary or artistic tales told in the first person are, for instance, "The Aspern Papers," "The Private Life," "The Real Thing," "The Death of the Lion," "The Next Time," and "The Figure in the Carpet." In most of these cases, the narrator is not so much a protagonist as an observer, or what James once called a "more or less detached, some not strictly involved, though thoroughly interested and intel-

25. For one such modernist assumption, see William Spengemann, *The Forms of Autobiography* (New Haven, 1980), 167–68.

ligent, witness or reporter'' (*AN*, 327). Thus, although he is ''the impersonal author's concrete deputy or delegate,'' this narrator is not primarily concerned with self-revelation or with the revelation of the author. Instead, he serves to tell someone else's story; to employ Gérard Genette's terms, he is a homodiegetic narrator (one who belongs to the fictional world he writes about), but not an autodiegetic one (one who writes about himself).[26]

Thus, paradoxically, the ostensibly first-person narrator in these short stories functions almost as a third person. This odd twist can be seen at work, for instance, in the notebook sketch for the story called ''The Friends of the Friends.'' After conceiving his main characters, a man, a woman, and a third party who is going to bring them together, James reflects on the narrative point of view to be adopted: ''There would be various ways of doing it, and it comes to me that the thing might be related by the 3d person, according to my wont when I want something—as I always do want it—intensely objective'' (*NB*, 231). By a curious shift in perspective, a first-person narrator (for that is what James actually refers to here) is named, according to his real function, as a third person, and the precious ideal of objectivity is saved. In fact the paradox involved here is quite transparent. James's avowed trepidation before ''the terrible *fluidity* of self-revelation'' ensures that, when he does use the narrative form most naturally associated with self-revelation, he will take special precautions against fluidity—that is, he will not allow his first-person narrator to write primarily about himself.

The question of person, then, and with it the question of self-reference or autobiography, falls in with other important distinctions in James's theory of fiction. The differentiations of narrative form and of genre interlock in a quasi-logical system, in accord with James's stated desire to ground the writing of fiction in laws, and to use a ''scheme of consistency'' (*AN*, 319). In large part, the laws of composition we have seen James pursue are derived through a series of binary oppositions between related concepts or categories: romance and realism, first-person and third-person narration, short tales and long novels, fictional and nonfictional autobiography. From these pairs there results a logical matrix or, to borrow a structuralist term, a *com-*

26. See Genette, *Narrative Discourse*, 243.

binatoire, in which either member of one pair can be linked up with members from the other pairs in order to create a composite form.

Theoretically the number of potential literary forms or genres James's matrix could encompass would be equal to the total number of such combinations. But in practice the permissible number of forms is never so large. Specific laws tend to prescribe certain combinations and to prohibit others; this is exactly the procedure we have seen James follow in forbidding the use of the first person for certain kinds of works. James's basic exclusionary rule is that, of the three categories of romance, the first person, and the "long piece" of fiction, no two may coexist in the same work. Thus for instance the ghost story, which is by its subject matter a type of romance, must be contained in the short piece, not the novel, and it must be narrated through an oblique, third-person form which provides it with a thickness of relations; only in this way can its innate tendency to romance be controlled. Or again, a first-person narrative must be short; it is also preferable that it not be an autodiegetic narrative since the latter tends toward fluidity. As a final example, James apparently finds it acceptable that genuine (nonfictive) autobiography be written in the first person, a combination of traits that is not allowable, as we have seen, in fictive autobiography.

How James can admit the first person in his own autobiography and still avoid "the darkest abyss of romance" is something I shall try to show while studying that work in the next two chapters. Chapter 4 will deal with a somewhat different work—the Prefaces—which lies on the borderline between two genres, autobiography and literary criticism, and thus calls for a unique employment of first-person narration. The last three chapters deal with examples of fiction either admitted or proscribed by James's *combinatoire* of genres. We have just seen that two of the outlawed forms are the ghost story told in the first person and the first-person novel. Yet no sooner do we name these transgressive forms than we realize that a notorious example of each exists in the Jamesian canon: these are, respectively, *The Turn of the Screw* and *The Sacred Fount*, which are treated together in Chapter 5. Chapter 6 deals with a set of short works often taken to be autobiographical in content, and in which James uses the first and the third persons alternately, with various stratagems for avoiding the "fluidity of self-revelation.'' Finally, in Chapter 7 we come full circle in *The Ambassadors*, the novel in which James's intimacy with the hero almost prompted him to adopt the autobiographical form until he changed his mind and avoided ''the darkest abyss of romance.''

2

THE AUTOBIOGRAPHY
Self and Others

H ENRY JAMES'S volumes of autobiography are works of the author's old age. The idea for composing them came to James after his final return from America to England in 1911, following the death of his brother William in August of 1910. Beginning the work of dictation in 1911, he was able to publish the first volume, *A Small Boy and Others*, in 1913, and the second, *Notes of a Son and Brother*, in 1914. A third volume, to be called *The Middle Years*, was projected but never completed; the hundred-odd pages James had written for it were published after his death, in 1917. The autobiography thus belongs not only to the very last stage of James's career (it postdates even the great novels of the "major phase" by about a decade) but also to the dawn of the modernist period in literature. *A Small Boy and Others* appeared in the same year as *Swann's Way; Notes of a Son and Brother*, just two years before *A Portrait of the Artist as a Young Man*. In the epistemological problems it raises and in its treatment of the distance between narrator and protagonist, the autobiography is much closer to these works than to the works of James's own early period. Along with the novels of Proust and Joyce, James's autobiography can be taken as belonging to the modern genre of the artistic *Bildungsroman*, the subjective study of the artist's consciousness. Like them it concentrates on the years of childhood and adolescence that lead up to the discovery of the literary vocation, and stops short of a treatment of the author's actual practice of his art.

The attention James devotes to his early years, even to his extreme childhood, also shows his autobiography to be at least as typical of the twentieth century as of the nineteenth. The fact that the autobiography stops before James reaches full adulthood is unusual. The first volume takes James up only to about his thirteenth year, and only on the final page of the *Notes of a Son and Brother* does he announce "the end of our youth." Thus both of the completed volumes depict a period from which James was removed, at the time of writing, by almost half a century. It is not only other people who appear alien to the small boy, as the title of the first volume suggests, but the small boy himself who has become distinctly other and remote from the elderly man who is reminiscing.

Yet the confrontation with the younger "I" that occurs in the autobiography is by no means critical in intent. James's autobiography has nothing in it of a confession in which the author attempts to apologize for or redeem the errors of his youth. Nor, although he is writing more than a decade after *The Interpretation of Dreams*, is James interested in tracing to childhood the roots of an adult's repressions. In fact, except for a natural tendency sometimes to correct the immature perspective he had as a young boy, he does not particularly care to demystify or debunk the small boy's view of life. He portrays the child's world (in the way that has frequently been noticed in the fictional world of his mature novels) as a world absolutely permeated by consciousness. The limits of James's narrative are for the most part the limits of what the small boy was aware of, and all of James's verbal mastery is directed toward recapturing, in an almost phenomenological spirit, the very quality of the boy's consciousness of his world.

James's concern, however, is not entirely with the world of his young self for its own sake. His autobiography is explicitly predicated on a postromantic belief in the genetics of the individual soul, on the belief that the child is father to the man. James writes with an implicit teleology as he traces the seeds of himself as a mature imaginative artist back to their origin. The entire story is written, like Hegelian history, in a future anterior tense. "I contend for nothing moreover but the lively interest of the view, and above all of the measure, of almost any mental history after the fact. Of less interest, comparatively, is that sight of the mind *before*" (*SBO*, 219). He stresses the importance of "our having with considerable intensity *proved* educable" (*SBO*, 217) and speaks of "my instinct to grope for the earliest aesthetic seeds" (*SBO*, 164). The autobiography is to be "the history of my fostered imagination" (*SBO*, 112), but it stops at the threshold of the period when that imagination was to come to fruition in the author's literary works.

In other words the autobiography is a success story, and James eschews all false modesty as he repeatedly asserts his belief that his youthful education was a success in more ways than one. James's personal success (with that of his brother William) constitutes one of the dramatic resources of the narrative, especially since it is set off against the calamities befalling other people around him. At the outset he tells us that his father's family history offered "such a chronicle of early deaths, arrested careers, broken promises, orphaned children" (*SBO*, 14), and indeed the next two volumes are heavily larded with stories of tragic, and often youthful, ends met by James's cousins and other relatives. The chronicle of early death comes to a head in the *Notes of a Son and Brother* in two separate events: first, the Civil War, which stunted or ended the careers of so many young men of James's own age, and second, the death of his favorite cousin, Minnie Temple, the reverberations of which in his later fiction are well known.

The contrast between James's success and Minnie's tragedy emerges strongly in a passage from the letter James wrote to his brother William just after receiving the news of Minnie's death: "Among the sad reflections that her death provokes for me, there is none sadder than this view of the gradual changes and reversal of our relations: I slowly crawling from weakness and inaction and suffering into strength and health and hope: she sinking out of brightness and youth into decline and death." [1] The catastrophes striking all these others act as a foil, putting into relief James's own future success, which is the necessary condition for the autobiography.

James posits, then, a genetic continuity between the young boy he was and the successful author he has become, and this continuity mitigates the sense of otherness he must feel toward the much earlier self. Yet, even if

---

1. Henry James to William James, March 29, 1870, in Henry James, *Letters*, ed. Leon Edel (4 vols.; Cambridge, Mass., 1974–84), I, 224.

James recognizes much sympathy for and identity with the young boy about whom he writes, he must recognize that this very continuity may pose a certain threat for the authenticity of his narrative. The continuity is in fact so strong that it produces a "blur" between memory and "fond fancy," that is, between what the boy actually experienced and what the present author is reading into that experience. "I reconstruct and reconstruct," he writes (*SBO*, 37), and from the start he confesses to a "soft confusion" of memory which makes it difficult for him now to distinguish the objective memory from his later imaginative reconstruction of it (*SBO*, 11, 13). Whereas a critical posture would have implied so great a distance between the present and past selves that the boy's consciousness had to be undermined by the adult's, "reconstruction" seems to threaten a collapse of distance so that the present and past visions may contaminate each other to the point of becoming indistinguishable.

While upholding his right to reconstruct his earlier experiences, James does not gloss over those differences between his two selves, narrated and narrating, which make the reconstruction necessary. The chief difference to which he points is simply his ignorance, as a young boy, of much that was happening around him. "It was only I who didn't understand," he writes in a characteristic passage that makes us feel the world's impenetrable otherness for the young boy's mind (*SBO*, 95). His upbringing, isolating him from the world of business, which he vaguely senses to be the only solid basis for existence in America, promoted his bafflement. "What happened all the while, I conceive, was that I imagined things—and as if quite on system—wholly other than as they were, and so carried on in the midst of the actual ones an existence that somehow floated and saved me even while cutting me off from any degree of direct performance, in fact from any degree of direct participation, at all" (*SBO*, 194). This state of being cut off from experience recalls the vocabulary of romance, and in fact the older James repeatedly affirms that his childhood seems to have been infused with the "last refinement of romance" (*NSB*, 244). It was the young Henry James's very ignorance, his inability to understand the interconnections of things—the whole state of mind that led him to believe all of the rest of mankind to be divided into "three classes, the busy, the tipsy, and Daniel Webster" (*SBO*, 49)—that made for romance.

Thus there is a great difference between the younger, "inevitably contracted consciousness" (*NSB*, 243) and the present, mature one. It is first of all a difference in the understanding and appreciation of his experience, a difference that gives him "the enormous advantage now (for this I should unblushingly claim), of being able to mark for present irony or pity or wonder, or just for a better intelligence, or again for the high humour or extreme strangeness of the thing" (*NSB*, 434–35). We may assume also that the difference is not only one of appreciation but one of literary mastery, which now allows James to express much more of the experience than he could have done at the time. As Alfred Kazin has written: "The fascination with childhood as a subject in contemporary narrative derives, I think, from the esthetic pleasure that the writer finds in substituting the language of mature consciousness for the unformulated consciousness of the child." [2] Although James does not explicitly discuss this linguistic difference in the autobiography itself, he did remark on a similar problem in his Preface to *What Maisie Knew*.

The technical problem James confronted in composing *What Maisie Knew* was in fact perfectly analogous to that posed by his autobiography. In each case he needed to render the consciousness of a child who was remarkably perceptive but not adult enough to understand or formulate his or her perceptions. Like the young Henry James himself, Maisie was to be granted " 'no end' of sensibility" (*AN*, 144). Yet James needed to portray in the novel not only this sensibility but the outside reality it exercised itself upon, a complex set of disingenuous adult relationships. The complexity of this world might be lost, he realized, if he restricted his picture to "what the child might be conceived to have *understood*—to have been able to interpret and appreciate." And he continues: "Further reflexion and experience showed me my subject strangled in that extreme of rigour. The infant mind would at the best leave great gaps and voids; so that with a systematic surface possibly beyond reproach we should nevertheless fail of clearness of sense" (*AN*, 144). Moreover, alongside the problem of Maisie's comprehension was the problem of her verbal ability to express what she under-

2. Alfred Kazin, "Autobiography as Narrative," *Michigan Quarterly Review*, III (1964), 214.

stood. "Small children have many more perceptions than they have terms to translate them; their vision is at any moment much richer, their apprehension even constantly stronger, than their prompt, their at all producible vocabulary" (*AN*, 145). Thus James is drawn to the only solution that allows him to salvage both surface consistency (in terms of point of view) and sense (or "completeness and coherency" of the represented subject matter—*AN*, 145). This solution consisted in supplementing Maisie's vision with the narrator's adult language. James stresses that the narrative would thus remain faithful to Maisie's point of view, "Only, even though it is her interest that mainly makes things interesting for us, we inevitably note this in figures that are not yet at her command and that are nevertheless required whenever those aspects about her and those parts of her experience that she understands darken off into others that she rather tormentedly misses" (*AN*, 146).

This entire argument applies to James's autobiography as well, despite the fact that the question of point of view might initially seem to be different in the two works. Paradoxically, in respect to the small boy, the autobiography is practically written from a third-person stance similar to that employed in *Maisie* and in the most of James's other novels. The narrative is of course technically first-person, with the author enjoying "the double privilege of subject and object." But the subject and the object, that is, the narrating and the experiencing selves, are separated, mainly by the great chronological gap between them. Thus the consciousness of the young boy is filtered through the language of a distinct narrator just as Maisie's is. The control that comes from indirect narration is thus not wholly sacrificed in the autobiography. Moreover, *Maisie* is comparable to the autobiography insofar as Maisie's ignorance of affairs around her threatens to convert the novel into romance, in those places where "gaps and voids" appear and the girl's experience "darkens off" into the unknown. James's narrative language rescues the novel from these abysses by filling in the picture, by displaying the complex relationships that make up the novel's plot. In James's terms, the author's own figures are superimposed on the surface of Maisie's consciousness. In the autobiography this means that the older James's reconstruction of the young boy's experience, his reading into it and finding appropriate language for it, is not a violation of that earlier experience but

41

is the only adequate way of expressing it, of developing its potential content.

Some passages in the autobiography use similar terms to describe the problematic relation between the child's original experience and the adult's translation of it. James's story of himself is a "recording and figuring act" (*NSB*, 369); the term *figure* here, as in the Preface, seems to refer to language superimposed on the original, recorded experience. Elsewhere James acknowledges the danger of imputing to the boy's experience more than it originally contained, of "treating an inch of canvas to an acre of embroidery." But he goes on in self-defense: "Let the poor canvas figure time and the embroidery figure consciousness—the proportion will perhaps then not strike us so wrong" (*NSB*, 481). Through the imagery of canvas and embroidery, James is implying that his present commentary is not exterior to the prime experience but is imbedded in it as a necessary part of the picture. Similarly, categories like "time" and "consciousness" are not opposites (as "past" and "present" might be); the implication is that time can be known, or come to fruition, only *in* consciousness. The charge James is defending himself against comes down to the same one he had confronted in the prefaces: that of overtreatment (*AN*, 98–99, 114–15). Now, as then, he suggests that it is impossible, or at least artificial, to separate a subject from its treatment. The small boy's experience is like the germ or the *donnée* of a story that expands miraculously as James watches it. The expansion of the given experience in the hands of the artist is natural to it, is even a part of its essence. Overtreatment may be an aesthetic problem concerning the formal proportions of a work, but it does not threaten to invalidate the "recording and figuring act."

James thus upholds the authenticity of his narrative, even in those cases where "fond fancy" may have led him to read something into the primal experience. In making this claim he stands squarely within a large autobiographical tradition that has been clearly defined by critics of the genre. As Roy Pascal has written, literal accuracy or inaccuracy is not a serious problem for the autobiographer.[3] Since the author is engaged in a double por-

3. Roy Pascal, *Design and Truth in Autobiography* (Cambridge, Mass., 1960), 18. Compare Jean Starobinski, "The Style of Autobiography," in Seymour Chatman (ed.), *Literary Style: A Symposium* (New York, 1971), 287.

trait, not only of his experiencing self but also of his narrating self, any statement he makes is bound to portray him authentically as he is. A complementary argument has recently been advanced by Philippe Lejeune, who points out that the autobiographical pact includes the author's claim to absolute identity with the self he is writing about, not just resemblance as in other genres (including biography) that can be submitted to outside verification. Such a principle of verification, which would depend on a strict resemblance between the self depicted in the literary work and the self known historically by other people, cannot hold for autobiography.[4] James's claim, then, for the truthfulness of his reconstruction is perfectly orthodox.

But it is possible to go one step further, to declare that James's childhood was uniquely suited to be treated, or reconstructed, by James's later imagination. His childhood was essentially romantic and imaginative: James as a boy had lived ignorant of and detached from reality and had relied heavily on his own "figurative faculty," as he labels the imagination (*SBO*, 123). This childhood, which lacked any literal definition and was chiefly figurative, is merely prolonged, not misrepresented, by the figures that James employs in writing the history of himself.

In the thematics of the autobiography, the figures of the imagination are opposed to a literality that James came to disdain. This disdain is directly attributable to the educational methods of his father, Henry James, Sr. "The literal played in our education as small a part as it perhaps ever played in any, and we wholesomely breathed inconsistency and ate and drank contradictions" (*SBO*, 216). The literal was associated with the merely *personal*, an abhorred term in the father's philosophy. The young Henry came to intuit that "by so much as you were individual, which meant personal, which meant monotonous, which meant limitedly allusive and verbally repetitive, by so much you were not literary or, so to speak, *largely* figurative" (*NSB*, 180). When James writes that his cousin Minnie Temple avoided dull "earnestness," because she was "much too unliteral and too ironic" (*NSB*, 78), he is offering high praise.

Thus James's upbringing taught him to deprecate literal truth and prefer

4. Philippe Lejeune, *Le Pacte autobiographique* (Paris, 1975), 39–40.

indirection, irony, and figures.[5] Relieved of the need to enter the business world or choose a profession, he was free to develop his ''figurative faculty.'' But by the same token his childhood became the very stuff of romance. Hence, his autobiography, in which he allows his imagination to reconstruct his past, continues the romantic spirit of the childhood. In fact it is finally impossible to decide whether the romance belonged to the early years themselves or whether it belongs only to the present, nostalgic view of those years: ''Those desperate days, nonetheless, affect me now as having flushed with the very complexion of romance'' (*SBO*, 155). The ''soft confusion'' of memory and imagination makes it impossible to pinpoint the exact source of the romance. Where there was no literal level in the first place, everything belongs to the figurative level of the imagination. James's autobiography is based on a kind of extended catachresis, that figure of speech which is forced or necessary because no literal term exists.

Yet James is not willing to permit this double layering of the imagination to take his autobiography into ''the darkest abyss of romance.'' He seeks to avoid romance by establishing relations between the parts of his experience, by providing it with a context and an order of which he was not aware at the time. For one thing, in the course of the narrative certain formal arrangements or symmetries lend the experience a satisfying aesthetic shape. The figure of Minnie Temple, for instance, is first planted in the opening pages of the first volume, to be evoked again at magisterial length only in the closing section of *Notes of a Son and Brother*. There, her untimely death is made into a pivotal date in the James brothers' own life, where it marks ''the end of our youth'' (*NSB*, 515). The event that lends unity to the second volume is the Civil War, on which James centers a number of episodes and impressions. Finally, all three volumes are organized around the image of Europe, which so strongly informed James's earliest years. Most of the first volume, recounting years that the child Henry passed in America, sees Europe as a far-off goal, the attainment of which ''would constitute success in life'' (*SBO*, 84–85). It is, thus, a culmination when, before the end of the volume, the family departs for England and the continent in 1855. Most of the *Notes of*

5. A good recent study of James's preference for figurative or metaphoric treatment of his subject matter is Ruth Bernard Yeazell, *Language and Knowledge in the Late Novels of Henry James* (Chicago, 1976).

a Son and Brother once again takes place in America, but the figure is re-introduced at the beginning of the unfinished *Middle Years* with Henry's embarkation on his first adult and solo trip to Europe, in 1869.

These discernible formal patterns provide only a skeletal underpinning for the long narrative, however, and surely do not approximate the more rigorous structure that governs most of James's novels. More important for the organization of the autobiography than any formal symmetry is James's practice of developing, almost ad infinitum, the associations that adhere to any single experience. The narrative expands by metonymy, one memory always calling forth an adjacent one until the chain of associations is exhausted or (more often) until James feels he must pass on to something else. The chapter divisions seem to be placed as a series of safety valves that allow James to release the pressure of a cluster of memories, to put an end to them and start afresh with a new topic in the next chapter. Following the metonymic drive of his memories, James freely violates the actual chronology of his past, presenting in one passage any number of experiences that belong together thematically, if not temporally.[6]

Thus the actual texture of the autobiography resembles not a well-laid-out formal plot but (to use James's own favorite images) a web or a woven fabric. In this way the narrative succeeds in imitating what is for James the very quality of consciousness, as some of the best-known passages in his essays remind us. "Experience is never limited and it is never complete; it is an immense sensibility, a kind of huge spider-web of the finest silken threads suspended in the chamber of consciousness, and catching every airborne particle in its tissue," he had written in "The Art of Fiction" (*FN*, 12). Later, in the first preface he wrote for the New York Edition, he refers to himself as an "embroiderer of the canvas of life" and writes: "Really, universally, relations stop nowhere, and the exquisite problem of the artist is eternally but to draw, by a geometry of his own, the circle within which they will happily *appear* to do so" (*AN*, 5). Similar images occur in the autobiography itself. On his second page James is already describing how he found "discrimination among the parts of my subject again and again dif-

6. On the organization of the autobiography, compare Millicent Bell, "Henry James and the Fiction of Autobiography," *Southern Review*, XVIII (1982), 463–79.

ficult—so inseparably and beautifully they seemed to hang together and the comprehensive case to decline mutilation or refuse to be treated otherwise than handsomely'' (*SBO*, 2). Later he notes his text's ''exhibition of the rate at which the relations of any gage of experience multiply and ramify from the moment the mind begins to handle it'' (*SBO*, 96). He even finds cause to lament his extraordinary power of recall, which had long before gotten him in trouble with his brother William, whom it exasperated (*SBO*, 68– 69). Yet it is clear that James revels in his marvelous power to produce a closely woven web of intricate experience. He admits to an ''almost fanatical aversion to loose ends'' (*MY*, 109), and his apparent ideal would be a narrative in which every element would relate to every other, so that it would be complete in itself, ''shut up wholly in cross-relations,'' as he had described one of his works in the prefaces (*AN*, 114).

Such an ideal not only permits but encourages the reading into an experience of new implications that are discovered only after the fact. A typical example occurs when James recounts his attendance at a school in Paris on the Rue Balzac, so named because it was the site of the house in which Balzac had died about five years before James arrived there. This coincidence leads him to speculate:

> I positively cherish at the present hour the fond fancy that we all soaked in some such sublime element as might still have hung about there—I mean on the very spot—from the vital presence, so lately extinct, of the prodigious Balzac. . . . The Pension Vauquer, then but lately existent, according to Le Père Goriot, on the other side of the Seine, was still to be revealed to me: but the figures peopling it are not to-day essentially more intense . . . than I persuade myself, with so little difficulty, that I found the more numerous and more shifting, though properly doubtless less inspiring, constituents of the Pension Fezandié. Fantastic and all ''subjective'' that I should attribute a part of their interest, or that of the scene spreading around them, to any competent perception, in the small-boy mind, that the general or public moment had a rarity and a brevity, a sharp intensity, of its own. (*SBO*, 374–75)

The passage reveals a certain embarrassment at the subjective character of the ''fond fancy'' that leads the author to invest the scene with a Balzacian aura even at a date when the young Henry had never heard of Balzac. Yet he easily persuades himself to do so, and it is obvious that he would have been unwilling to forgo the pleasure afforded by this association made retrospectively. For the association is, of course, a felicitous one because it places the young boy under the aegis of the novelist who was later to be one of his most important literary models and whom he was to call, even in late age, "the father of us all" (*FN*, 102). The link with Balzac thus contributes to the seed theory on which the autobiography is premised: it allows James to find one more genetic connection between his formative years and his mature artistry. The fact that this link belongs to James's embroidery as much as to his canvas does not matter, since his consciousness is essentially a complex unity that absorbs all the relations that are presented to it.

By such intervention of the "figurative faculty" as this, the canvas of James's text gets more and more filled up or covered over. There is no logical terminus to this process, except that imposed by the exigencies of space. James occasionally acknowledges that the infinitely expansive quality of his consciousness poses a threat to the aesthetic form of his narrative. "I feel that at such a rate I remember too much," he opens one chapter by writing (*SBO*, 92), and later: "I confess myself embarrassed by my very ease of recapture of my young consciousness; so that I perforce try to encourage lapses and keep my abundance down" (*SBO*, 276). But in fact he has a horror of such lapses (which are like the gaps and voids to which Maisie was prone), and his narrative might go on forever if an arbitrary stop were not put somewhere. Just how arbitrary a stop is required is suggested by the clever way in which James finally closes off *A Small Boy and Others*. Recounting a bout of sickness he had in Boulogne, he recalls a fainting fit, announced by a "strong sick whirl of everything about me, under which I fell into a lapse of consciousness that I shall conveniently here treat as a considerable gap. THE END" (*SBO*, 419). Relations will cease, and the narrative can halt, only with the extinction of consciousness itself.

The canvas of the autobiography can be completed, then, only through an act that is both recording and figuring. The figures supplied by the imagination do not, as might be feared, lead only to romance; the imagination does not cut James off from the conditions of reality. Instead, he is able to reconcile the representation of his childhood's romance with a strong sense of realism, for the imagination, in permitting him to develop and express all the relations inherent in any given experience, brings him to that very realism defined in the prefaces.

We can now see somewhat better what it means that the young boy Henry is both other and the same as the autobiographer. The older James knows more than the young boy, but what he knows seems now to have been latent within the latter's experience. Hence when he reinterprets the boy's experience he does not need to demystify the boy's mind, or belittle it, or even really to correct it. Instead, the effect of the reconstruction is to make the young boy's sensibility seem—like that of Maisie and the other fictional children in James's works—immense. Through the soft confusion of memory, the boy's mind seems to expand to meet the adult, magisterial mind of the late James; there is no clear demarcation between the two. This intermingling of the two consciousnesses is borne out, on the level of narrative technique, by the way in which James fuses the two modes of showing and of telling, or of *story* and *discourse*, as Benveniste would use the terms.[7] Although some passages are clearly commentary belonging to the narrating self (figuring acts) and others clearly belong to the boy's original experience (recording acts), at many times the distinction breaks down, or at least the two modes of narration are so minutely intermixed that it seems futile to try to separate them: "The 'first' then—since I retrace our steps to the start, for the pleasure, strangely mixed though it be, of feeling our small feet plant themselves afresh and artlessly stumble forward again—the first began long ago, far off, and yet glimmers at me there as out of a thin golden haze, with all the charm, for imagination and memory, of pressing pursuit rewarded, of distinctness in the dimness, of the flush of life in the grey, of the wonder of consciousness in everything" (*SBO*, 3). The boy's impressionistic awareness alternates here, almost phrase by phrase, with the nostalgic distance of the old man. In such passages James exploits the potential, inherent in all first-person discourse, to reconcile immediacy with distance, experience with reflection. He achieves the same effect that Gérard Genette has

7. Emile Benveniste, "Les Relations de temps dans le verbe français," in his *Problèmes de linguistique générale* (Paris, 1966), 237–50; *Problems in General Linguistics*, trans. Mary Elizabeth Meek (Coral Gables, Florida, 1971), 217–30.

pointed out in certain passages of Proust's novel, a fusion of ''the maximum of 'showing' with the maximum of 'telling.' '' [8]

James's autobiography is not a completely subjective narrative, with the only intersubjective complication arising in the question of the relation between the narrating self and the experiential or narrated self, although James's own description of the work as a history of his fostered imagination encourages this almost solipsistic perspective. In fact the text is far more complex, because the autobiographical self is from the start caught in a web of relations: it must narrate not only its own story but that of others as well. Indeed nothing is more striking in this autobiography than the way in which, from its very first page, it purports to be not autobiography at all but biography of the novelist's brother William. The opening sentences of *A Small Boy and Others* read:

> In the attempt to place together some particulars of the early life of William James and present him in his setting, his immediate native and domestic air, so that any future gathered memorials of him might become the more intelligible and interesting, I found one of the consequences of my interrogation of the past assert itself a good deal at the expense of the others. For it was to memory in the first place that my main appeal for particulars had to be made; I had been too near a witness to my brother's beginnings in life, and too close a participant, by affection, admiration and sympathy, in whatever touched and moved him, not to feel myself in possession even of a greater quantity of significant truth, a larger handful of the fine substance of history, than I could hope to express or apply. (*SBO*, 1)

The alternative presented here can be described as one between true autobiography and memoirs. As Philippe Lejeune has suggested, in memoirs the narrative self is on stage primarily as a witness of larger historical events that involve other people; in autobiography, he ''puts the accent on his in-

---

8. Gérard Genette, *Narrative Discourse*, trans. Jane E. Lewin (Ithaca, 1980), 166–67. Jean Starobinski, in ''The Style of Autobiography,'' 287–88, suggests that autobiography, because of its double narrative standpoint, may be an inherently mixed mode, a kind of ''discourse-story.''

dividual life, and particularly the story of his personality.''[9] In his opening paragraph, James is elusive: stating at first his intention to write memoirs of his brother, he is simultaneously explaining why this enterprise immediately took a turn toward autobiography. When, on the next page, he speaks of the recollected past as beginning to take shape ''round the primary figure,'' the reader is already unclear as to who that figure is, William or Henry. This ambivalence will continue to some degree through all three volumes, though the emphasis falls sometimes in one direction, sometimes the other. *A Small Boy and Others* is based entirely on Henry's own subjective memories. Consequently, although there is a certain amount of talk about William, this volume is predominantly autobiographical. One telltale sign is the frontispiece to this volume, a photograph showing the twelve-year-old Henry posing with his father. But in the *Notes of a Son and Brother*, the frontispiece shows a pencil-drawn self-portrait of William; furthermore this volume consists largely of memorials to Henry James, Sr., and William James, and includes ample extracts from the letters of each, to which Henry James appends his ''notes.'' As the title of this volume suggests, the novelist takes a subordinate position here, appearing only in his relationship to other figures.

The situation in the unfinished *Middle Years* is less clear. Opening with James's first solo trip to Europe, it describes him for the first time separated from his family and therefore seems to throw to the winds the pretense of being a memoir of William. But it is plausible to see in the very fact that this volume remained incomplete (in fact, was scarcely begun) a sign that James found it impossible to write overt autobiography, which no longer had the sanction of being a tribute to his brother. Leon Edel points out that no external necessity forced James to abandon this volume; he surmises that James simply had no desire to write ''personal autobiography'' that was ''removed from the frame of family.'' In a letter addressed to William's widow in late 1911, James spoke of his work as one ''almost of brotherly autobiography,

9. Philippe Lejeune, *L'Autobiographie en France* (Paris, 1971), 14–16. For a similar distinction between memoirs and autobiography, see Georges Gusdorf, ''Conditions et limites de l'autobiographie,'' in Günther Reichenkron and Erich Haase (eds.), *Formen der Selbstdarstellung* (Berlin, 1956), esp. 112–13.

and filial autobiography not less.'' [10] The phrase ''brotherly autobiography'' is ambiguous, if not paradoxical; it aptly expresses the two contrary tendencies of the work as a whole.

The tendency for memoirs (of William, for example) to veer over into actual autobiography—that is, for the objective story of another person to become the subjective story of the narrator himself—is parallel to something that happens repeatedly in James's fiction, where a story ostensibly concerning an objective set of circumstances or events turns into the subjective story of somebody's (the reflector's) appreciation of them. In the Preface to a volume of his ghost stories, James argued that supernatural events must always be represented in ''the field, as I may call it, rather of their second than of their first exhibition'' (AN, 256), meaning only as they are filtered through some character's consciousness. This field of second exhibition allows James to have his cake and eat it too, to have the romance of the ghost story as well as the realism of the reflecting character's psychology. In the fictional works, the field of second exhibition usually belongs to a third-person reflector, whereas in the autobiography it belongs to the author himself. In both cases James's technique allows him to bracket, in the phenomenological sense, the question of the objective existence of his fictional state of affairs and to concentrate instead on how the state of affairs appears to someone's consciousness.

The autobiography shows how this subjective turn was well suited to James's basic mental disposition; it also shows the dangers inherent in this disposition. We have already seen how James considers himself to have been removed from outside reality, to have existed in ''fond detachment'' from the world (SBO, 58). He was detached not only from the world of business but even, in a sense, from those members of his family who are nonetheless so important for his autobiography. ''I see myself moreover as somehow always alone in these and like New York flâneries and contemplations'' (SBO, 24), he informs us, and he pictures himself as ''lone and perverse even in my own sight'' (NSB, 108). Elsewhere, writing of himself momentarily in the third person: ''For there was the very pattern and measure of all

10. Leon Edel, *Henry James: The Master* (Philadelphia, 1972), 448; James to Alice James, November 13, 1911, in Percy Lubbock (ed.), *Letters of Henry James* (2 vols.; New York, 1920), II, 207.

he was to demand: just to *be* somewhere—almost anywhere would do—
and somehow receive an impression or an accession, feel a relation or a vibration'' (*SBO*, 25). There is here no genuine sense of others as others, no
entering into a true intersubjective relationship; the pressure of the outside
world is felt only as a vibration that impinges on the boy's organism, as we
might imagine the experience of a mollusk. ''It was also quaint, among us,''
James writes of himself and his brother, ''to have *begun* with the inward
life'' (*SBO*, 56), suggesting that the outer world was not naturally given but
had to be acquired. James maintains it is possible for the single subject to
exist, and to have an intuition of itself, before it becomes aware of the external world. As he wrote in his Preface to ''The Private Life'': ''to be truly
single is to be able, under stress, to be separate, to be *solus*, to know at need
the interlunar swoon of *some* independent consciousness'' (*AN*, 252). William and Henry's education was designed to enhance this pure self-consciousness: ''What we were to do . . . was just to *be* something, something
unconnected with specific doing, something free and uncommitted'' (*SBO*,
50–51). The stress upon the cultivation of the inner life and upon the superiority of being over doing seems to incline here toward the now familiar
danger of romantic detachment from experience. The independent or single
self would be the first-person narrator pushed to a logical extreme, one who
could recount only his own solipsistic history.

This movement toward solipsism is, however, only one of the two opposing tendencies to be found in the autobiography. The other, as I have
suggested, is the tendency away from pure autobiography toward narrative
focused on other people, in which the primary, narrating self is seen as existing in a web of interrelationships. Relying on phenomenological terms
we might say that, even if James's subjectivist bias makes him bracket or
reduce a belief in the objective existence of the outside world, his consciousness is still consciousness of objects, which transcend him and which
have more than a merely subjective existence, in the psychologistic sense
that phenomenology opposes. James's consciousness is never pure self-
consciousness; it is always portrayed as intending or aiming at objects, and
James never takes the idealist step of denying the existence of those objects.
On the contrary, the very titles of the first two volumes strongly assert the
importance of others. And if the small boy himself still figures in a central

role in the title to the first volume, in the title to the second he is no longer granted any independent existence but is present only in relation to others, as a son and brother.

At times James goes even further. Not only does he see himself as being in relation to others, but he evokes his childhood sense of being completely immersed in them, of merging his small ego with that of a larger group. The first and most natural such group is of course the family, whose members James describes as "fused and united and interlocked" (*SBO*, 2). It was a "homogeneous family group" centered on the mother, who not only held the family members together but seemed miraculously to embody all of them: "she *was* he [the father], *was* each of us, was our pride and our humility, our possibility of *any* relations, and the very canvas itself on which we were floridly embroidered" (*NSB*, 179–80). Although the family circle was undoubtedly the most important one for the young James, other circles later rivaled it. In adolescence James participated in a new group that coalesced around his cousin, Minnie Temple. Near the end of the *Notes of a Son and Brother*, he recalls the circle of friends among whom he saw Minnie in New Hampshire in the summer of 1865. "Our circle I fondly call it, and doubtless then called it, because in the light of that description I could most rejoice in it, and I think of it now as having formed a little world of easy and happy interchange" (*NSB*, 457–58). Just as the family circle had centered on the mother, this one centers on Minnie, its "heroine": "everything that took place around her took place as if primarily in relation to her and in her interest" (*NSB*, 461).

The need for such circles, for "communities of contemplation" (*SBO*, 382) continues into the present moment of James's writing. One of the purposes of the autobiography is precisely to recall those circles and to translate them, through the act of memory, into what James calls the "circle of my commemoration" (*SBO*, 2). In this he is perhaps most like his character Stransom, of "The Altar of the Dead," who brings together into one place his worship of the memories of all his dead friends. James's autobiography not only remembers but preserves and reconstitutes the "homogeneous" circles in which he had lived and in which he can at least temporarily lose his sense of separate selfhood.

The importance James attaches to being included in communities can best be appreciated when measured against the clear counterexample the autobiography offers. Just as the autobiography is James's personal success story set against a record of others' catastrophes, so his inclusion in a tightly knit family is set against the spectacle of other children who are orphans. The James family's "chronicle of early death" gives the young Henry plenty of occasion to observe children who were liberated from the parental ties he took for granted. He confesses he found the orphaned state thrilling and envied it: "I think my first childish conception of the enviable lot . . . was to be so little fathered or mothered, so little sunk in the short range, that the romance of life seemed to lie in some constant improvisation, by vague overhovering authorities, of new situations and horizons" (*SBO*, 14–15). To be orphaned was to enjoy "the happy, that is the romantic lot," because it meant being freed from the usual connections and rules governing experience. One of Henry's orphaned cousins appeared to him as "a pure gift of the free-handed imagination" (*NSB*, 143) because his life seemed undetermined and independent. But if such a state of romance is thrilling, it is also threatening: the orphan, unshielded by a family community, is exposed to external risks that Henry himself never had to fear (*SBO*, 48). Even if Henry may envy the orphaned cousins, it is safer for him to cling to family ties and to profit from the others' liberation only through his imagination.

In at least one instance, though, we see James stepping out of the family circle and trying to establish a relation with a larger group. This attempt occurs during the Civil War, which is the great public event forming the backdrop of the *Notes of a Son and Brother*. The young Henry found that the war could furnish him with a common cause in which to immerse his separate identity, while the autobiographer James finds in it a way to link his personal narrative to a public one. In Chapter 9 he recounts with considerable pathos a visit he paid to some Union soldiers encamped in Rhode Island shortly after the outbreak of the war. Mingling with the young soldiers he felt a sense of community, even of "homogeneity and its entailed fraternity"; he was able to "establish . . . a relation" with the soldiers "even to the pitch of the last tenderness of friendship" (*NSB*, 314–16).

Yet James is in an awkward position here, because his famous "obscure hurt," related some twenty pages earlier, had prevented him from entering the military himself. The autobiography, however, in bringing together

James's wound and the war, seeks to establish a connection between them. Commentators on the "obscure hurt" episode have not usually observed that the major significance of this passage within James's narrative is to provide a link between his private past and the national history. Two things, he explains, occurred at the same time—the outbreak of war and his own accident. After mentioning the war, he continues:

> The other, the minutely small affair in comparison, was a passage of personal history the most entirely personal, but between which, as a private catastrophe or difficulty, bristling with embarrassments, and the great public convulsion that announced itself in bigger terms every day, I felt from the very first an association of the closest, yet withal, I fear, almost of the least clearly expressible. Scarce at all to be stated, to begin with, the queer fusion or confusion established in my consciousness during the soft spring of '61 by the firing on Fort Sumter, Mr. Lincoln's instant first call for volunteers and a physical mishap, already referred to as having overtaken me at the same dark hour, and the effects of which were to draw themselves out incalculably and intolerably. Beyond all present notation the interlaced, undivided way in which what had happened to me, by a turn of fortune's hand, in twenty odious minutes kept company of the most unnatural—I can call it nothing less—with my view of what was happening, with the question of what might still happen, to everyone about me, to the country at large: it so made of these marked disparities a single vast visitation. . . . The twenty minutes had sufficed, at all events, to establish a relation—a relation to everything occurring round me not only for the next four years but for long afterward—that was at once extraordinarily intimate and quite awkwardly irrelevant. (*NSB*, 296–97)

James's juxtaposition of these two events exemplifies the way he often arranges his narrative in order to stress thematic connections he believes relevant. In this case he has had to violate chronology to do so, since, as Leon Edel has demonstrated, the "obscure hurt" must have occurred in the autumn, not the "soft spring," of 1861.[11] The passage I have just quoted goes to extraordinary lengths to convince the reader of the real, necessary relation between the two events, though the necessity of this relation seems to be in proportion only to its ineffability. It is a "queer fusion or confusion" (reminiscent of memory's "soft confusion"), "beyond all present nota-

11. Leon Edel, *Henry James: The Untried Years* (Philadelphia, 1953), 176–79.

tion,'' both too intimate and too irrelevant to be expressed. Through such evocation James seeks to create a single moment of consciousness that is a synthesis of two quite disproportionate affairs.

Yet it is only too obvious that James is not discovering a real relation but is intuiting one or conjuring one up after the fact. For once the ''soft confusion'' between the recording and figuring acts does not achieve a convincing synthesis of memory with fancy. The chief sign of this is the inordinately diffident and impressionistic style of the whole chapter. ''Vagueness at best attends, however, the queer experience I glance at,'' James writes, and he admits to stressing ''the prodigiously subjective side of the experience'' (NSB, 309). Or again, he writes, ''There are memories in truth too fine or too peculiar for notation, too intensely individual and super subtle'' (NSB, 318). Furthermore, the appeal to ineffability is not the only rhetorical strategy James uses to affirm a relationship that cannot be objectively proved. He also employs metaphor to assimilate his nonmilitary experience into that of the soldiers. Metaphorically, the ''obscure hurt'' serves as James's badge of courage; when he returns from the long day spent visiting the soldiers he recalls ''my acute consciousness of paying physically for my excursion— which hadn't answered the least little bit for my impaired state'' (NSB, 317). Forced to remain in bed with a book at Harvard law school during the first campaigns of the war, he yet insists: ''This was at least a negative of combat, an organised, not a loose and empty one, something definitely and firmly parallel to action in the tented field'' (NSB, 301).

This, finally, may be seen as the main goal of this chapter: to allay James's lingering sense of guilt over his failure to answer Lincoln's ''instant first call for volunteers.'' The guilt almost surfaces in his observation that ''to have trumped up a lameness at such a juncture could be made to pass in no way for graceful'' (NSB, 297). But the autobiography's attempt to parallel the obscure hurt to action in the field cannot really bridge the gap between two such contrary experiences. Even while mingling with the men in uniform, James has seen in each soldier ''a figure of romance,'' someone far removed from his own experience (NSB, 313). Instead of signing up, he distributes spare change among the soldiers, paying them off as it were for living his experience vicariously. We may be reminded of some moments in his fiction: Ralph Touchett paying for Isabel's adventures or Adam Verver buying the Prince for Maggie. Finally, James's marvelous rhetoric cannot mask the fact that the obscure hurt, far from uniting his history with the common destiny, was precisely the event that removed him from an extroverted role in public life; it was indeed the negative of combat. For the rest of the war, Henry would have to rely on the experiences of his two younger soldier brothers, taking from them "the mere borrowed . . . impression" and "vicarious sensation" of the war (*NSB*, 380–81). The relations James has with the outside world turn out to be both imaginative (vicarious) and imaginary (read into the past, not objectively present in it). But the intensity of his rhetoric in these pages is in direct proportion to his clear need to relate the tenuous thread of his personal history to a public history that could give it legitimacy. In this he achieves but a very qualified success.

James's most important relation to an other remains his relation to his brother William. The autobiography begins, as I have said, with a statement of the author's intention to compose memoirs of William, and the *Notes of a Son and Brother* are largely made up of documents for such memoirs. One reason these volumes continue to vacillate between biography and autobiography is the unusual relationship they depict. William's main role is that of a kind of alter ego, Henry's window on the world, who takes in experiences and impressions for him by proxy. As a younger brother, Henry takes on the interests of his elder brother: "William had only to let the light of *his* attention, his interest, his curiosity, his aversion even . . . visibly rest on them [other people] for me entirely to feel that they must count for as much as might be—so far at least as my perception was concerned, contact being truly another affair" (*NSB*, 323). So focused is Henry on his elder brother that, he admits, "What I really most apprehended, I think, was the circumstance of *his* apprehending" (*NSB*, 330). This epigonic position can become pitiable, as when James recalls that all he did was "to pick up . . . the crumbs of his feast and the echoes of his life" (*NSB*, 13).

With such images we have moved away from the view of James's autobiography as a purely subjective or solipsistic investigation into "the history of [his] fostered imagination." There is something disturbing in this spectacle of James, whose narrative was to be a phenomenological rendering of the quality of his own younger consciousness, abdicating his claim to have had personal perceptions at all and appointing his brother as his surrogate. His posture toward experience is now one of mediation, like that of the literary author toward the fictional characters and situations in his work. When he records William's lengthy boat trip to Brazil during the Civil War, James speaks of "our having him planted out as a reflector of impressions where impressions were both strong and as different as possible from those that more directly beat upon us" (*NSB*, 443). William, too, is a reflector; his role is exactly analogous to that of one of James's fictive centers of consciousness, "the impersonal author's concrete deputy or delegate" (*AN*, 327). William was Henry's delegate, sent to do his living for him, while Henry remained content "if I might live, by the imagination, in William's so adoptive skin" (*NSB*, 15). This relationship between the two brothers may remind us not only of the relationship between the Jamesian author and his fictional reflector but also of the one that sometimes pertains between one fictional character and another in the novels. Rowland Mallett lives in Roderick Hudson's "adoptive skin," Ralph Touchett in Isabel Archer's, the Princess Casamassima in Hyacinth Robinson's, and Lambert Strether in Chad Newsome's, in a way that allows the first member of each pair to economize his own expenses and minimize his personal dangers.

The relation of Henry James to William James in this work is just as paradoxical as the term "brotherly autobiography" would suggest. Purporting to use his own memories only as a vehicle of William's biography, James also shows how William's experience was, surreptitiously, a surrogate for his own. The autobiography takes on a rhythm defined by the alternate moments of William's presence or absence from Henry's sight. William was by no means always accessible. James recalls, "I never for all the time of childhood caught up with him or overtook him. He was always around the corner and out of sight, coming back into view but at the hours of his extremest ease" (*SBO*, 9). Henry came to accept "the ease of his disappearances," or what he also calls "W. J.'s eclipses." [12] Like the sun or moon (the image here recalls that of the "interlunar swoon of *some* independent consciousness"), William comes and goes, and his intermittences determine Henry's posture toward his own experience. When William is present he acts as Henry's reflector; when he leaves on a voyage Henry feels ex-

12. See Edel, *Henry James: The Untried Years*, 75–76.

posed, forced to face reality more directly (*NSB*, 412). Given William's repeated eclipses, it is hard to see how James's narrative can claim to be a biography of him at all. Yet James persists in treating his work as "brotherly autobiography" and even in using a first-person plural right up to the last page of the *Notes of a Son and Brother*, where he speaks for William and himself: "We felt it [Minnie's death] as the end of our youth" (*NSB*, 515). The alternative between memoirs and autobiography remains to the end a double bind that cannot be unraveled.

In retrospect, this double bind can be seen to have been implicit in the terms of the enterprise James set for himself. Having contracted to write the story of his own youth in the first person, James immediately sought to mitigate or avoid the "*fluidity* of self-revelation" by establishing a primary reference to his brother, and a general reference to the rest of the others with whom he had come into contact. But at the same time he found himself compelled to admit that his consciousness had been, first of all, an intense *self-consciousness*, both in the philosophical sense and in the sense of embarrassment over presenting himself as a spectacle for others. Throughout the autobiography, James conveys a strong feeling of his own isolation, even in the midst of family and friends. The relation that finally outweighs all others is James's relation to himself, that is, the relation that James the autobiographer discovers with his young self. In comparison, the relations he tries to establish with genuine others seem pallid and unconvincing. The fraternity he seeks with the soldiers or with his own brother William must be supported, as we have seen, by the rhetoric the autobiography summons up. At their most tenuous, these relations seem to be not only imaginative but imaginary. But it is time now to turn to the theme of the imagination itself, the faculty that sustains James's contact with the outer world.

3

THE AUTOBIOGRAPHY
The Imagination

T HE AUTOBIOGRAPHY presents itself as "the personal history, as it were, of an imagination" (*NSB*, 369), as though the imagination were to write its own story. James's discovery of himself as "the man of imagination " (*NSB*, 370) was what made the writing of the autobiography immediately possible. Thus, it is important to discover exactly what James means by the *imagination*. In fact, he uses the term in different ways, and it may help to begin by distinguishing three different definitions this key term can have for James.

In the classical tradition of empiricist psychology, the imagination commonly refers to the mental faculty responsible for forming images, as opposed to other mental representations such as sensations, perceptions, or concepts. William James, in his *Principles of Psychology* (1890), was squarely within this tradition.[1] In most discussions of this kind, the imagination is far from being Baudelaire's "queen of the faculties." Instead, images are usually seen as copies of sensations or perceptions, feebler than the originals, and the imagination itself is seen as a subordinate or derivative faculty. Of the three definitions, this one has the least currency in Henry

1. William James, *Principles of Psychology* (2 vols.; New York, 1950), I, 44–75.

James, although at least once in the autobiography he does use the terms *imaginative* and *reproductive* as synonyms (*NSB*, 482).

In a more common literary, and nontechnical, usage—the one according to which a critic may call a piece of writing *imaginative*—the imagination refers not so much to a single faculty as to an entire way of having any kind of experience. It defines any experience that is enjoyed vicariously, that is substituted for the direct or empirically real experience. In this sense *imaginative* is roughly a laudatory synonym for *imaginary*. This definition is very important for James, although he uses it in a somewhat special way. When James writes of his own living "by the imagination, in William's so adaptive skin," he is describing an experience that is imaginary for him even though it is real (empirical) for someone else. In *A Small Boy and Others* we learn that one of James's most inveterate childhood traits was envy of other people, not of what they had, but "simply of what they *were*, or in other words of a certain sort of richer consciousness supposed, doubtless all too freely supposed, in them" (*SBO*, 175). James's imagination grew in response to the question not just of what other people's lives were like but of how they experienced their lives. "They were so *other*—that was what I felt; and to *be* other, other almost anyhow, seemed as good as the probable taste of the bright compound wistfully watched in the confectioner's window" (*SBO*, 175). James distinguishes his envy from jealousy by saying that jealousy would have meant wanting to have the experience for himself, whereas envy meant that he was content with his "view of them as only through the confectioner's hard glass" (*SBO*, 176). The imagination, in this second sense, depends on the maintenance of this hard glass separating the real from the vicarious. There is never any confusion between the two realms, and the imaginary remains subordinate to the real, dependent on it for its nourishment.

In the final and most generous conception, which may for convenience be called the romantic one, the imagination is no longer a single mental faculty, nor is it something set off against the real and charged with vicariousness. It is now commensurate with consciousness itself, if consciousness is taken as a continuing *act* that perpetually calls the real world into existence. This formula, so close to Samuel Taylor Coleridge's definition of the primary imagination as "a repetition in the finite mind of the eternal act of creation in the infinite I AM'' (*Biographia Literaria*, ch. xiii), is, consequently, also close to Immanuel Kant's treatment of the imagination as the faculty that mediates between the understanding and the sensibility and allows the synthetic act of consciousness to occur.[2] Though it may seem strange to find James a bedfellow of Coleridge, there is good reason to place his notion of the imagination within the romantic tradition. Charles Feidelson, who has done just that, sums up James's usage of *imagination* thus: ''James is conceiving of 'imagination' as the total activity of the mind, not as a special psychological state, whether essentially reflective or essentially projective. . . . 'Imagination,' on this view, is essentially the coming-into-being of the significant forms of consciousness and life, self and world—the ontological *image*-ination, as it were, of reality.''[3]

Feidelson's formula is helpful, as long as we bear in mind that James is not always consistent in this usage. In fact, the final value of imagination in James's autobiography may be said to depend on a tension between the second and the third definitions just given. The second definition, in the most severe construal, would mean not only that James's imagination leads him to live vicariously, dependent on the experiences of others, but also that the objects of his imagination may be delusive, imaginary. The third definition, construed most favorably, would mean that James could not be deluded, because his entire world would be brought into existence precisely through his imagination. As we shall see, the world depicted in James's autobiography does tend to submit to the power of his imagination, though in the end the limits of that world point also to the possible limits of the imagination.

2. Samuel Taylor Coleridge, *Biographia Literaria* (2 vols.; Princeton, 1983), I, 124–25. For Coleridge's description of the imagination as an intermediate faculty between the mind's active and passive powers, see I, 304, and for Coleridge's description of the imagination as an intermediate faculty between the mind's active and passive powers, see I, 86. For a historical account of the origins of both Kant's and Coleridge's ideas of the imagination in the eighteenth-century empiricist and idealist traditions, see James Engell, *The Creative Imagination: Enlightenment to Romanticism* (Cambridge, Mass., 1981). For a much briefer account, see Jean Starobinski, ''Jalons pour une histoire du concept d'imagination,'' in his *La Relation critique* (Paris, 1970), 173–95.

3. Charles Feidelson, ''James and the 'Man of Imagination,' '' in Frank Brady, John Palmer, and Martin Price (eds.), *Literary Theory and Structure* (New Haven, 1973), 336. For an extended recent discussion of James's relation to romanticism, see Daniel Mark Fogel, *Henry James and the Structure of the Romantic Imagination* (Baton Rouge, 1981), esp. 1–13.

While keeping these different possible meanings of the imagination in mind, we can begin by asking whether James's autobiography can actually depict the imagination itself at work or whether instead it concentrates on the objects of the imagination, the images or the entire world it reproduces or calls into being. This is how James poses the problem: "I had in a word to draw him [the man of imagination] forth from within rather than meet him in the world before me, the more convenient sphere of the objective, and to make him objective, in short, had to turn nothing less than myself inside out" (*NSB*, 370).

The paradox involved in such an undertaking would seem to be that, for the imagination to become an *object* representable in a narrative, it would have to be divested of its true nature as a purely subjective power that takes other people or things as *its* objects. Conversely, insofar as the imagination remains purely subjective, it could have no history at all; nothing that happened to it could essentially affect it. James in fact often depicts himself as pure consciousness, specifically as an eye. As we have seen, he is frequently detached and alone. His most characteristic pose, especially in the first volume, is that of someone gaping at things around him.[4] "I had but one success, always—that of endlessly supposing, wondering, admiring" (*SBO*, 243). Indeed the young James often seems something of an Emersonian transparent eyeball. His posture of simply admiring can become ramified to an almost ludicrous degree, as during a comical passage in *The Middle Years* when James, who has gone to the National Gallery in London to see the paintings, suddenly finds himself just watching somebody else (it turns out to be Swinburne) who is in turn looking at a canvas (*MY*, 52–53).

But it is obviously difficult to construct a narrative out of such moments of pure vision. Insofar as James indulged only in "the so far from showy practice of wondering and dawdling and gaping" (*SBO*, 26), there is very little to *show*—least of all the observer himself. "Quel oeil peut se voir?" James might have asked, after Stendhal, and insofar as he remains pure eye, he tends to be lost to the reader's view. In *The Middle Years* James recounts how, on his trip to London in 1869, he was overawed to meet a number of

4. On James as simply "seeing," see Robert F. Sayre, *The Imagined Self* (Princeton, 1964), 140, 154–55.

"eminent gentlemen" in society. But his awe left him unprepared for the interest they expressed in getting to know him. "My identity for myself was *all* in my sensibility to their own exhibition, with not a scrap left over for a personal show" (*MY*, 29). The personal show remains absent because the pure subject, existing only as an immense sensibility, cannot at the same time appear as an object for other people or for himself.

The "history of [a] fostered imagination" (*SBO*, 112) seems to promise a picture of the actual growth of an imagination. As we saw earlier, the autobiography is founded on a principle of genetic continuity: it is to be a real-life *Bildungsroman*. But James's education, as it turns out, is no more showy that his habit of gaping. The actual results of his education "would be difficult to state" (*SBO*, 26). He repeatedly appeals to "the vague processes . . . of picking up an education" (*SBO*, 352). This does not mean that James casts doubt on the value of his education. On the contrary, we have seen that he considered it a success, a success that was to be made tangible in his literary works. But those concrete products of his imagination lie outside the scope of the autobiography. The process of growth itself is less tangible— especially so in his case, James suggests, because of the pedagogic methods of his father. In fact the father eschewed all method, just as he tried to discourage in his sons any concern for direct personal or literal success. He betrayed little interest in his son's "mastery of *any* craft or art" (*SBO*, 220), just as he disdained any outward signs of religiosity, so that even if a religious sense pervaded the James household, they had nothing "to show for it" (*NSB*, 167). In retracing his upbringing James is thus reduced to apologizing for the vagueness and "the tenuity of some of my clues" (*SBO*, 219). Although the memories of his education may be vivid enough for the author, yet "at the same time an exhibition of them to mere other eyes or ears or questioning logical minds may effect itself in no plain terms" (*NSB*, 319).

This is not to say that James's autobiography fails to represent the growth of the artistic imagination. In its way it succeeds brilliantly. Only, James realized that this representation could not be direct or literal; it could work only through evocative suggestion of the world that is the object of the imagination. "Tell me what the artist is, and I will tell you of what he has *been* conscious" (*AN*, 46). A definition of the artist necessarily passes through a description of the world he has known. Roy Pascal has written of

James's autobiography, "It is not an analysis of the imagination, or the feelings, but the story of the swarming world that filled his imagination."[5] James's own comments on his goal in the autobiography corroborate this view even while refining it. In a crucial passage of *Notes of a Son and Brother* James related his discovery of himself as the man of imagination. Referring to his "imaginative passion," he writes, "Fed by every contact and every apprehension, and feeding in turn every motion and every act, wouldn't the light in which it might so cause the whole scene of life to unroll inevitably become as fine a thing as possible to represent?" (*NSB*, 369–70). In this sentence, the grammatical balance between the *fed* and *feeding* phrases points to a mutual conditioning between the imagination and its objects. Furthermore, the subject of the sentence is neither of these but rather the light in which the world is bathed for the imagination that conceives it. James's theme, then, is to be neither the consciousness nor the "swarming world," in isolation from each other, but the synthesis in which both of these exist. Again, his position is the phenomenological one that defines consciousness as consciousness *of* something that exists as its necessary correlate. James's precision in defining this phenomenological stance can be appreciated if we compare another passage, this one from *A Small Boy and Others*: "What I find in my path happens to be the fact of the sensibility, and from the light it sheds the curious, as also the common, things that did from occasion to occasion play into it seem each to borrow a separate and vivifying glow" (*SBO*, 222). Once again, neither the sensibility nor the things themselves but the light in which subject and object coalesce is his theme.

Thus the alternative to the (impossible) portrayal of the consciousness in itself will not be a simple notation of the details or features of the world that floated into James's view. There will be no attempt to get at an essence of these objects, apart from the way they appear. James is uninterested in debunking the small boy's consciousness. Instead, by seeking the essence of the objects *in* the way in which they appeared to consciousness, James will be able to fuse his telling and his showing. The only way to render the quality of a particular imagination is to ask *how* the world appears to (and in) it.

James tells us repeatedly that he lived just for the sake of gathering ap-

5. Roy Pascal, *Design and Truth in Autobiography* (Cambridge, Mass., 1960), 141.

pearances, sensations, or—the favorite word—impressions. As we have seen, his only desire was "just to *be* somewhere—almost anywhere would do—and somehow to receive an impression or an accession, feel a relation or a vibration" (*SBO*, 25). James's consciousness does not exist apart from the impressions it receives; he becomes a "plate for impressions," or a "plate of sense," which becomes "overscored and figured" (*NSB*, 346, 332). At times he speaks as if only the quantity of these impressions matters (their quality presumably being taken for granted); he seeks "an impressional harvest" (*NSB*, 5). This harvesting of impressions is in fact the chief process James's narrative records; the question of what purpose the impressions ultimately serve is deferred. As a boy, James writes, he took in the sights of Second Empire Paris "as if to store up, for all the world, treasures of impressions that might be gnawed, in seasons or places of want, like winter pears or a squirrel's hoard of nuts" (*NSB*, 60–61). The autobiography scarcely hints that the final goal of all the impressions is to be literary composition. "To feel a unity, a character and tone in one's impressions, to feel them related and all harmoniously coloured, that *was* positively to face the aesthetic, the creative, even, quite wondrously, the critical life and almost on the spot to commence author" (*NSB*, 24–25). It is perfectly characteristic of James that the creative and critical aspects of authorship grow up inseparably. In this passage he seems to offer a glimpse of that conversion of impressions into a created form that was the prime goal of the father's pedagogic method (*SBO*, 214–15). But the autobiography never offers a full account of the conversion of art to life. Like Wordsworth or Proust, James is writing a prelude to his literary career proper, so he limits himself to a study of the harvesting of experience, excluding any account of how that experience was converted into nourishment for his art.

The autobiography does not confine itself, however, to a simple narrative of the accumulation of impressions, a process that might remain amorphous and bewildering. Instead it does pursue at least the stage of the conversion of impressions into something else at which they begin to jell into scenes. *A Small Boy and Others* tells the humorous story of the "epoch-making" moment when the notion of the scene first dawned on the young boy. Visiting the home of some relatives where he met a young female cousin, James witnessed some misbehavior on the part of this girl which moved her mother to cry, "don't make a scene!" The revelation for James was immediate: "The expression, so vivid, so portentous, was one I had never heard—it had never been addressed to us at home; and who should say now what a world one mightn't at once read into it? It seemed freighted to sail so far; it told me so much about life. Life at these intensities clearly became 'scenes'; but the great thing, the immense illumination, was that we could make them or not as we chose" (*SBO*, 186). James thus traces his famous scenic sense to its origin in an infantile misunderstanding of a common figurative expression. Trouble results from his taking our ability to make scenes as being literally true. But the real grain of truth in the expression—the truth concerning our active participation in the creation of the scenes we witness—is pursued in many of James's mature meditations scattered through the autobiography.

One conclusion we might expect James to draw is that, whereas impressions themselves are simply given, it is only our imaginative power that can shape them into scenes. But James's actual solution is not so clear or consistent. In *The Middle Years* he suggests that even the wealth of impressions he gathered in London was somehow deserved, that he himself must have been capable of "some doing, as we nowadays say, to make them so well worth having." He concludes that "the virtue of the business was repeatedly, no doubt, a good deal more in what I brought than in what I took" (*MY*, 53). But this kind of ledger-book arithmetic—where any addition on the side of the subject means a subtraction on the side of the object—is finally inadequate to the phenomenological description James is actually performing. A passage like the following, though it begins with the ledger-book approach, moves on to a more satisfactory formulation: "There was no need for curiosity—it was met by every object, I seemed to see, so much more than half way; unless indeed I put it better by saying that as *all* my vision partook of that principle the impulse and the object perpetually melted together" (*NSB*, 305–306). This is indeed a better way of putting the relation because it places the emphasis on that common medium, the light in which subject and object are inseparably fused.

Moreover, the imaginative consciousness is not simply a dramatic author or director who creates scenes for the stage while himself remaining detached from them. Rather, the consciousness is itself the stage on which the scenes appear. The "young mind," James writes, was "arranged as a stage for the procession and exhibition of appearances'' (*SBO*, 182). Elsewhere, as he shifts the vehicles of his metaphor, the mind becomes the canvas of a painting (*SBO*, 28) or, as we have seen, a plate for the inscription of impressions. Whichever art James uses for his analogue, the mind itself is seen, not so much as the author of representations, but as their field or instrument. The opposition between raw data and representations (or between impressions and scenes) does not operate. Consciousness deals only with its own appearances; it is even constituted by those appearances. Again the principle presents itself that the autobiographical self can never be false in the sense of misrepresenting its own case, because whatever appears to it is its truth.

We still need to consider exactly how a scene is constituted. The autobiography provides many examples of scenic representation, although these are usually not so pure or sustained as the scenes in many Jamesian novels because they are mediated by the presence of the reminiscing narrator. But one thing James can do here that he cannot do in his novels is to reflect on scenes *as* scenes, to show how they come into being. Perhaps the best example of such reflection occurs in the passage in *A Small Boy and Others* describing how James, on his first childhood trip to the continent, discovered spontaneously that whole ''sense of Europe'' he had so long hungered after (*SBO*, 283–85). Recovering from a sickness and riding in an ''absurdly cushioned state'' in a carriage from Lyon to Geneva, ''I took in, as I have hinted, by a long slow swig that testified to some power of elbow, a larger draught of the wine of perception than any I had ever before owed to a single throb of that faculty.'' The experience culminates in his perception of two separate objects, an old, ruined tower and a colorfully dressed peasant woman, ''the effect of whose intervention just then is almost beyond my notation.'' The choice of terms here underlines James's ambivalence concerning the respective contributions in a given impression of the subject and the object. The peasant woman's intervention seems predesigned, providentially beyond James's control; yet he has just called attention to his own ''power of elbow'' in drinking in impressions. In any case the particular scene that results is one that requires James to formulate it: ''Supremely, in that ecstatic vision, was 'Europe,' sublime synthesis, expressed and guaranteed to me—as if by a mystic gage, which spread all through the summer air, that I should now, only now, never lose it, hold the whole consistency of it: up to that time it might have been but mockingly whisked before me.''

Here James succeeds in representing the operation of his imaginative faculty, even if he has to appeal, in a way now familiar, to the ineffability of the experience. The scene of Europe is constituted by an act of synthesis that is typical of the romantic imagination. It is also closely akin to the epiphanic moments found in Joyce, Woolf, and Proust, sharing with them not only ineffability but also the quality of conferring on the experience a sense of eternity that makes it recapturable. Moreover, the scene is epiphanic because it depends on a sense of ''something far more deeply interfused.'' The ruined tower and the peasant are not literal shapes only; they point to a meaning that is quite incommensurate with them: they embody Europe. James has performed what he declared in ''The Art of Fiction'' to be the habit of the imaginative mind, which, ''when you give it an inch, takes an ell.'' In that essay, he cited the example of a female English novelist, ''a woman of genius,'' who, having once had a glimpse of some young French Protestants around a table, had converted this impression into a tale that contained a study of French Protestantism (FN, 12–13).[6] Similarly, the young James takes an almost ludicrously banal pair of objects and turns them into the signifier for a signified of inexhaustible importance for his later life and art.

This is the most important feature of the imaginatively constituted scene for James: it is accompanied by the notion of its own significance. In phenomenological terms, the scene is the product of an intentional act that must be meaningful because it originates in consciousness. James tells us that his was ''an imagination to which literally everything obligingly signified'' (NSB, 360). No impression he receives can remain a mere matter of surface; he must immediately plunge into its depth. Writing of the summers he passed in Boulogne, he says that it was a place where he had ''a lively felt need that everything should represent something more than what immediately and all too blankly met the eye'' (SBO, 411). This need, as he sometimes acknowledges, could lead him into the error of imputing to a given object or event

6. For a discussion of James's theory of knowledge as gained through impressions in terms of phenomenology, see Paul Armstrong, *The Phenomenology of Henry James* (Chapel Hill, 1983), esp. 37–68.

a meaning it did not really possess: "I have to reckon, I here allow, with the trick of what I used irrepressibly to read into things in front of which I found myself, for gaping purposes, planted by some unquestioned outer force: it seemed so prescribed to me, so imposed on me, to read more, as through some ever felt claim for roundness of aspect and intensity of effect in represented matters, whatever they might be, that the conscience of the particular affair itself was perhaps developed enough to ask of it" (*NSB*, 219).

This time the "reading in" is not performed by James as narrator. The danger is not that the present narrative might falsify the past, but that the past was already split between a surface appearance and a deep meaning. Peter Brooks has recently described the element of melodrama in James, the tendency to apply pressure to every experience, to make it yield up an unstated depth of meaning. (Brooks also points out that this melodramatic sense is intimately allied with James's sense of scene as the place where meaning is both concealed and revealed.)[7] Such a tendency was apparently innate in James. He recognizes that he has always exercised "so elastic a fancy, so perverse a little passion for finding good in everything" that the retrospective disengagement of a scene in itself from what he read into it seems now "almost an act of violence" (*NSB*, 332). Yet he cannot help thinking that these "visionary liberties" he constantly took were simply a "harmless extravagance," nothing to disturb the essential truth of his narrative.

Thus James always sees a given scene as the objective correlative of a meaning that lurks behind or, more precisely, in it. But the particular meaning that emerges for any one scene is not always a specific one. In this respect the example just cited, where the tower and the peasant woman yielded the meaning Europe, is atypical. More often in the autobiography the sense of meaning that accompanies a scene remains just that: a sense, abstract and portentous.

Still, the meaning of the past experience is not something read into it, merely subjective in the bad sense. Our experience is given as scenic, as representative of itself and something else. Since this quality is already part of the experience, any later act of reconstruction (as in the autobiography) is not a subjective misapprehension of the past but a repetition of the same

7. Peter Brooks, *The Melodramatic Imagination* (New Haven, 1976), esp. 153–97.

kind of meaning-giving act that created the original experience. In discussing James's grasp of history in *The American Scene*, John Carlos Rowe has argued that for James the historian gives history its meaning; history is nothing outside of "the artistic act of making the past meaningful."[8] The writing of history, whether public or private, is indeed an act that assigns meaning, but the historical past is not devoid of meaning until it is treated by the historian; history writing is not an exercise in subjective idealism that must animate with its own concerns an inert, lifeless matter. For James historical consciousness is not creative in this absolute sense. Any history—at least, that is, human history—is suffused with self-consciousness and already has meaning inherent in it. The historian's act is not so much a creation of meaning as its re-creation or reconstruction. Certainly, James's personal history, which has been so thoroughly a history of consciousness, is a re-creative act.

It might seem, if the scene is totally constituted and provided with its significance from the outset, that the imagination is left out. But just the opposite is true. James does not accept any clear contrast between a faculty of receptivity and one of activity; as we have seen, he uses terms like *critical* and *creative* as virtual synonyms. Consequently, the imagination need not be seen as a power of pure creation *ex nihilo* in opposition to the merely passive or reproductive mental faculties. In line with the romantic conception of the imagination, James tends to see the imagination as a co-agent in the emergence of reality itself, or as a power that re-creates, and maintains in existence, the *données* of experience. Instead of being the absolute creator of an alternative, vicarious, and imaginary world, the imagination participates in the coming-into-appearance of the real world.

To express this conception, James speaks of the grasping or appropriating imagination. When he writes in a famous letter of 1871 about the "really *grasping* imagination" required to make America a fertile field for the novelist, he is referring to the possibility of grasping the *real* America, not a separate, fictitious one.[9] The imagination does not have to create a new

8. John Carlos Rowe, *Henry Adams and Henry James: The Emergence of a Modern Consciousness* (Ithaca, 1976), 136.

9. Henry James to Charles Eliot Norton, January 16, 1871, in Henry James, *Letters*, ed. Leon Edel (4 vols.; Cambridge, Mass., 1974–84), I, 252.

America out of nothing but rather to re-create for art the American scene that is already in front of it. Such a statement reveals why James remained more receptive to the imaginative realism of Balzac than to the homegrown naturalism of William Dean Howells, whom Jame criticizes in his letter. Howells does not succeed as Balzac does in synthesizing the critical and creative faculties. For James, criticism is just as grasping as the imagination is. "To criticize is to appreciate, to appropriate, to take intellectual possession, to establish in fine a relation with the criticised thing and make it one's own" (AN, 155). Almost all the terms James applies here to the critical or intellectual faculty are ones we have already seen him apply to the sensibility or the imagination. Especially familiar are the impulse to establish relations wherever possible and the desire for quantity almost for its own sake.

The vocabulary of appropriation is present in the autobiography as well. Everywhere James is interested in establishing a special relation to his experience, in making it his. "We seize our property by an avid instinct wherever we find it," he writes (SBO, 279). Of the mystery of "Parisianism" he says: "It was at all events, this mystery, one's property—that of one's mind; and so, once and for all, I helped myself to it from my balcony and tucked it away" (SBO, 281). Like the scene that becomes an epiphany, such experience becomes our property forever. This seizing and making into our own of objects from the outside world suggests a new kind of relation between the self and others. In seizing people or things outside of him, James makes them familiar, or as he also puts it, he assimilates them to himself. The narrative of the autobiography is called "a tale of assimilations small and fine" (SBO, 182).

The fact that many of the people James is writing about are dead seems to facilitate their assimilation. To a degree, the autobiography is, as I have said, a memorial to the circles of people in the midst of which James had lived. But to memorialize them means to reconstruct them, to give them a second life in represented form. James repeatedly imagines the dead as "beckoning ghosts" who solicit his attention as he passes among them, demanding that he use his literary memory to revivify them (NSB, 261). James becomes a latter-day Aeneas or Dante, descending to the underworld: "I confess I feel myself drag my mantle, right and left, from the clutch of suppliant hands" (NSB, 439). They turn to him lugubriously and ask, "What are you going to do for me?" (*NSB*, 283). What James can do for them is simply to "do" them, to render them for art, just as he "does" his fictional characters. Once he has translated them into a represented form, they have become his; he has appropriated them. Remembering his long-dead friend James Russell Lowell, James interrupts his narrative in order to observe: "For I can only see the ghosts of my friends, by this token, as 'my' J. R. L. and whoever; which means that my imagination, of the wanton life of which these remarks pretend but to form the record, has appropriated them, under the prime contact—from the moment the prime contact has successfully worked—once for all, and contributed the light in which they were constantly exposed" (*MY*, 95). The appropriation by the imagination thus works as well in the present as in the past. James must continue to appropriate *his* ghosts for his present narrative, and in doing so he repeats his appropriation of them while they were alive.

Appropriation, thus, is essential to representation, the process of making objects enter into new relations and become meaningful. "My face was turned from the first to the idea of representation—that of the gain of charm, interest, mystery, dignity, distinction, gain of the importance in fine, on the part of the represented thing (over the thing of accident, of mere actuality, still unappropriated)" (*SBO*, 263). Thus the appropriation of reality performed by the imagination is close to artistic representation, but it operates not in a fictive realm but upon the real itself. Consciousness is constantly converting impressions into scenes, raw objects into representations. Appropriation is the most innate impulse of imaginative consciousness.

As the appropriative faculty, the imagination is not simply a faculty that deals with a subordinate mode of experience, with the subjective or vicarious realms. Likewise, appropriation cannot be limited to that kind of behavior that some critics have isolated as the greatest moral crime that can be committed in James's universe.[10] The appropriation of one person by another—of the kind practiced by Gilbert Osmond, or perhaps by Adam Verver—is no doubt reprehensible, but only because it is a version of aesthetic appropriation that has gone wrong. (Both Osmond and Verver, we

10. See, for example, Quentin Anderson, *The American Henry James* (New Brunswick, 1957), 146–49.

may note, are degenerate artists: Osmond is a dilettante painter, Verver, a collector.) But for James, the man of imagination, imaginative appropriation of the world is a way of life. So, at any rate, the experience of the boy and young man represented in James's autobiography is depicted.

There are, however, limits to this kind of experience. Such a total identification of the imagination with consciousness would mean, as Charles Feidelson has pointed out, that James is making a claim for himself more extravagant than any put forward by the romantic poets.[11] If James's imagination were able to appropriate the whole of his world, then he could never possibly be in error about any event occurring in that world. He would never be forced to admit—as he does in *A Small Boy and Others*—that "what happened all the while, I conceive, was that I imagined things—and as if quite on system—wholly other than as they were" (*SBO*, 194). That such an error is possible shows that the imagination is not in such "*supreme* command" (*AN*, 310) as James might want to believe.

Another way to put the problem is that, if the impressions among which James lives are always already scenes and representations of themselves, then he is living his life as an "aesthetic phenomenon," to use Nietzsche's phrase, in *The Birth of Tragedy*, when he speaks of the only way life can be justified. Here, the word *aesthetic* has a meaning halfway between its etymological sense relating to perception and its modern sense relating to art. The aesthetic way of life for James is not necessarily to be equated with the production of works of art; on the contrary, the young James is not yet an active artist, and if his life takes on an aesthetic guise, it does so through the spontaneous, unconscious operation of his imagination. Yet the autobiography also shows that works by *other* artists did much to condition James's consciousness as an aesthetic one and even to promote a certain confusion between art and life. For how long can the autobiography depict this as benign confusion sponsored by the imagination before raising the question of whether it is an adequate or even a possible mode of existence?

Literature and the arts enter the life of the young Henry James at a precocious age. Even if in the opening pages of *A Small Boy and Others* he can remember a past that was "still bookless," later in the same paragraph his

11. Feidelson, "James and the 'Man of Imagination,'" 336–37.

principal memory concerning his grandmother is of her passion for reading popular novels (*SBO*, 4). Later, this volume is filled with a veritable stream of memories pertaining to the arts, especially novels and the stage. The latter was for the young Henry a particular source of wonder; he remembers how even the street placards announcing new plays appeared to him as "founts of romance" (*SBO*, 100). The central figure of the artistic world for Henry was Charles Dickens, "the great actuality of the current imagination" (*SBO*, 120). Not only were Dickens' novels familiar in the James household (he recalls not being able to hold back his tears one evening when he overheard his parents reading *David Copperfield* out loud—*SBO*, 118), but the theater too seems to have been dominated by dramatic adaptations of his works. The general onslaught of drama and fiction was so seductive and so rapid that James was unable to keep a critical distance. Dickens, he recalls, was thought to be beyond reproach; any criticism of him would have been "futile and tasteless" (*SBO*, 177).

Nor was aesthetic distance encouraged when, as sometimes happened, he met the authors of the books he was reading. Emerson and Thackeray, for example, visited his father in New York. James even met Dickens, at a literary dinner, and saw him as shrouded in a "sublimity of authorship" (*NSB*, 253–55). The real man appeared inseparable from the artist.

No wonder, then, that James inclined to confuse real people he met with fictional characters from books. "I doubtless put people 'into books' by very much the same turn of the hand with which I took them out," he writes (*NSB*, 145). James often sought to understand people he knew by finding fictional counterparts for them, that is, by taking them out of books. Thus his cousin Henry Wyckhoff and his aunt Helen, in their relation to each other, remind him of Mr. Dick and Miss Trotwood from *David Copperfield* (*SBO*, 145). The boardinghouse he lived in while a law student at Harvard is converted by his imagination into an American "maison Vauquer," out of *Le Père Goriot* (*NSB*, 306–307). In other cases, James put people into books, inventing fictional stories for them that would round out his imperfect knowledge of their lives. So, for example, the two Wyckhoffs and a third relative take roles in a private drama that James creates for them as he goes along, using for his own ends the few pieces of information about them he actually recalls. "So for the spectator did the figures distribute themselves; the three principal, on the large stage—it became a field of such spreading interests—well in front, and the accessory pair, all sympathy and zeal, prompt comment and rich resonance, hovering in the background" (*SBO*, 133–34). James's scenic imagination takes its cue from both real life and art (Thackeray had been invoked earlier) to convert an actual situation into a dramatic, representational one. Even people whose lives offer no apparent dramatic interest are considered for their scenic potential. James refers to one uncle who, try as hard as he might, presented no drama, no "case." He was a "blank," a "shade of nullity," a "spectral" figure (*SBO*, 135–36), resisting any attempt to convert him into a represented character.

These reciprocal shadings of life and art into each other can involve not only individuals but also an entire scene or place, especially in Europe, the sense of which was so deeply imbedded in James's imagination. He describes how his family arrived in Paris on one trip and, despite their belief in the supremacy of the Comédie-Française, neglected the theater almost entirely because "life in general, all around us, was perceptibly more theatrical" (*SBO*, 354). (In *The Ambassadors*, as we shall see later, Strether, when he gets to the Comédie-Française, finds life in the loges just as dramatic as what is on stage.) Conversely, when he visited the Louvre, James went not only for the art but for the rich spectacle of life it offered: "the house of life and the palace of art became so mixed and so interchangeable" (*SBO*, 351). As Stephen Donadio has written of the Louvre passage, "The details of actual experience seem to exist in two realms simultaneously, and the border between those realms no longer appears distinct: in this way the quality of actual experience is altered in direct proportion to the enhancement of the artistic illusion." [12]

Since life and art already overlap, the transporting of figures from real life into fiction does not constitute a unique case for the imagination. Beyond the example of Gilbert Osmond, who James admitted was modeled on his friend Francis Boott (*NSB*, 481–83), James discusses this kind of translation only once, and then it is in order to stress what was for him "the constant quick flit of association, to and fro, and through a hundred open doors,

12. Stephen Donadio, *Nietzsche, Henry James, and the Artistic Will* (New York, 1978), 255.

between the two great chambers (if it be not absurd, or even base, to separate them) of direct and indirect experience'' (*NSB*, 436). So far is James from feeling a gulf between art and life that he considers it an intellectual and moral error to contrast them. Instead he believes in the ''interpenetration,'' the mutual ''borrowing and lending,'' between the two realms (*NSB*, 435).

This attitude accords with what I have already described as James's romantic conception of the imagination. If the role of the imagination is not only to build a vicarious world of fancy but also to aid in constructing the real world, then James indeed has the power to ignore the division between art and life, to invent fictional dramas to explain the lives of his acquaintances, or to see them as analogous to figures he has met in art. He has given such absolute authority to his imagination that he is no longer obliged to distinguish what is present from what is absent, what is perceived from what is fancied. But is there no limit to this hegemony of the imagination? Is there no case where an imaginative construct of reality might come up against something that resists it or challenges its interpretation of what is true?

We can witness the increasing urgency of these questions in the way James treats the important theme of Europe. This theme is also a good test case for the imagination and its ability to appropriate reality, because Europe exists both as a sense of something in the child Henry's mind and as something ''out there,'' which he eventually visits. It can be confronted both in the imagination and in the flesh, both *in absentia* and *in praesentia*. As we have seen, during most of James's childhood, Europe is a goal in the distance. It is finally attained in the two trips (depicted in the autobiography as one long trip) made by the family between 1855 and 1860. But at age seventeen James returned home to America, not to cross the sea again until he made his first adult voyage to Europe at the end of the 1860s. The difference between these two trips as represented in the autobiography, then, seems to be roughly the difference between an episode belonging to childhood and one belonging to adulthood; they represent two different situations for the imagination.

When the twelve-year-old Henry accompanied his family to Europe, he had a head start on the experience. Even in America he had attended to ''the 'European' value'' of objects around him, sometimes to the neglect of things that were ''close at hand'' or domestic (*SBO*, 240, 84). The James household was saturated with European memories, allusions, and culture. Life in New York was almost an extension of life in London or Paris; the boy could read the latest issue of the *Revue des deux mondes* or meet Thackeray in his father's parlor. To live in America under these circumstances was already in part to live vicariously in Europe. Thus the first sojourn in Europe, when it actually came, was something the young boy was ready to assimilate with ease. As we have seen, the first scene of Europe coalesced immediately, by synecdoche, out of two meager data. It was the well-prepared imagination that allowed for this economical grasp of the whole concept of Europe. The direct experience of the old world, finally, did not differ from the indirect experience of it already acquired in America: what the young James saw in London when he finally got there was "extraordinarily the picture and the scene of Dickens" (*SBO*, 304).

The later trip recounted (abortively) in *The Middle Years* came after childhood, even at the end of youth. The *Notes of a Son and Brother* had ended with the death of Minnie Temple in 1870, which was said to mark "the end of our youth." But when he began to dictate the third volume, James quickly qualified this abrupt periodization of his life: "If the author of this meandering record has noted elsewhere that an event occurring early in 1870 was to mark the end of his youth, he is moved here at once to qualify in one or two respects that emphasis. Everything depends in such a view on what one means by one's youth—so shifting a consciousness is this, and so related at the same time to so many different matters" (*MY*, 1). Even while James changes *our* youth to *his* youth, thus separating himself from William and suggesting the greater degree of independence in which he would live thenceforth, he hesitates to assign the subsequent events to his adulthood; they still, perhaps, seem to him too other. This ambivalence suggests that the 1869 trip to England formed a transitional moment between youth and adulthood and thus stands for a pivotal moment in the life of the imagination. There is in fact good reason in the narrative to regard it as such.

At the outset the tone of this trip resembles that of the first, although it is a bit more self-conscious. Even more than the first time, Europe is already familiar to the youthful James: it is felt "in no degree as strange or obscure," and as "far from impenetrable" (*MY*, 8). James enjoys an almost Platonic sense of recollection or recognition of the London displayed before him, which derives from two sources: "Recognition, I dare say, was what remained, through the adventure of the months to come, the liveliest principle at work; both as bearing on the already known, on things unforgotten and of a sense intensely cultivated and cherished from my younger time, and on the imagined, the unimagined and the unimaginable" (*MY*, 7). Memory and imagination are the two sources of the recognition, but in the "soft confusion" (as he had put it before) of the retrospective consciousness, they become indistinguishable. Whichever faculty was at work, London seemed familiar, even transparent to him, so that "appropriation became thus eager and romance thus easy" (*MY*, 6). James recalls possessing "a consciousness not other than that of a person abruptly introduced into a preoccupied and animated circle and yet so miraculously aware of matters conversed about as to need no word of explanation before joining in" (*MY*, 8–9). Whereas James earlier seemed to resemble his own character Stransom in his dedication to the memory of the dead, he now behaves like Ralph Pendrell of *The Sense of the Past* when the latter is plunged back into the past through a peculiar sort of metempsychosis and finds that he has a double consciousness allowing him to live alternately in the present and the past. The romance of James's situation consists in this almost supernatural expansion of the individual consciousness to fathom and assimilate a reality that would normally be alien and recalcitrant to it.

But this early familiarity, so like his childish first impressions of Europe, soon gives way to a feeling of less transparency, of less perfect adequation between his imagination and reality. Already in Chapter 1, James begins to cast doubt on his own claim to total understanding: "It was doubtless a part of total fatuity, and perhaps its sublimest mark, that I knew what everything meant, not simply then but for weeks and months after, and was to know less only with increase of knowledge" (*MY*, 8). What is meant by this paradoxical knowledge that grows smaller and larger at the same time? The implication is that the knowledge furnished by his imagination or memory of London did not conform to the new knowledge presented through actual perception. The real, current London, as he comes to know it, undermines his supposed foreknowledge of it. James's appropriation of London turns out to be reversible; he can after all be dispossessed of his intellectual and imaginative property.

James's meeting with Alfred Lord Tennyson later in the volume corroborates this inference and gives a concrete example of the process involved. It is all the more telling because it counterbalances the meeting with Dickens in the *Notes of a Son and Brother*, where, as we saw, Dickens was described as beyond criticism, as "the great actuality of the current imagination." James encountered not the man but the legend; he captured "the essence of the hour," and his "subsequently panting imagination" could scarcely catch up with all that had been implied in the "prodigious glimpse" (*NSB*, 255–56). The imaginary Dickens swept the real Dickens along with him and survived the meeting.

In contrast to the almost elegiac solemnity of the Dickens passage, the meeting with Tennyson in the final volume is narrated in a tone of easy satire. James tells the humorous story of attending dinner in the home of Tennyson, and of the poet's failure to recognize the American ambassador, James Russell Lowell, who was one of his dinner guests. But the climax of the Tennyson recollections comes when James is treated to a private reading of "Locksley Hall" by its author. The reading, however, fails of its desired effect on James: "He had not got a third of the way through Locksley Hall . . . before I had begun to wonder that I didn't wonder, didn't at least wonder more consumedly; as a very little while back I should have made sure of my doing on any such prodigious occasion" (*MY*, 104). The trouble was, James concluded, that the poet "was not Tennysonian" (*MY*, 105). James devotes several pages to explaining the effect upon himself of this peculiar discovery. "I remember that I saw the Tennyson directly presented as just utterly other than the Tennyson indirectly," and he was obliged to recognize that "there had been folly somewhere." He draws the moral: "The fond prefigurements of youthful piety are predestined more often than not, I think, experience intervening, to strange and violent shocks; from which no general appeal is conceivable save by the prompt preclusion either of faith or of knowledge, a sad choice at the best" (*MY*, 87–92).

The Middle Years breaks off not long after this episode, and it is tempting to see more than a coincidence in this fact. It is as though the autobiography had to stop at this point not only because James found it impossible to narrate his story as an individual, separate from his family but also because the moment of disenchantment that his story was beginning to touch upon was radically out of harmony with the story of childhood imagination he had told so far. With experience intervening, he could no longer have relied on the adequation of imagination to reality that had made the narration of his childhood such a pleasure for him. The new Europe, that of his adult years, eluded the grasp of his imagination and might have asserted itself at the expense of his narrative.

The autobiography thus narrates only the child's consciousness, with its otherness and its romance steeped in the imagination. The division between the childhood and the adult experience is not necessarily easy to locate, however. The equivocation James displayed at the end of the second and the beginning of the third volumes as to where to place the limit of his youth suggests that this division is not strictly chronological but is a function of the individual's particular way of seeing the world. A similar confusion between the different stages of the imaginative life can be found in many of James's fictional characters. Several of the precocious children in the novels, like Maisie in *What Maisie Knew* and Nanda Brookenham in *The Awkward Age*, reach a distinctly adult vision while some of the nominal adults, of whom Strether is perhaps the preeminent example, still have the imagination of the child.

In his autobiography, James prefers to remain within a single stage of the imagination, a stage represented as belonging to the child. The autobiography shows little of the critical spirit that animates the novels when they analyze, and partially undermine, the childlike or otherwise limited consciousness of protagonists like Isabel Archer, Maisie, or Strether. If we compare the autobiography to the fiction in this respect, it must be admitted that the autobiography retains a certain flavor of romance, which the fiction usually avoids and which stems from James's acquiescence, or indulgence, in his own childhood vision of the world. The great benefit of such an acquiescence, no doubt, lies in James's brilliant rendering of his earlier consciousness and its world, but this success must be weighed against a difficulty inherent in the autobiographical narrative of which James was well aware, at least in works of fiction. The "double privilege of subject and object" can be abused when the subject is unwilling or unable to separate itself

distinctly from the object of its investigation. Toward the end of the autobiography, in the interrupted *Middle Years*, James appears on the brink of
such a step, but in the end he prefers the note of elegy, romance, and pathos
to that of critique.

4

THE PREFACES
Criticism and Autobiography

J AMES WROTE the Prefaces for the New York Edition of his works
between 1906 and 1908; chronologically they come between the three
novels of his "major phase" and the three volumes of autobiography.
These Prefaces, which accompanied James's rewriting of practically his
complete works, have rarely been viewed as a literary work in their own
right.[1] Instead, critics have usually gone to them either for the author's own
comments on specific novels or tales or for a Jamesian theory of the novel.
The Prefaces do lend themselves to both of these uses, but only in limited
ways. As commentaries on the fictional works, they can be maddeningly
elusive; they focus far more attention on technical, often abstract questions
than on the thematic content of the work at hand. Even when James does
discuss this content, he often does so with reference to the source or germ
of the story (for instance, to the way it took shape in his notebooks) rather
than to the finished version.[2]

1. The most important exception to this tradition is Laurence Holland, who devotes a section of his work on James to the Prefaces. Holland, *The Expense of Vision: Essays on the Craft
of Henry James* (Princeton, 1964), 155–82. Leon Edel discusses the writing of the Prefaces in
his *Henry James: The Master* (Philadelphia, 1972), 330–33. See also Mutlu Konuk Blasing,
The Art of Life: Studies in American Autobiographical Literature (Austin, 1977), 55–76.

2. For James's use of his notebooks while composing his Prefaces, see F. O. Matthiessen's Introduction to the *Notebooks* (*NB*, xi–xii).

Critics from Percy Lubbock to Wayne Booth and beyond have been interested in extracting from the Prefaces a general theory of the novel. Most of the Jamesian concepts now enjoying wide currency—point of view, the organic form of fiction, and the center of consciousness, for example—come from the Prefaces. This borrowing of concepts is certainly legitimate on its own terms, but it does not do full justice to the Prefaces themselves. It presupposes that the rhetorical mode of these essays is purely expository, so that an enumeration of their topics and themes is sufficient to exhaust their interest.

On the contrary, at least ever since R. P. Blackmur brought the Prefaces together in book form in 1934, it has been possible to see that they do indeed form a single work, which does not merely present an argument but enacts a story of its own. In fact these essays make up not simply a book of criticism about James's fictional works but a new narrative that in many ways repeats or prolongs those earlier fictional works. The Prefaces explicitly assume the character of a narrative, even in their opening paragraph, where James calls them a "thrilling tale" or (later) when he refers to them as "the story of one's story" (AN, 313).[3] Moreover, the Prefaces use certain common novelistic devices: a first-person narrator, who is of course James himself (a point to which I shall return), and an abundance of invented dialogue.[4] Finally, they contain a rich imagistic and figurative language that is comparable in scope and function to that found in James's late novels.

There is good reason, then, to regard the Prefaces not as a critical metalanguage but as a new version of a literary narrative, which not only comments on but repeats the devices of the earlier language of the author's fiction. Yet, if we begin to read the Prefaces as a new literary fiction, we rapidly run up against yet another aspect of the essays' rhetorical mode. Throughout the Prefaces, James is clearly asserting that his language is not fictional, that it has an authentic referential function. The narrative the Prefaces embody is intended to be the story of the author, Henry James, as a creator of literary

3. All references to the Prefaces, in this chapter, are to *The Art of the Novel*, cited parenthetically in the text by page number only.

4. Dialogue can be found on *AN*, 3–4, 64, 106, 112, 116, 134, 168, 173–74, 182, 222–25, and 269.

narratives. The story of the novels' composition is not only their story but James's too, the "history of the growth of one's imagination" (47).

This last phrase, virtually identical to the expression James would use in the *Notes of a Son and Brother*, reveals this series of essays as a preface not only to the novels and tales but also to the more formal autobiography James was to begin writing a few years later. The Prefaces are meant to be genuine—if partial—autobiography, not just a new fictional narrative. It is for this reason, presumably, that they, like the later autobiography, can use the first person with relative impunity, whereas long works of fiction cannot; despite the first person, James has no intention of wallowing in the romance of his own isolated selfhood. We have seen that one important way in which he tempered the romance of the autobiography was by insisting on his relations with others, to the point of claiming to write filial and brotherly autobiography. In the Prefaces, James is equally intent on finding an objective topic or external occasion for writing about himself. Here the occasion is offered not by other people but by the reappearance of his own works.[5] His novels and stories are outside of him—hence objective—but they are also uniquely related to him. On the final page of the Prefaces James will argue that artistic works have a unique value for the artist's personal history because "our relation to them is essentially traceable" (348). This relation, rather than the novels and tales in themselves, is what the Prefaces are mainly about.

Consequently, the status of the Prefaces is even more complicated, in its own way, than was that of the autobiography. In the Prefaces James is practicing both an intrinsic, formalist criticism of his works and an extrinsic, referential history of himself as imaginative author. This mixed situation accounts for the diverse, even diametrically opposed, appraisals of the Prefaces made by their readers. At one extreme Leo Bersani has been able to see them as a kind of protostructuralist manifesto: "James should be continually proposed as a model for structuralist criticism. For the Prefaces are the best example I know of a criticism that constantly draws our attention away from the referential aspect of a work of art—its prolongations into reality—

5. *Cf.* Charles Feidelson, "James and the 'Man of Imagination,'" in Frank Brady, John Palmer, and Martin Price (eds.), *Literary Theory and Structure* (New Haven, 1973), 347.

and toward its structural cohesion, which is taken as its principal source of inspiration.'' At the other extreme René Wellek, looking to the Prefaces for a theory of criticism, has found their theory overshadowed by autobiographical intrusions: ''The *Prefaces*, as a totality, judged as criticism, are disappointing; they are, no doubt, of great interest to the student of James's life and career as a writer, and they have the almost unique distinction of being an author's extended commentary on his own work. But the *Prefaces* are primarily reminiscences and commentaries and not criticism.''[6]

That both of these reactions have their grain of truth can be seen from the way James intermingles formal and autobiographical concerns even in the first paragraph of the first Preface, where he sets out what will be his relation to his former works in the essays that follow:

> This revival of an all but extinct relation with an early work may often produce for an artist, I think, more kinds of interest and emotion than he shall find it easy to express. . . . This accordingly is what I mean by the contributive value—or put it simply as, to one's own sense, the beguiling charm— of the *accessory* facts in a given artistic case. This is why, as one looks back, the private history of any sincere work, however modest its pretentions, looms with its own completeness in the rich, ambiguous aesthetic air, and seems at once to borrow a dignity and to mark, so to speak, a station. . . . Addicted to ''stories'' and inclined to retrospect, he [the artist] fondly takes, under this backward view, his whole unfolding, his process of production, for a thrilling tale, almost for a wondrous adventure, only asking himself at what stage of remembrance the mark of the relevant will begin to fail. He frankly proposes to take this mark everywhere for granted. (3–4)

The judicial image of accessory facts shows that, however great may be their contribution to the formalist study of narrative technique, the primary interest of the Prefaces for James lies outside the pale of intrinsic criticism. The fictional stories have their own ''private history'' that necessarily connects them with their author, whose ''process of production'' is involved. It is the retelling of this story of the genesis of the novels that becomes the

6. Leo Bersani, ''Le Mensonge jamesien,'' in *Poétique*, XVII (1974), 51, my translation; René Wellek, *A History of Criticism, IV: The Later Nineteenth Century* (New Haven, 1965), 213–14.

"thrilling tale" told in the Prefaces and makes them both critical and autobiographical at once.

The coexistence of these two goals produces an ambivalence in the mode of the narrative. As critical essays discussing works of fiction, the Prefaces take artistic representation as their principal theme. Notions like realism, intensity of illusion, and representational value almost always underlie the more particular qualities James attributes to successful fiction—economy, organic form, consistent point of view, and the rest. As autobiographical essays, they are premised on the referentiality of their language, that is, their ability to refer to the history of James and his career as an imaginative author. The strategy of the essays is to conflate these two kinds of narrative. On the one hand, the Prefaces claim to represent James the author, just as his novels represented fictional characters; on the other hand, they seek to place his fictional representations (the novels and tales) squarely within the real, referential history of the author. In other words, James himself appears to be drawn into the realm of fiction even while his fictional works are being resituated as events in reality. James seems to point to this conflation of the two dimensions of the essays when he calls them "re-representation" (335). The result is that artistic representation, or mimesis, is the performative mode of the Prefaces as well as their principal subject matter; they accomplish an act of mimesis even while discussing mimesis as a technical and aesthetic issue in the novels.

The central position of mimesis within the theory of fiction presented in the Prefaces has often been recognized, of course. But it has been less often recognized that, on an explicit thematic level, James subjects his theory of mimesis to numerous qualifications and even contradictions. If in his earlier critical essays James always saw the novelist as the "painter of life," in the Prefaces he appears more conscious than ever that literary mimesis is an illusion produced by a set of highly self-conscious technical devices and dependent upon the particular qualities of the verbal medium. For example, even while he continues in the Prefaces to uphold an organicist theory according to which the work of art imitates life by being formed like a natural object, he puts this very theory into question by constantly referring to artifice and technique, to the necessity of various nonorganic devices like foreshortening, misplaced middles, and dissimulation. Or again, his assertion that art springs from the "garden of life" (312) is contradicted else-where when he describes art as an "alchemical" transformation that arises only out of the negation of the "form" of life (230; see also 337). Thus the Prefaces taken as a whole exhibit a tension between mimetic and antimi-metic hypotheses comparable to the tension between a critical metalanguage and a literary or fictional language.

This ambivalence in the theoretical discussions is bound to affect the au-tobiographical goal James is pursuing at the same time. His antimimetic de-scriptions of literary artifice may also put into question the authenticity of his present claim to be portraying or representing his own history as a cre-ative author. The factual accuracy of James's narrative is not the primary issue. (There are in fact several inaccuracies in dating and other matters, but these do not seriously jeopardize the value of the story James tells.) The real issue is whether the present James, as narrating self, can be a faithful re-porter on the earlier James, the experiencing self who wrote the novels. Can he understand that former self, both coincide with it and dominate it so as to be able to tell its story as a coherent narrative containing a teleological pattern?[7] James's relation to his earlier self must be an intersubjective one, as it would later be in the autobiography, but in the Prefaces this intersub-jectivity is further complicated by the fact that James's access to his former self must work through the path of literary criticism; the occasion for his self-representation must be the discussion of his works.

Because of this close relation in the Prefaces between literary criticism and autobiography, it will be convenient to begin by looking at an issue cen-tral to James's criticism of his novels that will also have repercussions for the question of his own autobiographical relation to his former self. This is the issue of subjectivity as it operates in the novels and particularly as it is embodied in the centers of consciousness. What James says of these char-acters and their mode of consciousness will turn out to be doubled at the level of James himself in his two roles as author of the novels and narrator of the Prefaces.

The importance of the reflector or center of consciousness for the theory

7. *Cf.* Blasing, who argues that James's retrospection itself produces the sense of a nec-essary pattern in his career. *The Art of Life*, 58–59.

of fiction of the Prefaces is too well known to require much demonstration. A typical statement is James's admission that "I never see the *leading* interest of any human hazard but in a consciousness (on the part of the moved and moving creature) subject to fine intensification and wide enlargement" (67). This consciousness becomes the center of the fictional work, which "remains in equilibrium by having found its centre, the point of command of all the rest. From this centre the subject has been treated, from this centre the interest has spread, and so, whatever else it may or may not do, the thing has acknowledged a principle of composition and contrives at least to hang together" (15). As structural center, the leading consciousness is responsible for the formal integrity of the work, and James also implies that it is fundamental to the very possibility of representation. All mimetic virtues, such as clarity, intensity, and visibility, depend upon it (254–56).

This insistence on the technique of point of view thus turns the fiction into a phenomenology of the subject. At the most basic level, James reads his novels as exercises in a phenomenology of perception. His reflecting characters are "intense perceivers" (71). Of Strether he says that "he now at all events *sees*: so that the business of my tale and the march of my action, not to say the precious moral of everything, is just my demonstration of this process of vision" (308). From *The Portrait of a Lady*, James singles out a scene (the famous Chapter 42) which, he claims, is worth more than twenty incidents because it is a sustained act of pure consciousness: "It is a representation of her motionlessly *seeing*, and an attempt withal to make the mere still lucidity of her act as 'interesting' as the surprise of a caravan or the identification of a pirate" (57). Passages like these obviously reflect James's preference for being over doing, a preference of which we saw ample evidence in the autobiography. *Seeing* clearly stands for a state that has more to do with self-consciousness and understanding than with physical vision, but the metaphor of seeing is striking precisely because it equates cognition with lucidity of perception.

This identification of consciousness with perception also applies, in the language of the Prefaces, to the situation of the novelist himself. The vision belonging to the fictional character is not only his but also the author's window on the world. This window belongs to the house of fiction, the most famous image in the Prefaces for the author's relation to his fictional world:

> The house of fiction has in short not one window, but a million—a number
> of possible windows not to be reckoned, rather; every one of which has been
> pierced, or is still pierceable, in its vast front, by the need of the individual
> vision and by the pressure of the individual will. . . . The spreading field, the
> human scene, is the "choice of subject"; the pierced aperture, either broad
> or balconied or slit-like or low-browed, is the "literary form"; but they are,
> singly or together, as nothing without the posted presence of the watcher—
> without, in other words, the consciousness of the artist. (46)

This passage forcefully claims that the subject matter of the fiction and its form are secondary to the quality of the artist's vision, which is clearly the ultimate source and prototype for the perceptions achieved by the characters within the work.

The author, like his reflecting characters, is essentially a viewer, posted at the window of his consciousness, and just as the character sees his experience as an object, the author sees his characters. In some instances this act is all that is required for the germination of a fictional work in the author's mind. Of the inception of his story "The Pupil," James writes, "No process and no steps intervened; I *saw*, on the spot, little Morgan Moreen" (151). Again, of Hyacinth Robinson in *The Princess Casamassima*, he remarks, "I had had for a long time well before me, at any rate, my small obscure but ardent observer of the 'London world,' saw him roam and wonder and yearn" (71). Just how long James had had this figure before him and just how closely the experience of Hyacinth was modeled on his own, can be measured once we recognize in this description the young Henry James himself, the young boy who was forever taking in London in *A Small Boy and Others*. James is explicit about this autobiographical link: "I arrived so at the history of little Hyacinth Robinson—he sprang up for me from the London pavement. To find his possible adventure interesting I had only to conceive his watching the same public show, the same innumerable appearances, I had watched myself" (60). In the case of Hyacinth most explicitly perhaps, but in the case of all the other reflectors too, these characters become the author's "concrete deputy or delegate" because he delegates to them his own power of imaginative vision (327).

One more crucial step remains to be taken, the step that leads from James at the moment he wrote the novels to the present James who is composing an autobiographical narrative built up out of those acts of authorship. It is here that the thematic discussion dealing with the art of writing fiction is doubled at the performative level of James's enterprise in the Prefaces. We have seen that James underscores this doubling by describing his current endeavor as a rerepresentation, raising the author's original mimetic act to a second power. This chain of representations is kept intact because the business of the Prefaces is, once again, a simple act of vision, or rather of ''revision.'' The Prefaces themselves and the monumental rewriting of much of his earlier fiction amount to a ''revision'' in the punning senses of ''editing, correcting,'' and of ''seeing again.''[8] James's ploy is to reduce the first of these meanings to the second: ''To revise is to see, or to look over, again—which means in the case of a written thing neither more nor less than to re-read it. I had attached to it, in a brooding spirit, the idea of re-writing—with which it was to have in the event, for my *conscious* play of mind, almost nothing in common. . . . Where I had thus ruefully prefigured two efforts there proved to be but one—and this an effort but at the first blush'' (339).

These lines signal the crucial moment when the Prefaces turn back upon themselves as James seeks to define the status of his current writing and his relation to his former authorial self. His manifest desire is to reduce, if not annihilate, the gap separating him now from that previous self. The prospect of rewriting, with its suggestion of great effort and, more important, of a possible infidelity to or misrepresentation of the past text, had provoked a strong sense of foreboding. Just as in the autobiography, however, where the threat of a violation of the past was overcome by the realization that the present and the past were essentially related in such a way that the former was only an outgrowth of the latter, here the threatening act of rewriting has turned out to be nothing more than an act of rereading, that is, reading what was already there on the page.

This theory of rewriting as a simple, passive act of rereading, or seeing again, thus lends support to an important theme of the autobiographical practice in the Prefaces, that of the organic connection between James's past

8. On James's rewriting as a form of rereading, see Walter Benn Michaels, ''Writers Reading: James and Eliot,'' *Modern Language Notes*, XCI (1976), 827–49.

and present selves. The perusal of his old works allows the author to ''retrace the whole growth of one's taste'' and to ''hold the silver clue to the whole labyrinth of his consciousness'' (340). The literary work is the result of an act that is not over once and for all but is as ''continuous and persistent and unquenchable'' as consciousness itself (347). Among the acts due to our intelligence there exist ''no arbitrary, no senseless separations'' (347). Thus the present rewriting is by necessity faithful to the original text, even while altering it. To express this faithful continuity between the stages of composition, James uses the organic image of a flower. ''The act of revision, the act of seeing it again, caused whatever I looked at on the page to flower before me as into the only terms that honorably expressed it'' (339), and again, ''The term that superlatively, that finally 'renders,' is a flower that blooms by a beautiful law of its own'' (342).

This argument for the organic necessity of the revisions James made of his earlier novels has not always convinced his critics. One rather well known example of a revision of *The American* will suffice to show why. Where in the original version (1876) James had written of his hero that ''he was cleanly shaved,'' the description that spontaneously blossomed into view for him thirty years later was: ''he spoke, as to cheek and chin, of the joy of the matutinal steel.''[9] There is room for differing critical opinion about the aesthetic success of such apparently arbitrary rewriting as this. Yet we are in a sense forced to accept James's word that such revision presented itself to him not as an arbitrary or aggressive act of rewriting but as a mere rereading of what was already there. ''The 'old' matter,'' James insists, ''is there, re-accepted, re-tasted, exquisitely re-assimilated and re-enjoyed'' (339). If any act is involved, it is what the author calls ''this infinitely interesting and amusing *act* of re-appropriation'' (336). *Appropriation* here, as in the autobiography, is the act of consciousness that grasps what is outside of it, but in a way that does not violate or misrepresent its data. In the present passage, *reappropriation* means, first, repossession of the work by its author who re-creates or reassimilates it and claims it again for his own. But just as important, it means also a reappropriation by the author of his own past, or his past self. Appropriation, then, complements and completes the task

9. Cited by Leon Edel, *Henry James: The Master*, 328.

of representation. The autobiographical mission of the Prefaces is not only to represent the past self in the form of a narrative but to reintegrate that self into the larger present consciousness of the reminiscing author.

So far we have remained within a phenomenology of perception that has led from the reflector's grasp of his fictional surroundings to the author's grasp of his fictional world and, finally, to James's present "revision" of his entire imaginative history. But the Prefaces cannot remain totally within such an "*absolute* of perception" (151). They cannot construct a narrative out of acts of pure vision, any more than the autobiography could. In order to write "the story of one's story," James needs conflict, he needs different moments to form a linear pattern, whether or not those moments can then be dialectically subsumed or taken up into a retrospective order. But the narrative James ends by constructing is a peculiarly complex and ambivalent one, in part because of the ambivalent status and goals of the Prefaces themselves and also because of the intractable nature of James's subject matter and his unwillingness to conceal or simplify the problems of narrative with which he is dealing. James is clearly confronting in these essays the difficulty of constructing any narrative whatsoever. At the level of the composition of the original novels, he must deal with the relation between character (conceived primarily as consciousness) and plot (everything that hems in, or opposes, consciousness). At the level of composition of the Prefaces, he must confront their reliance on the notion of authorial intention and the respective roles of memory and imagination in recovering that intention. Finally, James is concerned about the central notion of representation itself and the tension between the ways in which representation operates in the Prefaces at the levels of thematic statement and performance.

We have already begun to see how James privileges consciousness over the incidents that impinge upon it and how this privileging leads to his account of the way in which a fictional character may see, or cognitively grasp, the entire situation in which he finds himself. The Prefaces appear, indeed, to have a large stake in maintaining this priority of character over its determination by outward plot.

It is instructive to compare James's treatment of character and plot in the Prefaces with his treatment of the same topic in his earlier writings. In the essays collected in *Partial Portraits* (1888), where he developed the view of the novel as an organic whole, James argued basically for the mutual determination of character and plot. As a well-turned dictum from "The Art of Fiction" puts it, "what is character but the determination of incident? What is incident but the illustration of character?" (*FN*, 15–16). In the chapter on Ivan Turgenev, he raised the question of the proper balance to be struck between portraits of individuals and composition, or plot structure, in a novel.[10] Noting the Russian's self-proclaimed method of starting a novel with nothing but "the figure of an individual, or a combination of individuals," James recognizes the "want of 'architecture' "—in other words, of composition—that may attend this method. He praises Scott and Balzac because they keep character and composition in equilibrium, a virtue no doubt related to that other great merit we have already seen James point to in the same authors, their success in steering a middle course between romance and realism (*PP*, 314–15).

Another early discussion of character versus plot or structure occurs not in an essay but in *The Portrait of a Lady* (1881). This example is especially instructive because we can compare it directly to what James had to say in the Preface to this novel, a quarter century later.[11] In the famous debate between Isabel and Madame Merle in Chapter 19 of the novel, Isabel upholds the absolute independence of the self against Madame Merle's insistence on "the whole envelope of circumstances" in which one lives. Although the debate does not concern plot in the strict sense, it is certainly centered on the opposition between character as a pure, self-subsistent consciousness and the external circumstances or structure of events in which character finds itself. In essence, it is the same debate that James conducted with himself in the autobiography between the concept of an autonomous self and that of a self dependent for its definition on others. In the novel, it is Madame Merle who has the last word and appears to dominate, while Isabel is made to look somewhat naïvely idealistic.

10. For a description of this conflict in terms of the contrast between pictorial and dramatic modes or, more broadly, between pictorial mimesis and structural integrity, see Holland, *The Expense of Vision*, 120–26.

11. For a discussion of the tensions in the Prefaces and *The Portrait of a Lady* between the novel of consciousness and the social novel, see Feidelson, "The Moment of *The Portrait of a Lady*," in *The Portrait of a Lady*, ed. Robert D. Bamberg (New York, 1975), 741–51.

This makes it all the more interesting that, in the much later Preface, James sides with Isabel. He does so, not by referring expressly to the dialogue between his heroine and Madame Merle, but by constructing a narrative about how he composed the novel that repeats the terms of his characters' debate. "Trying to recover here, for recognition, the germ of my idea, I see that it must have consisted not at all in any conceit of a 'plot,' nefarious name, in any flash, upon the fancy, of a set of relations . . . but altogether in the sense of a single character" (42). After invoking (once again) the example of Turgenev, for whom a novel always began with "the vision of some person or persons," James feels sufficiently emboldened to put forth the priority of character over plot as a general principle: "I was myself so much more antecedently conscious of my figures than of their setting—a too preliminary, a preferential interest in which struck me as in general such a putting of the cart before the horse" (44).

As against the careful, almost classical balance maintained between character and plot in the essays from *Partial Portraits*, James has now decidedly tipped that balance in favor of character. It is not that the ideal of organic wholeness has altered for James in the intervening quarter century but only that its source and locus in the fictional work have changed. Whereas in the earlier essays the fusion of character and plot ensured the organic quality of the novel, in the Prefaces character itself becomes the prime category in which form and content, or consciousness and incident, are united. In calling plot a "nefarious name" and in siding (in effect) with his own character Isabel in support of the priority of her self-consciousness, he is not only making a comment on the formalist issue of point of view in the novel. His comments also work on the level of the representational task in the Prefaces, that is, the level of the story of the author's composition of his novels. At this level, the priority of character becomes a temporal priority, which turns James's account of his composition into an authentic narrative containing at least two moments: the germ of character precedes plot. This small narrative thus contributes to what James shortly afterward calls the history of his imagination. Moreover, it serves that history well by suggesting that the creative imagination always deals originally with something that is akin to it—character or pure consciousness—rather than with the opaque matter of plot or incident.

Yet, despite his desire to assert the priority, both temporal and formal, of character over plot, James has been forced to bring up the latter's ''nefarious name'' and has in fact made it into one of the constituent moments in his story of the novel's germination. From this point on, it will be difficult for him to preserve character in a pure, undetermined state in which plot can merely befall it as an accident from outside. In fact, even in this same discussion, James admits that a character seen in total isolation from any ''set of relations'' would have difficulty in attaining a positive identity. And this admission forces him to reopen the question of the narrative of composition he has just composed: ''If the apparition was still all to be placed how came it to be vivid?—since we puzzle such quantities out, mostly, just by the business of placing them. One could answer such a question beautifully, doubtless, if one could do so subtle, if not so monstrous, a thing as to write the history of the growth of one's imagination'' (47).

This is a strange confession: that the history of his imagination he has undertaken in the Prefaces, far from being a self-assured enterprise, can only be envisaged as monstrous. The confession results from James's realization that the priority of character over plot, or plot over character, is undecidable. At the time of *Partial Portraits*, this undecidability or mutual involvement of the two terms appeared benign; it pointed in fact to the achievement of a classical synthesis of the two. But now, in the context of the Prefaces, the question of priority becomes more disturbing. Since he is committed to telling a story with a chronological order, it is imperative for James to be able to assign priority and secondariness. When he finds himself unable to do so, his narrative discourse is forced to question its own grounds.

If the alternative between character and plot leads to one kind of problem for the narrative in the Prefaces, the notion of authorial intention raises another kind. This narrative is indeed based on James's belief that criticism must take the author's intention into account: ''What matters, for one's appreciation of a work of art, however modest, is that the prime intention shall have been justified—for any judgment of which we must be clear as to what it was'' (134). Therefore in these essays James continually commits the supposed fallacy of intentionalism, believing that the identification of his original intention for a given novel will both prove the work's integrity and contribute to the autobiographical narrative of his own imagination's history.

This is yet another reason why it would be wrong to see James in the Prefaces exclusively as a formalist critic. For James, the origin of the work is outside of it, in the author's mind.

Another premise behind James's intentionalist criticism is that the work is an adequate expression of that mind. The author's intention is written into his work and can be recovered, at least ideally, from the very surface of the text. Once again, James is seeking to reduce the process of reading (or rereading himself) to an act of simple perception. The old work need not be interpreted but only glanced at or read off and the enduring presence of the author's subjective intention will emerge. Whatever depth the text may have, it can be plumbed by the faculty of sight and need not be submitted to a strictly hermeneutic construction.

In arguing that the intention remains visible in the text—at least to himself, as author—James is doing away with the disjunction in time that would allow for the possibility of misconstruction or misinterpretation. *The Ambassadors*, which James took to be his best work, is also, not coincidentally, the one that best embodied and preserved the intention that grounded it. "Never can a composition of this sort have sprung straighter from a dropped grain of suggestion, and never can that grain, developed, overgrown and smothered, have yet lurked more in the mass as an independent article" (307). James goes on to reveal that the grain of intention is actually contained in Book 5 of the finished novel, in the scene in Gloriani's garden where Strether exhorts Little Bilham to "Live!" This point in the novel, identified by the author himself as its germ, is also its thematic center, "the idea of the tale." Germ and flower, intention and performance coincide in a classic genetic and teleological pattern.

But *The Ambassadors* is, by James's own admission, an exceptional case. Usually the author's first intention does not remain intact in the completed work, nor is he able to recall it to memory in every case, even with the aid of outside evidence such as his notebooks.[12] In these straits James is reduced to the awkward position of an intentionalist critic who must prove the presence of the author in his work through textual evidence alone—even when

12. Susanne Kappeler, *Writing and Reading in Henry James* (New York, 1980), 174–90, maintains that James makes virtually no use of the private materials he could draw upon as author of the novels. *Cf.* Matthiessen, Introduction to the *Notebooks* (*NB*, xi–xii).

this evidence is apparently lacking. At this point, the process of his memory is typically cast in a hypothetical mode or a conditional past tense as in this account of the origins of *The Spoils of Poynton*: "I still make out, between my reconsidered lines, as it were, that I must . . . have assisted at the growth and prominence of Fleda Vetch. For something like Fleda Vetch had surely been latent in one's first apprehension of the theme: it wanted, for treatment, a centre, and, the most obvious centre being 'barred,' this image, while I still wondered, had, with all the assurance in the world, sprung up in its place" (126). James's virtual appeal here to a subconscious (he reads between the lines to find what is latent there) is not warranted by his own phenomenology of perception. Therefore he tries to represent as a conscious process a discovery he cannot literally recollect. What begins as hypothesis ("I must . . . have assisted") ends up in an indicative pluperfect ("this image . . . had . . . sprung up"); conjecture has been turned into history. This sleight of hand is essential to the birth of the narrative in this Preface, but it also shows that this narrative is based on a circle formed from the twin terms of text and intention. James has in fact simply posited the principle that there can be no text without its adequate intention. Once this is granted, then even negative evidence in a given work (the absence of any clear germ) can be converted into a positive proof of intention. Since it is not just any critic but the author himself who is working in this circle, there is a presumption that the conclusions he reaches will legitimately account for the work in question. As in the autobiography, James is here upholding his right to read back into his own history.

But if in some cases the missing intention can still be reconstructed on the basis of the finished work, in others the author can only observe how his intention failed to enact itself in the text. Edward Said has written of the molestation that mars all authority.[13] James writes of the "treacheries of execution," the ways in which the author's original intention is distorted or betrayed in the very act of composition. At his most extreme, James even describes this betrayal as not just contingent but necessary. After recalling his elaborate initial plans for *The Wings of the Dove*, he writes:

Yet one's plan, alas, is one thing and one's result another: so I am perhaps

13. Edward Said, *Beginnings: Intention and Method* (New York, 1975), 84.

nearer the point in saying that this last strikes me at present as most characterised by the happy features that *were*, under my first and most blest illusion,
to have contributed to it. I meet them all, as I renew acquaintance, I mourn
for them all as I remount the stream, the absent values, the palpable voids,
the missing links, the mocking shadows, that reflect, taken together, the early
bloom of one's good faith. Such cases are of course far from abnormal—so
far from it that some acute mind ought surely to have worked out by this time
the ''law'' of the degree in which the artist's energy fairly depends on his fallibility. How much and how often, and in what connexions and with what almost infinite variety, must he be a dupe, that of his prime object, to be at all
measurably a master, that of his actual substitute for it—or in other words at
all appreciably to exist? (297)

This new recognition does not only represent a serious obstacle for intentionalist criticism. As plan and result come to be torn apart from one another, so do intentionalist criticism and textual criticism. By implication
James is commenting here on the delicacy of his effort to bring together two
different exercises in the Prefaces, autobiography and formalist criticism. If
his own past design for his novels appears in them only negatively as absent
values, voids, and missing links, then it is hard to see how those works can
furnish evidence for the history of his imagination. The intention underlying
each novel now stands only as its negative. But whereas even a photo-
graphic negative at least bears a homological resemblance to the finished
product, in the art of fiction the executed work now appears to be a necessary skewing of the prime intention, so that neither of the two can legitimately be deduced from the other. James's own authority or mastery as an
artist now seems to rest, paradoxically, on nothing other than his skill in
submitting to the ''treacheries of execution'' and in becoming the knowing
dupe of the process of narration itself.

The exercise of the memory, then, as it seeks to recover an original authorial intention, results in an aporia or a vicious circle where text and intention can be only posited as present but not really shown to be so. The way
out of this dilemma for James is to invoke another method than that of memory, one that he attributes to the imagination.

The function of the imagination in the Prefaces can be approached through
the question of relations, a theme that links these essays to James's auto-

biography and, indeed, links art and life, criticism and autobiography. At the very outset of the Prefaces, in an effort to delimit the issues that are pressing on him from all sides and to "organise, for convenience and cheer, some system of observation," James lays down as an axiom: "Really, universally, relations stop nowhere, and the exquisite problem of the artist is eternally but to draw, by a geometry of his own, the circle within which they shall happily *appear* to do so" (5). The central problem for artistic representation is to imitate life's complex web of relations but at the same time to delimit it by giving it an artificial order. This problem remains the same whether the representation is fictional (as in the novels) or autobiographical (as in the Prefaces). As for the latter, we have seen that on the first page of the essays James describes them as "this revival of an all but extinct relation with an early work" and that on the last page of the last Preface he returns to this salient point of the connections or the "whole chain of relation" that binds the author to his works.

But if the task of reviving old relations at first seems to be a matter of passive recollection, other passages show it to be a much more active, even creative, assignment. "To criticize is to appreciate, to appropriate, to take intellectual possession, to establish in fine a relation with the criticized thing and make it one's own" (155). This famous sentence points not to the revival of preexisting relations but to the creation of new ones, thanks to an appropriative power, which in his autobiography James explicitly labeled as the imagination. As in the autobiography, here too the imagination's power to establish relations is absolute, so that, like the associations that come to the mind of the Freudian patient, anything that floats into James's consciousness ipso facto earns a place in the web of his experience:

> Who shall say thus . . . where the associational nimbus of the all but lost, of the miraculously recovered, chapter of experience shall absolutely fade and stop? That would be possible only were experience a chessboard of sharp black-and-white squares. Taking one of these for a convenient plot I have but to see my particle of suggestion lurk in its breast, and then but to repeat in this connexion the act of picking it up, for the whole of the *rest* of the connexion straightway to loom into life, its parts all clinging together and pleading with a collective friendly voice that I can't pretend to resist: "Oh but we too, you know; what were *we* but of the experience?" (182–83)

This organic unity of the subject's experience is not objectively present in the past itself; it comes into view only retrospectively, from the vantage point of the autobiographer. Memory alone cannot account for it but only an imagination that acts upon the past materials of life and creates them as it goes along. James introduces the term *imagination* immediately after defining this "associational nimbus" of experience: "Nothing more complicates and overloads the act of retrospect than to let one's imagination itself work backward as part of the business." He goes on to explain apologetically that this overloading or overdetermining of the narrative process by the imagination cannot be prevented because the "natural caretakers" of the imagination, "the judgment, the memory, the conscience," have been "occupied, as it were, elsewhere." The result has been the apparent formlessness of his narrative: "The effort to reconstitute the medium and the season that favoured the first stir of life, the first perceived gleam of the vital spark, in the trifle before us, fairly makes everything in the picture revive, fairly even extends the influence to matters remote and strange. The musing artist's imagination—thus *not* excluded and confined—supplies the link that is missing and makes the whole occasion (the occasion of the glorious birth to him of still another infant motive) comprehensively and richly one" (183). These lines evoking the birth of the novels are reminiscent of that early page in *A Small Boy and Others* where the author's imagination reached back to the first moment of consciousness, "the flush of life in the grey" (*SBO*, 3). In the Prefaces, however, James is acknowledging that the "first" is not there, that the imagination must supply "the link that is missing" (the missing link, for instance, of his intention) and thus create for the first time the relations, hence the narrative, of the past life. To represent the past, then, is not just to revive or make present again what was already there. In filling in the blank spaces of the past, in supplying the missing links, the imagination acts like the figure of catachresis, the forced metaphor that provides a needed term where none previously existed. This filling in of James's past is parallel to the process of the revision of his works performed concurrently with the writing of the Prefaces. In one sense (as we have seen James claim), this revision entailed only a vision of what was already there on the page, but in another sense it clearly involved a reworking, an elaboration and addition of new figures to the texts. In both cases, then, to represent means to figure, and James indeed uses these two terms as virtual synonyms in the phrase "the very terms and possibilities of representation and figuration" (319).

It is this exercise of the imagination, "thus *not* excluded and confined," that prevents the Prefaces from being in any way a failure—for instance, from being that monstrous thing that James at one point predicted. In writing "the history of the growth of his imagination," James must rely on that imagination; the imagination writes its own history. It is this self-representation on the part of the imagination that saves the narrative in the Prefaces from the charge of being fictive or self-deluding. Only the imagination is capable of writing this history. The perfect coincidence between the story's subject matter and its mode of narration allows it in practice to transcend the dichotomy of the fictive and the real.

The "story" of the novels themselves (the order of character and plot) and the narrative composition of the Prefaces (authorial intention and its recovery) correspond to the two chief goals of the series of essays—criticism and autobiography. But these two pursuits cannot be kept entirely separate. James's critical comments on the art of novel writing form at the same time stages in his autobiographical narrative. This interdependence is nowhere more evident than in the crucial theme of representation. Certain passages that describe the earlier act of representation involved in the fiction of the novels at the same time represent James himself as the subject of the new autobiographical narrative. This double role allows these passages to function as an allegory of narrative, or as an allegory of the process of representation that is implied in any narrative.

In these passages, James's novels are studied not for their content but for the light they can shed on the history of his imagination. James uses these novels for the purpose of "glancing at the *other*, the extinct actualities they hold up the glimmering taper in. They are still faintly scented, doubtless, with something of that authenticity, and a living work of art, however limited, pretends always, as for part of its grace, to some good faith of community, however indirect, with its period or place" (213). The novel indeed fulfills a mimetic function but not just the one the common reader might expect. The work is a representation not only of the outside world but also of the author's subjectivity; thus James writes that his fiction is "in the highest degree documentary for myself'' (196). The work's authenticity depends on the authority of the writer who created it, and its very survival as a ''living'' word depends on the link it maintains with the history of that writer. At the same time, the author now depends on his works to help him reconstruct his past, for which they offer the prime testimony.

Each novel, then, becomes not so much a mimetic copy of an external reality as a palimpsest. The visible surface of the palimpsest is the text as we have it, the text literally construed as the story of Isabel Archer or Lambert Strether; the hidden, partially obliterated layer is the history of the author and his imagination. Thus each novel performs two quite different semiotic operations, one for the ordinary reader and the other for James. To its readers, the novel produced a signified whole, which is the image of a fictional world. To the author, that level of meaning is not the only or even the most important one. The signs of the text also point to a referent that coincides with the real world of the author's past. Moreover, the levels of the signified and of the personal referent have nothing necessarily in common. James's own memories have little to do with the novel's literal images or content; the relation between the two is contingent and unpredictable. James's ability to summon up memories, whose relevance to the novel his reader would have no way of judging, gives him a privilege tantamount to that of a private language. This discordance between the (fictional) signified and the (real-life) referent not only complicates the functioning of the literary work as a semiotic system but also suggests that there may be no common measure, no necessary connection, between the two pursuits of the Prefaces, their formalist analysis of the novels and their autobiographical story. The two endeavors exist alongside each other in a relation difficult to clarify, and once again we glimpse the potentially formless or even monstrous character of these essays.

The metaphor of the text as a kind of palimpsest is not my invention but James's. In the Preface to *The American*, he describes how a view of the novel's surface (its finished, manifest form) leads on to a view of its depths: ''It is a pleasure to see how again and again the sunken depths of the old work yet permit themselves to be sounded or—even if rather terrible the image—'dragged': the long pole of memory stirs and rummages the bottom, and we fish up such fragments and relics of the submerged life and the extinct consciousness as tempt us to piece them together'' (26). This piecing together serves to fabricate a continuous narrative out of the fragmentary materials the author's former works yield up. The layers of density of the text correspond to the meaningful depths of the author's mind, of which the text is supposed to be the faithful representation.

In another image, these aqueous depths of the work become a more transparent kind of interior space. The ''shrunken concomitants'' of one novel, James writes, meaning the scraps of evidence the novel contains from his own past, ''lurk between the lines; these serve for them as the barred seraglio-windows behind which, to the outsider in the glare of the Eastern street, forms indistinguishable seem to move and peer; 'association' in fine bears upon them with its infinite magic'' (125). In this metaphor the spaced bars of the window stand for the actual appearance of the printed page, with its black lines on a white background. James again upsets our normal notion of the role of the literary sign; this time he ignores the arbitrary nature of language and instead imagines writing as a sort of pictography that operates in a spatial, perceptual field rather than a semantic or interpretative one. Once again, he is consciously minimizing the basic relation between the signifier and the signified in order to stress a putative relation between the text and its referent, a relation that, although it may be held to be necessary to the author, is also private to him.

As this passage proceeds, the literary work continues to be represented as a kind of palimpsest, so that the author looking into its interior space immediately looks *through* its surface: ''Peering through the lattice from without inward I recapture a cottage on a cliff-side, to which, at the earliest approach of the summertime, redoubtable in London through the luxuriance of still other than 'natural' forces, I had betaken myself to finish a book in quiet and to begin another in fear'' (125). The lattice and the earlier seraglio, however different they may be, work together to define the text as an enclosed, protected space. This motif of protection is reinforced by James's narrative account of his retreat from the distractions of London to the calm and isolation of the rural scene to which he retired in order to write his novel. For James, as a retrospective reader of his own works now embarked on an autobiographical venture, one value of those works lies in their power to enclose and preserve the traces of his former self. In another preface he again describes the role the old novel plays in summoning up his past: "I find this ghostly interest perhaps even more asserted for me by the questions begotten within the very covers of the book, those that wander and idle there as if in some sweet old overtangled walled garden, a safe paradise of self-criticism" (10). The work appears as a self-contained, organic object, but what James is describing is not a true version of intrinsic or formalist criticism since the novel is not being considered as an entity in its own right but as an aid to self-criticism. The author's works become the *locus amoenus* within which he can withdraw in order to accomplish his act of self-appropriation. The interior of the literary texts has absorbed and preserved from oblivion the outer, referential reality of the author's past.

What is described is thus the process of representation itself, the process whereby a literary work can appropriate the presence of an external reality and save it from destruction by giving it a second, interiorized life. The passage in the Preface is an allegory of the act of representation, in the sense that it puts into a linear, narrative account the structure of the mimetic act involved in the writing of a fictional work. The enterprise of the Prefaces is a repetition, but also a raising to the second power, of the mimetic enterprise of the novels they discuss. Hence, as we have seen, James calls these essays a rerepresentation. The "*act* of re-appropriation" in the Prefaces (the author stresses the performative role) carries the act of representation in the novels one step further.

The dualistic imagery of inside and outside, as a metaphor for the process of representation, has obvious relevance to the house of fiction from the Preface to *The Portrait of a Lady*, as well as to the many other houses James describes in these essays. In fact the narrative the essays develop is made up largely of a series of literalized versions of the metaphoric house of fiction. As early as the Preface to *The American* (the second essay), James describes the house in Paris in which he wrote most of that novel. The Parisian scene is the referent, the earliest writing on the palimpsest. The deep content of his memory, James writes, "makes for the faded page to-day a sort of interlineation of sound." This sound is, quite literally, the sound that rose to the author's windows from the Parisian street:

This sound rises to a martial clatter at the moment a troop of cuirassiers charges down the narrow street, each morning, to file, directly opposite my house, through the plain portal of the barracks occupying part of the vast domain attached in a rearward manner to one of the Ministères that front on the Place Vendôme; an expanse marked, along a considerable stretch of the street, by one of those high painted and administratively-placarded garden walls that form deep, vague, recurrent notes in the organic vastness of the city. I have but to re-read ten lines to recall my daily effort not to waste time in hanging over the window-bar for a sight of the cavalry the hard music of whose hoofs so directly and thrillingly appealed; an effort that inveterately failed. (26–27)

The present-tense verbs of the first sentence suggest how vivid is the reappropriating and representational power of James's memory, but while the passage accomplishes an act of representation, it also describes one. As with the house of fiction, the author's sight is directed outward from within, and this gaze stands for the act of representation itself, the transmission of the force of the active life outside to the interiority of the work of art. Moreover, the house in this passage is associated with the *locus amoenus*; it is an enclave situated in the heart of the larger "organic vastness of the city." The garden walls are there to indicate the line that separates the protected space of the text from the frenetic life of Paris. The contrast between the protected, passive pursuit of the artist and the vigorous activity of life is underscored by the choice of military maneuvers to represent the latter. James's remark that this spectacle "thrillingly appealed" is a capsulized formula for the author's fundamental ambivalence toward the outside world, an ambivalence parallel to that of his theoretical statements about the mimetic function of fiction. Although the world is the artist's sole source of material, it poses an unmistakable threat. The suggestion that this threat, embodied here in a military scene, is that of a certain form of death is perhaps counterbalanced by the fact that the military parade is after all only a form of make-believe or play (like the work of art). Still, the danger hinted at is not to be taken lightly.

The most important immediate result of the present passage, however, is that the effort at an artistic appropriation of external life is essentially a failure. James comments retrospectively that the only result of his endeavors was to waste time, not only because the author may never, as far as the passage tells us, have succeeded in seeing the spectacle anyway but because the artist's desire to appropriate life in so immediate a way was misguided in the first place. A key element in James's narrative is the window-bar that separates the writer from the scene outside. This bar is significantly different from the windows or niches of the house of fiction, which provided transparent points of view for looking outside. In semiotic terms, the window-bar of the Preface to *The American* can be construed as the bar that separates the signifier from the signified or, *a fortiori*, as the bar that separates the total, arbitrary sign from its referent.[14] James's desire for artistic representation (on the peformative level of the Prefaces, his desire for genuine autobiography) is a desire for the sign and the referent to coincide or at least to stand in a necessary relation to each other. However, the Preface shows that desire being frustrated by the arbitrary nature of the sign. James's repeated failure, in the narrative, to overcome the obstacle of the window-bar thus means he cannot ensure the classic mimetic relation between art and life.

As the narrative ends in apparent frustration, James adopts a more didactic tone to express the moral of his story: "I have ever, in general, found it difficult to write of places under too immediate an impression—the impression that prevents standing off and allows neither space nor time for perspective. The image has had for the most part to be dim if the reflexion was to be, as is proper for a reflexion, both sharp and quiet: one has a horror, I think, artistically, of agitated reflexions" (27). This argument in favor of mediated reflections over real-life images seeks to make a virtue of what his narrative has shown to be a necessity. But James's method of compensation implies a definite loss for his art, since he is confessing that his literary text stands in a secondary relation to the immediacy of life's image, which the mere text cannot hope to render in its original vividness. Thus the literary work, which James had optimistically called "the living work of art," finds itself strangely cut off from its life source. James even writes that his novel had to turn its back on Paris "to save as it could its own life" (27). This unsettling conclusion evokes once more the threat, already implicit in the

14. See Ferdinand de Saussure, *Cours de linguistique générale* (Paris, 1972), 97–102, on the arbitrary nature of the sign. The bar, which is already visible in some of Saussure's diagrams, is made explicit by Jacques Lacan in "L'Instance de la lettre dans l'inconscient," in his *Ecrits* (Paris, 1966), 493–528.

military parade, that real life, far from being the bounteous source of all art, is potentially the death of the work of fiction.

The Preface to *The American*, then, does preserve one important mimeticist tenet—that of the priority of life over art—but only at a great cost to the work of art, which seems cut off from the richness of life. The Preface to *The Portrait of a Lady*, the next essay, constructs a narrative that reaches the same conclusion (40–41). Some later essays, however, point to a way out of this dilemma, not by restoring lifelike qualities to the work of art but by putting into question the absolute priority of life. The Preface to *The Spoils of Poynton* at first seems to resemble the Preface to *The American*. This time, James tells us, he wrote his novel in Venice, where his room ''looked into the shade of a court where a high outer staircase, strikingly bold, yet strikingly relaxed, held together one scarce knew how; where Gothic windows broke out, on discoloured blanks of wall, at quite arbitrary levels, and where above all the strong Venetian voice, full of history and humanity and waking perpetual echoes, seemed to say more in ten warm words, of whatever tone, than any twenty pages of one's cold pale prose'' (136). The richness of life is asserted in terms almost embarrassing to the artist. Never has James seemed more removed from reality. His only window looks out not directly onto life but onto a courtyard, which itself stands in a mediated relation to the outside. As before, art and life are not continuous but opposed to each other. Over against the ''warm words'' of the voice of life stands the deathly pallor of the author's ''cold pale prose.'' James seems to subscribe here to a dualist metaphysic according to which the presence of the spoken word possesses life, while the written text is on the side of death.

Another look at the passage, however, complicates this scheme of priority and secondariness, life and death. The ''strong Venetian voice,'' standing for the immediacy of life, also, curiously, contains ''waking perpetual echoes'' that would seem to belong on the side of art and its reflections. The fact that the echoes are perpetual suggests that they cannot be easily deduced from the warm words of the city but are caught in a series of repetitions. Also, James's perception of the note of history suggests that the voices are not fully present but are mediated by the past, which they still bear within them.

In fact, the house of fiction has here turned in upon itself. No longer seeking a view of the outside field, the author looks only onto a doubly interior space that has become cut off from the outside world and sufficient to itself. What this narrative represents is the fictional work's liberation from its derivative relation to life. Paradoxically, this liberation results from the fact that "the romantic and historic sites of Italy" are so rich for the imagination (41). They are in fact too rich, James explains, to be of use for the work of art. The imagination cannot adapt Venice for fiction; it can only experience Venice as something that is already a fiction, a work of art in its own right.

The same conclusion can be drawn from the Preface to "The Siege of London." Here James describes his London chambers as having "a view of the Green Park," a name that symbolically links this vista to life itself. The house in which James found himself was "continued by the high wall of its ample court, opposite my open-eyed windows, gloomed, in dusky brick, as the extent of my view, but with a vast convenient neutrality which I found, soon enough, protective and not inquisitive" (212). The ambivalence of the relation between inside and outside is underscored here. The novelist's attitude is open-eyed as always but not inquisitive. The outside at which he peers for inspiration is not a thriving urban scene but a mere blank, neutral wall—like the white page he must fill up with his own words. This view protects him from the great life of London as much as it connects him with it.

But what is that life? "The big human rumble of Piccadilly . . . was close at hand; I liked to think that Thackeray's Curzon Street, in which Becky Sharp, or rather Mrs. Rawdon Crawley, had lived, was not much further off: I thought of it ponderantly, in my comings and goings, as Becky's and her creator's; just as I was to find fifty other London neighborhoods speak to me with the voice, the thousand voices, of Dickens" (212). The blankness of the wall he faces leaves James room—in fact compels him—to fill it up with images recalled from fictional experience. This vision of a Thackerayan or Dickensian London is akin to that passage in A Small Boy and Others where James conceived himself as living in a Balzacian Paris. Once again fond fancy is at work, but this admission on James's part ("I liked to think") does not undermine his imaginative construction of the city. He cannot see it as anything but the London of those earlier novelists whose works he absorbed in his youth. Life itself—what appeared earlier as the

referent, the deepest level of the textual palimpsest—exists only as a representation; it is indeed already experienced as a text: "The teller of a story
is primarily, none the less, the listener to it, the reader of it, too; and, having
needed thus to make it out, distinctly, on the crabbed page of life, to dis-
engage it from the rude human characters and the more or less Gothic text
in which it has been packed away, the very essence of his affair has been
the *imputing* of intelligence" (63). Of course the rude quality of life and the
artist's obligation to impute intelligence to it remind us of James's belief
that art must be an improvement, in economy and beauty and sense, on life.
But equally important is the shift James is making here from teller to listener
or reader, which recalls again his desire to depict his role in the Prefaces,
and in the entire New York Edition, as a passive one. Passivity now extends
to the original storyteller; just as Balzac once claimed to be a mere secretary
writing under the dictation of French society, James claims that as a writer
of fictions he merely transcribes the already composed text of life.[15] Narrative is not the invention of the novelist but is inherent in life itself.

James's argument about the representational value of his fictions has, in
this way, come full circle. Starting from the premise that his novels were a
kind of palimpsest allowing him access to the real world that had sustained
his imaginative activity, he has told in the Prefaces a series of stories whose
final burden it is to show the fictional work growing more and more distant
from the source of life, which threatens to overwhelm or extinguish it. Having reached this point, yet being unwilling to abandon the connection between life and art, James saves his argument by finally drawing life into the
camp of art. He pushes to its logical extreme the model of the palimpsest
and now reveals that life itself is only a layer of the text, even if it is the
deepest, most primary one. Fiction does furnish access to life, because life
is already constructed and experienced as a work of fiction.

If James's imaginative life as an author is already shaped as a narrative,
then his project of composing the Prefaces in the form of narrative is vindicated. In fact the Prefaces, as we have seen, are a double narrative. They
are "the story of one's stories" and also "the history of the growth of one's

15. Honoré de Balzac, Avant-propos to *La Comédie humaine* (12 vols.; Paris, 1976–81),
I, 11.

imagination.'' But, as we have also seen, James has never taken the success of his narrative for granted; instead, a questioning of the very grounds of narrative has been woven into the themes of the Prefaces. In all three areas we have just surveyed—the relations between character and plot, memory and imagination, life and art—he has confronted the dangers that challenge representational narrative, and his essays have met these dangers not by excluding them but by absorbing them. The Prefaces have exposed the fictions on which their narrative is based: the fiction of character's precedence over plot, the fiction that the imagination supplies for the failing memory, the fiction that allows the literary work to represent and reappropriate life. Thus James keeps open the possibility that the writing of the history of his imagination may be a monstrous thing. Yet at the same time he clearly stakes much on his ability to write such a narrative even while containing its monstrosity. What is at stake is the same thing that was at stake in the autobiography, the recovery of his past self. Like the autobiography, the Prefaces redefine the possibility of such a recovery and invent a new form to achieve it.

5

THE TURN OF THE SCREW and *THE SACRED FOUNT*
The Perils of the "I"

THE TWO great problem pieces for James criticism have always been *The Turn of the Screw* (1898) and *The Sacred Fount* (1901). They have called forth critical essays with titles like "The Ambiguity of Henry James" (Edmund Wilson) and *Jamesian Ambiguity and the Sacred Fount* (Jean Frantz Blackall). One way in which critics have tried to get a grip on these two works is to assume some sort of generic resemblance between them and other works James wrote around the same time, ones presumed to be less ambiguous, like *What Maisie Knew* (1897), *In the Cage* (1898), or *The Ambassadors* (1901).[1] I shall argue, however, that the best

1. For critics who relate *The Sacred Fount* to other works with limited "reflectors," and especially to *In the Cage*, see Jean Frantz Blackall, *Jamesian Ambiguity and "The Sacred Fount"* (Ithaca, 1965), 1–36; Tony Tanner, "Henry James's Subjective Adventurer: *The Sacred Fount*," in Lyall H. Powers (ed.), *Henry James's Major Novels: Essays in Criticism* (East Lansing, 1973), 224–40; Philip M. Weinstein, *Henry James and The Requirements of the Imagination* (Cambridge, Mass., 1971), 97–120. For comparisons between *The Sacred Fount* and *The Ambassadors*, see Julian B. Kaye, "*The Awkward Age, The Sacred Fount*, and *The Ambassadors*: Another Figure in the Carpet," *Nineteenth-Century Fiction*, XVII (1963), 339–51; Bernard Richards, "*The Ambassadors* and *The Sacred Fount*: The Artist Manqué," in John Goode (ed.), *The Air of Reality: New Essays on Henry James* (London, 1972), 219–43; Arnold L. Weinstein, *Vision and Response in Modern Fiction* (Ithaca, 1974), 69–90. Many of the most important essays on *The Turn of the Screw* are conveniently collected in two volumes: Gerald Willen (ed.), *A Casebook on Henry James's "The Turn of the Screw"* (2nd ed.; New York, 1969); and Henry James, *The Turn of the Screw*, ed. Robert Kimbrough (Norton Critical Edition) (New York, 1966).

context in which to study these two works is the context they offer each other, for they are both first-person narratives of a peculiar kind within James's oeuvre. Each of them is written in a form that combines the use of a first-person narrator with one other trait that, according to James's own critical rules, should never be found in conjunction with that narrator. In *The Turn of the Screw*, that incompatible trait is the presence of romance (or the ghost story); in *The Sacred Fount*, it is simply the work's length, its necessary classification as a longer piece.[2]

In works like *What Maisie Knew, In the Cage*, and *The Ambassadors*, the center of consciousness—Maisie, the telegraphist, Strether—is encaged in a focalized narrative that ensures objectivity and prevents fluidity. Such is not the case with *The Sacred Fount*, or even with *The Turn of the Screw*, even though this story's frame might be seen as encasing the governess' narrative in a way that saves it from the worst dangers of subjectivity. Actually, the frame functions to put the first-person narrative into stark relief and make its subjectivity all the more dangerous. Whereas the unreliability of the reflector in works like *What Maisie Knew* is a matter of degree and nuance only and does not disrupt the basic sense of the narrative, the problem with the narrators of *The Turn of the Screw* and *The Sacred Fount* goes far beyond unreliability and calls into question our ability even to state what the works are about.[3]

This problem is what is involved in the self-revelation with which James identified first-person narration. James does not mean that this kind of narrative necessarily takes an overtly autobiographical form; indeed the problem is rather that the self-revelation in this mode is unintentional and unforeseen. The governess and the Narrator (as I shall call the anonymous narrator of *The Sacred Fount*) tell us very little about themselves directly; they prefer to treat themselves as marginal characters in other people's dramas—a position that is in fact typical of the first-person narrators in James's shorter fictions. But if the comparative lack of definition of the two narrators

2. The most complete discussion of James's problem with the length of *The Sacred Fount* remains that of Claire J. Raeth, "Henry James's Rejection of *The Sacred Fount*," *ELH*, XVI (1949), 308–24.

3. For a similar distinction between ironic and truly ambiguous narrative in James, see Shlomith Rimmon, *The Concept of Ambiguity—the Example of James* (Chicago, 1977), 15.

is intended to make them seem unproblematic and inconspicuous and to reduce the element of autobiography, it can have the opposite effect as well.
The governess' and the Narrator's lack of definition ("My values are all
blanks," writes James in the Preface to *The Turn of the Screw—AN*, 177)
becomes a mystery that invites the reader's speculation and suggests that
these narrators may have blind spots toward their own character. In fact, the
narrators' apparent lack of self-revelation may turn out to mask the fact that
everything in their narratives, even the thematic material that seems most
remote from autobiography, is a projection of their own character and ob-
sessions.

Thus the posture of the two narrators leads directly to the ambiguity of
their two narratives. Both works conform to the rigorous definition of Jamesian ambiguity that Shlomith Rimmon has recently proposed. This ambiguity consists of an alternative between two contradictory answers to a
question, for the resolution of which the reader is not provided with adequate information.[4] In the case of these two works, the question has been
the fundamental one: what is the story about? One answer is that the story
is about what it appears to be about, that is, a certain notion or theory held
by the narrator: that two ghosts are menacing two children or that the law of
the sacred fount governs the relations between partners at a weekend gathering. But the second, contradictory answer is that the works are really about
the narrators themselves and why they hold their theories. This alternative
is radical because it means that the final interpretation of the story may be
oriented toward either of two quite distinct levels: in Benveniste's terms, the
level of the story (the actions represented in the narrative) or the level of the
discourse (the act of narration as it is identified with the narrator in his here
and now). The result is the kind of duck-or-rabbit alternative that has led
Charles Thomas Samuels to speak of *The Sacred Fount* as being two novels
at the same time.[5] It would be difficult to think of any narrative works writ-

4. *Ibid.*
5. Charles Thomas Samuels, *The Ambiguity of Henry James* (Urbana, 1971), 29. For similar statements, see Blackall, *Jamesian Ambiguity and "The Sacred Fount,"* 15; Philip Weinstein, *Henry James and the Requirements of the Imagination*, 98; Dorothea Krook, *The Ordeal
of Consciousness in Henry James* (Cambridge, 1962), 167; Raeth, "Henry James's Rejection
of *The Sacred Fount*," 320–22.

ten before James that pose exactly the same problem. The abundance of works after or contemporary with him that do so—for example, *The Heart of Darkness, Lord Jim*, or *Absalom, Absalom!*—suggests how central are these works of James to a certain modernist tradition.

This radical ambiguity in conjunction with the first-person narrator has a number of other correlatives or consequences. Foremost among these is a certain incompleteness of the narrative, which might be explained in James's terms as an inadequate objectification. The texts do not seem self-contained or self-subsistent. This sense of incompletion is most evident, formally, in the unresolved endings of both stories and also, in *The Turn of the Screw*, in the fact that the governess' narrative is explicitly said by the frame narrator not to be whole in itself but to require, "for a proper intelligence, a few words of prologue."[6] At the end, the reader is tempted to say that the story might also have required a few words of epilogue, but none are forthcoming.

But the dubious closure of both works should not be understood only as a formal problem, a matter of proportion or roundedness. When James writes about "the terrible *fluidity* of self-revelation," he is referring less to the problem of dramatic construction (both *The Turn of the Screw* and *The Sacred Fount* are dramatically tight works by most standards) than to the extratextual question of the relations between author, reader, and work. The lack of objectivity of these works, consequently, has the additional effect of implicating the author in his work. It is as if an insufficiently organic or objective work is one that is still attached to its author as by an umbilical cord and must to some extent be autobiographical for him. It is certainly no coincidence that many readers have detected the figure of the author in each of these two fictions, most apparently in *The Sacred Fount*, where the Narrator has often been taken as a version of James (whether serious or parodic). In *The Turn of the Screw*, James has been felt to be present in the figure of the master (or uncle) who sends the governess on her mission, and he has also been identified by at least one critic with the governess herself.[7]

6. All references to *The Turn of the Screw* are to the Norton Critical Edition, ed. Kimbrough, the text of which is that of the New York Edition. It is hereinafter cited parenthetically in the text by page number only.

7. See Maurice Blanchot, "Le Tour d'écrou," in his *Le Livre à venir* (Paris, 1959), 155–64.

Such equations between James and his characters make the fictional works appear to be much more directly autobiographical for their author than James, with his aversion to self-revelation, could have desired.

Similarly, the same lack of objectivity and closure in the narratives may be responsible for an unusual involvement of the reader as well, first, in the sense that both narratives incorporate characters who seem to be not only "the reader's friend," as James said of his *ficelles* (*AN*, 322), but actual surrogates or doubles of the reader, characters whose function is precisely to read the story being told them by the narrator. (These are Mrs. Grose in *The Turn of the Screw* and Mrs. Brissenden, Ford Obert, Lady John, and perhaps others too in *The Sacred Fount*.) But in a second sense we, the actual readers, are drawn into the story in ways many critics have found peculiar and even alarming. Critics as diverse as Leon Edel and Shoshana Felman have spoken of these two works as laying a trap for the reader, especially by forcing him to construct a meaning for the text, to commit himself to a single interpretation that may—or even must—turn out to be wrong.[8]

Radical ambiguity, the sense of incompleteness, the implication of the author, and a trap laid for the reader—this is the constellation of traits exhibited by these two first-person narratives, anomalies in the Jamesian canon. My goal in this chapter is not to explain away the ambiguity (I shall be taking sides on the famous questions as little as possible) but to show how it and the other disturbing qualities of these works are inevitably linked to the peculiar use of the first person. Ultimately, the ambiguity of these narratives must also lead us to question the sanity of their narrators. Madness is in a sense the final issue raised by the first-person narrator in James; along the way we shall see that this narrative method also raises fundamental questions of the artistic imagination and narrative authority.

The problematic, incomplete nature of *The Turn of the Screw* and *The Sa-*

8. See Leon Edel, Introductory Essay to *The Sacred Fount* (1953; rpr. New York, 1979), xxv. This is the edition of the novel to which I shall refer by page number in my text. For a much more elaborate discussion of the trap laid for the critics and readers of *The Turn of the Screw*, see Shoshana Felman, "Turning the Screw of Interpretation," *Yale French Studies*, LV/LVI (1977), 94–207. This stimulating essay, heavily dependent on Jacques Lacan's reading of Freud, is the most exhaustive and theoretically advanced study of *The Turn of the Screw* I have read.

cred Fount has almost without exception led critics to seek help from James's own comments about these works. This, again, is evidence of how the first-person narrative compromises the author's detachment from his work. In his private correspondence, however, James protects his detachment by refusing to divulge his real judgment as to the value of the two works. The similarity between the ways in which he deflects questions about each of the works is striking. In a reply to H. G. Wells, who had written James of his reaction to *The Turn of the Screw*, James ends by saying, ''But the thing is essentially a pot-boiler and a *jeu d'esprit*.''[9] After the publication of *The Sacred Fount* three years later, he writes to a correspondent of his new work as ''a profitless labyrinth . . . fantastic and insubstantial,'' as ''the merest of *jeux d'esprit*'' and ''a consistent joke.''[10] These evasions of serious criticism belie a certain uneasiness, a sense that something has gone wrong, especially in the case of *The Sacred Fount*, which James excluded from the New York Edition and therefore never discussed in a sustained way. The author seems to be dropping a red herring to prevent his readers from knowing what these works are about or even whether they are about anything serious at all.

James's notebooks, which have also been ransacked for clues to the meaning of the two stories, are not much more helpful. The notebooks tend to record the raw, ancedotal *donnée* for a story, but this can rarely be taken as evidence for the interpretation of a finished story since, by his own admission, James's working out of an idea so often deviates from his earliest intention. Moreover, this deviation usually operates in a certain direction, as Wayne Booth has noted. Booth has described a ''transformation of a 'subject,' through the development of a 'reflector' not important in the original conception, into something quite different. . . . often [James] gradually develops the reflector until the original subject is rivaled or even overshadowed.''[11]

The truth of Booth's remark can be shown through the example of *The Turn of the Screw*, possibly of all James's works the one most fully docu-

9. Henry James to H. G. Wells, December 9, 1898, in Henry James, *Letters*, ed. Leon Edel (4 vols.; Cambridge, Mass., 1974–84), IV, 86.
10. Quoted by Edel, Introductory Essay to *The Sacred Fount*, xxx.
11. Wayne Booth, *The Rhetoric of Fiction* (Chicago, 1961), 340–41, and *cf.* 346.

mented by an abundance of authorial comments made both before and after its composition, in the private notebooks and letters as well as in the public Prefaces. These comments show, first, that "the lesson of the master" is not simple or unequivocal but also that the ambiguity of this work is not accidental but is the logical result of the rules and conditions governing its composition. If we read James's comments closely we can uncover the rigorous theoretical reasoning that—perhaps despite the author's conscious intention—produces ambiguity in James's work.

Much of the Preface to *The Turn of the Screw*—as well as the Preface to "The Altar of the Dead" and other tales in another volume of the collected edition—is devoted to a theory of the ghost story. This genre, which is for James "the most possible form of the fairy-tale" (*AN*, 254), is of course a variety of romance. As we saw, however, the best romance disguises itself as realism. Thus it is not surprising that James's rules for the ghost story make it into a game of compromise that must balance alternative tendencies. "We want it clear, goodness knows, but we also want it thick" (*AN*, 256). On the one hand, the ghost story must not abandon its investment in the supernatural, or it risks becoming like "the mere modern 'psychic' case" and losing its power to arouse "the dear old sacred terror" (*AN*, 169).[12] On the other hand, it must be tight like the work of realism; it must display closeness, with "fewest loose ends dangling and fewest features missing" (*AN*, 255–57). The only way James can see to reconcile these dual requirements is to present the supernatural through the experience of an acute observer who can give it credibility. He calls this the technique of the "field of second exhibition":

12. In light of this statement, modern critics' attempts to explicate *The Turn of the Screw* through reference to James's acquaintance with the Society for Psychical Research seem of limited value. See for example Francis X. Roellinger, "Psychical Research and *The Turn of the Screw*," in James, *The Turn of the Screw*, ed. Kimbrough, 132–42; Ernest Tuveson, "*The Turn of the Screw*: A Palimpsest," *Studies in English Literature*, XII (1972), 783–800. For an account of the reasons that led James to reject the "psychic case" treatment of the supernatural, see Martha Banta, *Henry James and the Occult* (Indianapolis, 1972), esp. 42–50. James's view of the ghost story as a genre that hovers between a naturalistic explanation of its events and a supernatural one is similar to a recent theory of the fantastic proposed by Tzvetan Todorov. See his *The Fantastic: A Structural Approach to a Literary Genre*, trans. Richard Howard (Cleveland, 1973).

By which, to avoid obscurity, I mean nothing more cryptic than I feel myself to show them [the supernatural events] best by showing almost exclusively the way they are felt, by recognising as their main interest some impression strongly made by them and intensely received. We but too probably break down, I have ever reasoned, when we attempt the prodigy, the appeal to mystification, in itself; with its "objective" side too emphasized the report (it is ten to one) will practically run thin. We want it clear, goodness knows, but we also want it thick, and we get the thickness in the human consciousness that entertains and records, that amplifies and interprets it. That indeed, when the question is (to repeat) of the "supernatural," constitutes the only thickness we do get; here prodigies, when they come straight, come with an effect imperilled; they keep all their character, on the other hand, by looming through some other history—the indispensable history of somebody's *normal* relation to something. (*AN*, 256)

The ghost story thus can partake of both romance and realism, of the supernatural and the normal. (A similar balance is struck in one of James's statements in a letter on *The Sacred Fount*, which could as well apply to *The Turn of the Screw*: "As I give but the phantasmagoric I have, for clearness, to make it evidential."[13]) As for the ambiguity of the resulting work of fiction—the feature we are most interested in—this definition has another, most notable consequence. The "field of second exhibition" virtually guarantees the ambiguity of the text because it ensures that the reader will never witness the immediate representation of the supernatural element, which he will thus always be free to put into question. The narrative technique of such secondary, or indirect, presentation can be compared to a phenomenological *epoché* whereby the external reality of the objects of consciousness is bracketed and only the quality of the intentional experience itself is taken into account. In this case, *The Turn of the Screw* would become a phenomenological study of the governess' consciousness where the objective reality of the ghosts has been suspended as a question.

This description of the tale is inadequate, however, insofar as the reader still feels a compulsion either to believe or to disbelieve in the reality of the ghosts. Several generations of critical debate have shown that this compulsion is in fact incontrovertible for the reader, who cannot make sense of the

13. Quoted by Edel, Introductory Essay to *The Sacred Fount*, xxxi.

story as he reads it without positing one state of affairs or the other. The copresence of the phenomenological *epoché* and the continuing compulsion exercised on the reader to decide the issue may well be what constitutes the trap set for the latter.

It should be noted that, although James's theory of the "field of second exhibition" thus guarantees his text's ambiguity and the reader's dilemma, it does not necessarily stipulate that the story be told by a first-person narrator. A focalized, third-person narrative limited to one center of consciousness might have been consistent with the same objective; the ghost in "The Jolly Corner," for example, is represented under these conditions. It may be true, however, that in choosing a first-person narrator James chose (whether he meant to or not) the form that ensured the most perfect suspension of judgment.

The theory of the field of second exhibition can help to account for the changing sequence of James's remarks on *The Turn of the Screw* both before and after he wrote the novella. That series of remarks is noteworthy for heading in the direction of a more and more problematic understanding of the governess' role in the story. In his notebook entry for January 12, 1893—the main recorded source for the story—James made only one allusion to the problem of the narrator, at the every end of his notation: "The story to be told—tolerably obviously—by an outside spectator, observer" (*NB*, 178). The casualness of this is surprising enough. What is more surprising, however, is that even after the tale was composed and published James was still able to suggest that the governess was only a neutral observer. In the letter to H. G. Wells, he wrote, "I had to rule out subjective complications of her own—play of tone, etc.;—and keep her impersonal save for the most obvious and indispensable little note of neatness, firmness and courage—without which she wouldn't have had her data." [14] A decade later, in the Preface for the New York Edition, however, James tells a different story. Recalling the complaint of an early reader (Wells?) that "I hadn't sufficiently 'characterised' my young woman engaged in her labyrinth," James formulates this response:

> It was "déjà très-joli," in "The Turn of the Screw," please believe, the gen-

14. James to Wells, December 9, 1898, in James, *Letters*, ed. Edel, IV, 86.

eral proposition of our young woman's keeping crystalline her record of
so many intense anomalies and obscurities—by which I don't of course mean
her explanation of them, a different matter; and I saw no way . . . to exhibit her in relations other than those; one of which, precisely, would have been
her relation to her own nature. We have surely as much of her own nature as
we can swallow in watching it reflect her anxieties and inductions. It constitutes no little of a character, indeed, in such conditions, for a young person,
as she says, "privately bred," that she is able to make her particular credible
statement of such strange matters. She has "authority," which is a good deal
to have given her, and I couldn't have arrived at so much had I clumsily tried
for more. (*AN*, 173–74)

In this marvelously guarded passage, James is flirting with the very question
I am pursuing: that of the degree to which the governess' narrative is actually autobiographical, a story about herself. But it is difficult to see where
he comes down on this question. In accusing his reader of paying too little
attention, he is suggesting that he did characterize his narrator sufficiently,
and indeed he insists that "we have surely as much of her own nature as we
can swallow." But he also appears to claim that he has purposely avoided
going into "her relation to her own nature," which was not, after all, his
original subject, as the notebook entry showed.

The passage also maintains an ambivalence on the crucial issue of the
narrator's authority. First, in distinguishing between the governess' "keeping crystalline the record" and her explanation of her experience, James
suggests that narrative authority in this story is double edged or is split in
two. This split imposes an unusual burden on the reader, who must learn to
distinguish between two different kinds of evidence, and it obviously contributes to the ambiguity of the story. Furthermore, the issue is not resolved
by James's seemingly definite statement at the end: "She has 'authority,'
which is a good deal to have given her." In the light of the earlier equivo-
cations, this use of *authority* in quotation marks does not necessarily mean
that the governess must be taken as a reliable narrator. The use of the quotation marks may in fact mean that James is simply quoting the use of the
term that occurs in *The Turn of the Screw* itself (just as he quoted the words
privately bred from the story two lines earlier). In the frame of the narrative,
Douglas uses the term *authority* to describe the governess' position at Bly:

"There were plenty of people to help, but of course the young lady who should go down as governess would be in supreme authority." If this is the only authority James has in mind in the Preface, then it does not refer so much to the governess' reliability as simply to the fact of her centrality for the storytelling. As first-person narrator, she has usurped the place of the author (or the master) and taken his authority, but this usurpation is *de facto* rather than *de jure*.

In sum, this passage from the Preface helps us locate the central question of autobiography for *The Turn of the Screw*, but it does not decide that question. James's guarded conclusion—"and I couldn't have arrived at so much had I clumsily tried for more"—is very much in the spirit of compromise that we saw governing his definition of the ghost story. James's remarks also point to a compromise on the issue of the two stories of *The Turn of the Screw*, the story of the governess' relation to the ghosts and that of her "relation to her own nature." His comments at least support the possibility that the governess' entire narrative is autobiographical, that all of her seemingly outward preoccupation really reflects, as he puts it, "her own nature." At the same time, he is unwilling to admit that autobiography, with its "*fluidity* of self-revelation," is the actual mode of the tale.

The obscurities in the governess' position and the important distinction between two kinds of authority introduce a disturbing note that James cannot ignore. Although he seems pleased in his Preface by the "perfect homogeneity" of the story, its conformity to the laws he laid down for it, he also calls it an "irresponsible little fiction" and "a full-blown flower of high fancy" (*AN*, 169) (just as *The Sacred Fount* was a "small fantisticality"). If we look closer at the Preface, we find that this risk of irresponsibility— a possible abuse of authority—comes from the conjunction of romance or fancy and the first-person narrator, with his inevitable subjectivity. In short, the danger is that the romantic imagination will get out of control.

At first, it is true, James speaks of the function of the imagination in this story as an asset. *The Turn of the Screw*, he writes,

> had for me the immense merit of allowing the imagination absolute freedom of hand, of inviting it to act on a perfectly clear field, with no "outside" control involved. . . . I find here a perfect example of an exercise of the imagi-

nation unassisted, unassociated—playing the game, making the score, in the phrase of our sporting day, off its own bat. To what degree the game was worth playing I needn't attempt to say: the exercise I have noted strikes me now, I confess, as the interesting thing, the imaginative faculty acting with the *whole* of the case on its hands. (*AN*, 170–71)

The first question to ask of this passage is: whose imagination is concerned? The most obvious—and no doubt correct—answer is: that of the author himself. James is writing in the Prefaces of his own relation to the story. But a second, perhaps equally valid answer is that the imagination is that of the governess. As we have just seen from the frame of the tale, the phrase "no 'outside' control" defines the governess' situation perfectly. The chief function of the frame may be, as I have suggested, precisely to point to the elimination of control. In effacing itself before the end of the text, the vanishing frame underlines the "supreme authority" bestowed on the first-person narrator. That authority, as we shall see presently, will be appropriated largely by her imagination. Already in Chapter 3 of her narrative she describes her situation at Rye as "a trap—not designed but deep—to my imagination" (14).

The imagination, then, can not only supply a merit but lay a trap. The reason for this is apparent from the passage just quoted from the Preface. The terms James uses to describe the role of the imagination in *The Turn of the Screw*—"absolute . . . a perfectly free field . . . the *whole* of the case on its hands"—are terms that, up to now, we have never seen him use for works of fiction, but only for his own autobiography. The contrast between Strether and James himself in his autobiography was described as the difference between a relative and an absolute power of the imagination. Narrative fiction did not dare represent the supreme but only the comparative case of the imagination, and even then the imaginative Strether ran the risk of being wrecked (*AN*, 310). All of this makes it clear once again how *The Turn of the Screw* (and *The Sacred Fount* no less) involves a violation of James's self-imposed rules.[15] By endowing the governess with total imag-

15. Certain critics of *The Sacred Fount* have made exactly the same claim for that work, as being a pure product of the imagination, that James makes for *The Turn of the Screw*. See, for example, Philip Weinstein, *Henry James and the Requirements of the Imagination*, 118. *Cf.* Arnold Weinstein, *Vision and Response in Modern Fiction*, 74.

ination, James is in effect removing her from the ranks of his other fictional characters and is equating her with his own condition. The problem is that, unlike James, she cannot write real autobiography, not only because she is a fictional character but also because the narrative form within which she functions is arranged to discourage direct self-revelation. The case of the governess, then, confounds the categories of the fictive and the real, for which James sought such different stipulations. It is no wonder, too, that her dilemma seems to implicate James, so that he gets drawn into the autobiographical romance of her narrative.

The description of the trap that *The Turn of the Screw* lays for the imagination is not yet complete. If the author's and the narrator's imaginations are both implicated, so is the reader's. In his Preface, James speaks of this novella as a kind of trap for its audience, "an *amusette* to catch those not easily caught" (*AN*, 172). That the instrument of this trap was to be the reader's own imagination James makes clear a few pages later, as he describes his unwillingness to specify the exact nature of the evil that was threatening Miles and Flora: "Only make the reader's general vision of evil intense enough, I said to myself—and that already is a charming job—and his own experience, his own imagination, his own sympathy (with the children) and horror (of their false friends) will supply him quite sufficiently with all the particulars" (*AN*, 176). James prides himself on his reticence, his refusal to "expatiate" in the text: "There is not only from beginning to end of the matter not an inch of expatiation, but my values are positively all blanks save so far as an excited horror, a promoted pity, a created expertness—on which punctual effects of strong causes no writer can ever fail to plume himself—proceed to read into them more or less fantastic figures" (*AN*, 176–77).

This passage brings into play several of the terms that James regularly associates with romance and the imagination, notably, the images of reading in (the surplus of meaning supplied by the subject) and figures. The imagination, or figurative faculty as *A Small Boy and Others* called it (*SBO*, 123), has as its specific function to create a meaning that is not literally in the object but is added to it by a process James compares to that of figurative language. In his autobiography, James did not necessarily associate this process with error. In the present context, though, where the figures are ''more or less fantastic'' and where the entire story is designed to catch the sophisticated reader, the intervention of the figurative imagination is closely linked to the possibility of error and misreading.

The reader's imagination thus plays a role basically identical to that played by the author and the governess. One might almost speak of a redundancy of effect, where author, narrator, and reader all conspire to create the text (or its meaning) out of values that are initially blanks.[16] The governess' dilemma cannot leave the reader untouched any more than it can the author.

Although the personal motives of the first-person narrators of *The Turn of the Screw* and *The Sacred Fount* are never explicitly stated, both narratives are conducted mainly in a spirit of apology or self-defense. Each narrator feels the need to relate a disturbing set of events from his or her own point of view, in a light that will vindicate his or her conduct and interpretation of events as far as possible. (Here, as elsewhere, the governess shows a stronger, less compromising or self-critical character than the Narrator.) The reason behind this need is not far to seek. Both narrators are isolated from the people around them, a condition that becomes aggravated during the course of the stories they tell. In a sense, the very fact of being a narrator is for them already a sign of isolation, and of a unique burden placed on them as individuals in opposition to their society. To be a first-person narrator is already to be singled out as a potential scapegoat. This is most clear near the end of both narratives, where we witness the series of frustrating, sometimes humiliating, events that lead to their virtual ostracism. But it is also perhaps apparent, as I have already hinted, in the relation between the governess' written text and the frame of *The Turn of the Screw*. The frame is an oral storytelling scene, full of dialogue, with give-and-take between tellers and listeners. The ''voice'' of the governess, by contrast, comes out of the grave and is inscribed in a text that does not invite a real dialogue with its readers—hence the disturbing silence at the end of the narrative. The governess is as isolated from Douglas and his audience as she is, by the end, from the master, Mrs. Grose, and Flora.

In a state of growing isolation, then, both narrators are plunged into a sit-

16. On the reversibility of the roles of reading and writing in *The Turn of the Screw*, see Walter Benn Michaels, ''Writers Reading: James and Eliot,'' *Modern Language Notes*, XCI (1976), 827–49.

uation that offers special privileges but also risks. They are subjected to a test both of their behavior and of their ability to read the signs of the behavior around them. Each feels the novelty and expresses his or her portentous sense of this in strikingly similar terms. First, the governess speaks at the end of her Chapter 1: "I had the view of a castle of romance inhabited by a rosy spright, such a place as would somehow, for diversion of the young idea, take all colour out of story-books and fairy-tales. Wasn't it just a story-book over which I had fallen a-doze and a-dream?" (10). Now the Narrator, before his meeting with May in Chapter 8, writes: "I scarce know what odd consciousness I had of roaming at close of day in the grounds of some castle of enchantment. I had positively encountered nothing to compare with this since the days of fairy-tales and of the childish imagination of the impossible. *Then* I used to circle round enchanted castles, for then I moved in a world in which the strange 'came true' " (128). The reference to childhood is important, pointing to the model for the governess' and the Narrator's entire experience. For James himself, childhood proved to be the privileged ground for the practice of autobiography; these first-person narrators, too, have an affinity for the age in which imagination can so easily overshadow reality. Both narrators indulge in a belief in what Freud labeled "the omnipotence of thought," a primitive (and, by extension, childlike) belief in one's ability to will events to happen.[17] The Narrator continues: "It was the coming true that was the proof of the enchantment, which, moreover, was naturally never so great as when such coming was, to such a degree and by the most romantic stroke of all, the fruit of one's own wizardry. I was positively—so had the wheel revolved—proud of my work" (128–29).

Just as the strange can come true in *The Sacred Fount*, so imaginings can turn into reality in *The Turn of the Screw*. These are the terms in which the governess presents her first view of Peter Quint, which comes when she has been daydreaming about a possible sudden appearance of the master: "What arrested me on the spot—and with a shock much greater than any vision had allowed for—was the sense that my imagination had, in a flash, turned real" (16).

17. See Sigmund Freud, "The Uncanny," in James Strachey (ed.), *The Standard Edition of the Complete Psychological Works of Sigmund Freud* (24 vols.; London, 1953–74), XVII, 219–52.

Passages like these have led some critics to see in the Narrator (and more rarely in the governess) a figure of the artist, who does not simply concoct a theory to match the facts he sees but who makes the facts conform to the theory he is creating to contain them. If this is true—if the Narrator can be called an artist at all—then he is not just any artist but the absolute, romantic one who creates his work out of a free imagination, as James says he created the materials of *The Turn of the Screw*. That the Narrator does not really exercise such total freedom, however, is strongly hinted by Lady John, who responds to his claim to be a providence for the other characters by saying: "You can't be a providence and not be a bore. A real providence *knows*; whereas you . . . have to find out" (176). Lady John's equation of a true providence with a bore resembles James's statement, in the Preface to *The Princess Casamassima*, that a human drama must rely on the presence of fools—who, unlike providence, can be mistaken—to be a drama at all (*AN*, 67). Indeed, whatever drama *The Sacred Fount* possesses can only be a measure of the Narrator's mistakenness.

If both narrators display so strong an imagination that they tend to confuse the imagined with the real, what exactly is it that they imagine they see? What is the nature of the imagined or perceived world they inhabit? Paradoxically, the free imagination James said was operating in *The Turn of the Screw* tends to express itself in both works only in rigid, symmetrical schemes, or laws. "I was just conscious, vaguely," says the Narrator at the outset, "of being on the track of a law, a law that would fit, that would strike me as governing the delicate phenomena—delicate though so marked—that my imagination found itself playing with" (23). This mark of the imagination, to play out its freedom only by submitting it to law, conforms with James's desire to avoid fluidity, to temper romance with realism, the phantasmagoric with the evidential. The fantasy devised by these narrators is intended, as James put it, to be firm (*AN*, 173).[18]

In fact, the schemes invented by the two narrators to account for their ex-

18. For the view that the Narrator's passion for symmetry and law disqualifies his theory as an accurate description of existential reality, see Robert J. Andreach, "Henry James's *The Sacred Fount*: The Existential Predicament," *Nineteenth-Century Fiction*, XVII (1962), 197–216. For a more balanced appraisal of the Narrator's predilection for symmetry, in both his theory and his narrative style, see Rimmon, *The Concept of Ambiguity*, 209–26.

perience can be expressed by the same arithmetic: two times two. In both works, one pair of figures is given; a second pair, to be matched up with the first, must be deduced by the narrator. For the governess, the given pair is Miles and Flora; the second pair she discovers to be linked with them is Peter Quint and Miss Jessel.

The Narrator's scheme is not quite so stable. He seeks a symmetry among the principal characters like that which underlies the four main characters of Goethe's *Elective Affinities*, but for those mainly benign affinities he substitutes the vampire motif of the sacred fount. The two characters he assumes as given at the outset are Gilbert Long and Grace Brissenden, both of whom are the apparent beneficiaries of their partners' sacrifices. The second pair is more problematic. Grace's corresponding figure seems to be her husband Guy, but for Gilbert Long's partner there are several candidates, the choice among whom takes up much of the novel. The Narrator's theory, however, is seriously challenged only near the end of the narrative when Grace Brissenden suggests that one of his original *données*, Long's intellectual development, may never have existed (266–96).

This challenge corresponds, in *The Turn of the Screw*, to the governess' periodic worry that the children may not be evil after all; if they are not, then there is no need to posit the ghosts: "If [Miles] *were* innocent what then on earth was I?" (87). Yet the governess manages at least to uphold her theory against her one interlocutor, Mrs. Grose, whereas the Narrator actually depends on several interlocutors (Mrs. Brissenden, Ford Obert, Lady John, even Long and Guy Brissenden) to piece together his theory, which is always in a state of flux. To adapt a distinction made by Claude Lévi-Strauss, the Narrator acts like the tinkerer (*bricoleur*), who arbitrarily uses the materials he finds around him to construct an object he needs, whereas the governess resembles more the engineer who invents the pieces she needs to fit her preestablished intention.[19] As a *bricoleur*, the Narrator seems more modest and even critical of his own system building, whose arbitrary nature he fully recognizes at one point: "These opposed couples balanced like bronze groups at the two ends of a chimney-piece, and the most I could say

19. On the Narrator as a *bricoleur*, see Peter Brooks, *The Melodramatic Imagination* (New Haven, 1976), 176.

to myself in lucid deprecation of my thought was that I mustn't take them equally for granted merely *because* they balanced. Things in the real had a way of not balancing; it was all an affair, this fine symmetry, of artificial proportion'' (182–83).

Once the grand theory is glimpsed, however, both narrators evince intellectual and emotional commitment to it; a belief in the theory comes to dictate their every move. There is even a moral commitment in the way the narrators feel it their duty to save, protect, or screen one or more of the characters who are the potential victims of the system that they have laid bare. For the Narrator, there is the duty to protect May Server from public exposure, a duty that ironically threatens to interfere with the perfect elaboration of his theory, for at times he feels compelled to deny May's involvement in the sacred fount even though he is convinced of it. For the governess, the duty is of course to save the children from the ghosts, at one point by almost literally becoming a screen herself, so that "by offering myself bravely as the sole subject of such experience [the ghosts' visits], by accepting, by inviting, by surmounting it all, I should serve as an expiatory victim and guard the tranquillity of the rest of the household. The children in special I should thus fence about and absolutely save. . . . I was a screen— I was to stand before them'' (26–28).

But the narrators are not the only ones who screen others. They suspect that other characters are screening each other or are generally concealing things from the peering glance of the narrator. One corollary to the Narrator's theory is that the "agents of the sacrifice" desire to hide their impoverished state, while the governess of course constantly fears that Miles and Flora are concealing their communion with the ghosts from her. These beliefs foster an attitude of deep suspicion, if not paranoia, which in turn produces a perverse notion as to what constitutes evidence for the narrator's theory. Since (as the narrators presume) the persons actually involved with the ghosts or with the sacred fount must hide their involvement, the most significant signs will be negative ones. By a reversal similar to that at work in Freudian denial or negation (*Verneinung*), signs of omission or negation will be read as their opposites, as avowals.

In *The Sacred Fount*, of course, the Narrator's entire theory exhibits a negative reasoning because it is based on analogy, that is, on inferring the

absent and unknown from what is or is thought to be known. But these in-
ferences are made especially difficult because of the victims' presumed motive for dissimulation, "for as the appearance is inevitably a kind of betrayal, it's in somebody's interest to conceal it" (33). The Narrator's evidence
will be confined to what Ford Obert calls psychological signs, as opposed
to "the detective and the keyhole" (66). In practice, this means the Narrator's main opportunities for developing and propounding his theory will
be limited to those devious dialogues where the unspoken is often as important as the spoken. This tendency of the dialogues to operate by omission
as much as by statement reaches its apex in the final confrontation with Mrs.
Briss, where the Narrator sums up the quality of the talk thus: "It could *not*
but be exciting to talk, as we talked, on the basis of those suppressed processes and unavowed references which made the meaning of our meeting so
different from its form" (272). This breach between form and meaning, disturbing in the light of James's often-expressed belief in the organic union of
form and content, derives from a deep, unstated dimension of language that
escapes and surpasses the literal meaning of the words used.

In *The Turn of the Screw*, the governess has a similar penchant for separating the apparent form of language from its meaning and for taking the
unspoken as positive proof of what others are thinking or intending. Again
the governess relies, unknowingly, on a Freudian line of reasoning when
she sees the children's silence concerning their former servants as proof of
their complicity with the latter's ghosts: "*Never*, by a slip of the tongue,
have they so much as alluded to either of their old friends" (48; *cf.* 26). In
the two scenes where the governess is with Flora when Miss Jessel appears,
she takes Flora's failure to acknowledge her former mistress' presence as
proof that she is aware of it. When the governess and Mrs. Grose rush to the
lake in the second of these scenes and find the boat missing, the governess
rapidly concudes: "Our not seeing it is the strongest of proofs" (69). In the
later stages of the narrative, this reasoning by reversal becomes so pervasive
that relations between the governess and the others become like the conversation between the Narrator and Mrs. Brissenden; as the governess says,
"The element of the unnamed and untouched became, between us, greater
than any other" (50). Only in the final pages, with "the supreme surrender
of the name" of the ghosts (88), will the situation change, and then for the

worse. The governess' way of perceiving the world, then, like the Narrator's, depends less upon the seen than the unseen—at least, what is unseen by other people.

The Narrators do not, however, abandon their attempt to find objective evidence for their theories, to "make it evidential," as James wrote of *The Sacred Fount*. On the contrary, the tenuous and even negative quality of much of their evidence only stimulates the narrators' drive to see their beliefs vindicated. But they are both working under a major handicap indicated by the distinction Ford Obert makes between psychological signs and the keyhole. In *The Sacred Fount*, the impossibility of an appeal to concrete signs (the keyhole) is a self-imposed rule; in *The Turn of the Screw* it is rather an external constraint dictated by the intangible nature of the ghosts and by what the governess sees as the children's stubborn duplicity.

This exclusion of external, objective signs thus reinforces the method of the field of second exhibition. Both of these conditions imply that the realm of factual, objective signs has been excluded or bracketed; the only permitted drama will be concerned not with facts but with meanings, or Husserlian intentions. The truth of a theory, under these conditions, becomes less a matter of factual verification or even of predictive capacity than one of persuasive power. As Harold Tolliver has written of *The Sacred Fount*, " 'Truth' exists only in persuasion: it is carried only by personal force and conviction." [20]

The model of persuasion suggests the importance of dialogue in both works. In alternation with the pictorial mode of recollected meditation, dialogue is one of the two major modes of presentation used in these works. But there is always a question as to whether this dialogue embodies a genuine communication between two people or whether it is only an extension of the narrators' introspective monologue, a sort of ventriloquism where both voices ultimately belong to the first-person narrator. [21]

20. Harold Tolliver, *Animate Illusions* (Lincoln, 1974), 304. *Cf.* Sally Sears, *The Negative Imagination: Form and Perspective in the Novels of Henry James* (Ithaca, 1968), 36.

21. See Walter Isle, *Experiments in Form: Henry James's Novels, 1896–1901* (Cambridge, Mass., 1968), 217–24, for a good discussion of dialogue in *The Sacred Fount* and the ways in which it affects the subjective and objective orientations of the novel. On the ambiguity of dialogue in this work, see Rimmon, *The Concept of Ambiguity*, 168.

Both narrators want to believe that their conversations afford a real corroboration of their theories. But the narrative form in which the dialogues appear makes such corroboration difficult to obtain. Since the dialogue is embedded in the first-person narrative, it is never conducted between two equal and independent partners but is always one-sided, particularly in the governess' dialogues with Mrs. Grose. These are never pure dialogues, limited to direct discourse; the speech is always amply punctuated by stage directions of various kinds, supplied by the governess, and is usually introduced and concluded by the governess' own reflections. Furthermore, Mrs. Grose is no match for the narrator in eloquence or reasoning power; most of the conversations show the governess cajoling or browbeating her. Under these circumstances, it is rare that Mrs. Grose can offer independent evidence to confirm the governess' theories.

The Narrator of *The Sacred Fount* does not manipulate his interlocutors to the same extent, but he does face the same uncertainty as to how much of their thought is the product of his own suggestion. His theory is much more a result of collaboration with Ford Obert and Mrs. Brissenden than is the governess' of her dialogue with Mrs. Grose, but it is still the Narrator who instills in them the germ of his basic analogy, and as he watches them give new twists to it he cannot be sure whether their belief in his theory is independent of his influence. Moreover, the Narrator likes to feel that the theory is still his own and that the others are only playing with it within the boundaries he has prescribed. Even of Mrs. Briss, probably his most brilliant and dangerous accomplice, he remarks: "I felt a little like a teacher encouraging an apt pupil; but I could only go on with the lesson" (35). With this attitude, the Narrator can never really take others' hypotheses as corroborations of his own. Yet he, like the governess, sometimes conveniently forgets that he has planted the seed of his theory in others' minds and acts as though they have arrived at the same conclusions independently. Discussing Guy Brissenden's deterioration with Gilbert Long, the Narrator worries that they may already have betrayed their knowledge to the victim: " 'He knows we've noticed.' Long wondered again. 'Ah, but I haven't!' He spoke with some sharpness" (23). In the same way, during the Peter Quint identification scene, the governess tries to get Mrs. Grose to admit that she knows more than she is saying. "But now that you've guessed" (who the unknown intruder is), she begins—but Mrs. Grose checks her: " 'Ah I haven't guessed!' she said very simply. 'How can I if *you* don't imagine?' " (22). Mrs. Grose's curious answer calls attention to the fact that her knowledge, as well as that of the governess, depends primarily upon the latter's power of imagination.

The narrators' quest for the truth, then, relies not on objective knowledge but on pressure, the amount of physical and psychological pressure they can exert on the people around them. The governess tries to "keep [Mrs. Grose] in the grip" of her theory; she physically squeezes Flora and, later, Miles, with unfortunate consequences. The Narrator, as we might expect, is less violent and less successful in pressuring others, but he does his best. He puts pressure on Gilbert Long, gets a grip on Ford Obert, and tries to get a hold on Mrs. Brissenden (24, 214, 256). As he tells Mrs. Brissenden, even his relation to truth itself is based on force: "That has remained all day the same—to get at the truth: not, that is, to relax my grasp on that tip of the tail of it which you so helped me this morning to fasten to" (260).

In a sense, this almost Nietzschean notion of the truth as something to be conquered supports those critics who see in the Narrator a figure of the Jamesian artist.[22] The Narrator's peculiar expression about pursuing the truth strongly echoes some phrases James wrote in his notebooks when in pursuit of a germ for a possible story. "Last night, as I worried through some wakeful hours, I seemed to myself to catch hold of the tail of an idea that may serve as the subject of the little tale I have engaged to write," he wrote on one occasion (*NB*, 143). "Another little possibility dances before me—I only just catch the tip of its tail," he wrote another time (*NB*, 184).

This curious parallel brings us back to the disturbing element in the comparison that must be made between James himself and his first-person narrators. While the author in his notebooks knows full well that he is inventing a plot that will serve in his fiction, the "I" narrators have lost sight of the reality or fictionality of their hypotheses concerning the truth. Dialogue cannot lend them a means of distinguishing truth from fiction or what is outside from what is inside. Instead of getting outside of themselves through dia-

22. For an extended comparison of James's and Nietzsche's notions of the artist, see Stephen Donadio, *Nietzsche, Henry James, and the Artistic Will* (New York, 1978).

logue, the narrators use these confrontations only to subsume the other, to translate the other's language into terms that so closely resemble their own language and thought that it cannot be distinguished from their own creation. Occasionally, a genuinely alien voice makes itself felt, as in the case of Gilbert Long's and Mrs. Grose's resistance and, at more length, in the case of Mrs. Brissenden in the closing chapters of *The Sacred Fount*. When this happens, the new voice almost always challenges the assumptions under which the narrator is operating. Moreover, the narrator has no real way of integrating these challenges but must either suppress them or succumb to them, allowing the unraveling of the whole narrative web he has spun. But we have not yet come to the moment of this final self-destruction of the story.

Dialogue in the two works, then, raises but does not resolve the question of whether the narrator can reach out beyond his or her subjectivity and recognize the other *as* other. Insofar as the narratives are autobiographical, this question poses a fundamental obstacle to their success, since an autobiographical narrative must presumably be predicated on the ability to tell the self and its creations from the outside world. This problem not only is manifest in the dialogue; it also permeates the imagistic language of both narratives, especially perhaps *The Turn of the Screw*. In this novella the imagery that most directly raises the question of self and other, inside and outside, is that of water, with the related images of glass and mirror.[23] In studying James's terminology, we have already seen that fluidity is related to subjectivity. For the governess, the question raised by the imagery is whether she is actually able to confront others, as through a window, or whether she is confronting only her own nature, as in a mirror. More specifically, the issue is her ability to identify the ghosts as something outside of herself, rather than as reflections of herself.

On the very first page of her manuscript, the governess introduces, perhaps unwittingly, the theme of reflexivity. In the bedroom she is assigned at Bly, she is especially struck, among other things, by "the long glasses in which, for the first time, I could see myself from head to foot" (7). Here is a symbolic promise that her adventures at Bly will entail a degree of self-

23. Curiously, the fullest available treatment of James's imagery, Robert L. Gale, *The Caught Image: Figurative Language in the Fiction of Henry James* (Chapel Hill, 1964), never mentions the water imagery of *The Turn of the Screw*.

knowledge she has not heretofore attained. The word *glasses*, at the same time, already contains the fundamental ambiguity of her story, since it can refer not only to a mirror (as here) but also to a transparent medium—a window, for instance—through which one sees something exterior.

Along with the alternate motifs of mirror and window, the central image of water also enters early. The governess ends her first chapter with a foreboding sense of her responsibilities at the house at Bly, "in which I had the fancy of our being almost as lost as a handful of passengers in a great drifting ship. Well, I was strangely at the helm!" This sense of drifting is intensified toward the end of her narrative when her position has weakened after the climactic scene at the lake with Flora and Mrs. Grose. After Flora deserts her, she says, "It was in short by just clutching the helm that I avoided total wreck" (79). From this point on, water and movement on water become her chief source of metaphor: "How . . . could I make a reference without a new plunge into the hideous obscure? . . . I seemed to float not into clearness, but into a deeper obscure. . . . I felt a sick swim at the drop of my victory and the return of my battle" (80–88). If window and mirror are a pair of alternate terms related to outside and inside, water simply expresses the governess' sense of the burdens and the fluidity of her subjectivity.

The ghost sightings, however, function as the real cruxes in the text by forcing her—and the reader—to choose beween images of windows and of mirrors. The first scene that forces such a choice is that of Peter Quint's second appearance, in Chapter 4. Quint appears on the other side of a window, "his face . . . close to the glass." But the governess is not satisfied by this view of him. Her immediate impulse is to run outside to the other side of the window, as if to test whether it is a real window or a mirror with nothing behind it. Her doubt as to whether she has seen him is expressed in a peculiar, self-defeating formula that already suggests that Peter Quint exists only for her: "He was there or not there: not there if I didn't see him." Her next move is even more interesting, though its significance is obscure to the governess herself: "It was confusedly present to me that I ought to place myself where he had stood. I did so; I applied my face to the pane and looked, as he had looked, into the room." At this point Mrs. Grose shows up, somewhat patly, and assumes the governess' former position, thus offering to the latter "the full image of a repetition of what had already occurred" (21).

It is a repetition with a difference, of course. While Mrs. Grose now stands where the governess stood, the governess stands where Peter Quint stood, unintentionally identifying herself with him. The repeated scene, like the original, finds people both inside and outside and thus confirms the two-sidedness of the window, which was still in doubt in the first scene. But if the two scenes could be collapsed into one (as "the full image of a repetition" would seem to warrant), then we would find the governess on *both* sides, and the apparent window would revert to being a mirror that confines the governess to a specular relation to herself. This is not, of course, the interpretation that the governess accepts. In fact she is so far from accepting it that she seeks, in the end, to deny her own position in the structure altogether. This surprising conclusion transpires when Mrs. Grose, seeing the governess' face pressed up against the glass, turns white from fear, and the governess' reaction is: "I wondered why *she* should be scared" (21). To wonder about this is, of course, to suppress the fact that she herself is the cause of Mrs. Grose's scare. It is in effect a desire to efface her own role, to reduce the autobiographical element in her narrative.

No subsequent scene offers quite so full an image of the governess' dilemma of specularity. But the components of this scene—the confusion between window and mirror, the symbolic identification of different characters with each other, and finally, the governess' desire to efface the signs of her own involvement—can all be traced in later episodes with the ghosts. The next two sightings both make use of water or glass. The governess first sees Miss Jessel, in Flora's presence, across the reflecting surface of the lake ("the Sea of Azov"—29), and Quint once again appears through a window (41). The next ghost encounter after this, the night scene with Miles on the lawn, again involves a confusion of the governess' position with that of the ghost (43–45).[24] But the crowning episode is the long scene in which the governess and Mrs. Grose confront Flora, and Miss Jessel, at the lake (68–74).

Even before the governess ventures onto the surface of the lake in the boat

24. For a discussion of this scene, see Juliet McMaster, "The Full Image of a Repetition," *Studies in Short Fiction*, VI (1969), 377–82.

with Mrs. Grose, the water image is introduced metaphorically, in application to the narrator: "I scanned all the visible shore, while Mrs. Grose took again, into the queer element I offered her, one of her plunges of submission" (69). More strongly than before, the governess now *is* the watery element, the fluidity in which Mrs. Grose is invited to lose herself. The metaphorical and literal scenes become confused, so that the real "sheet of water," with "its extent and its agitation" (68), seems to merge with the depth of the watery element the governess has become.

If water imagery provides the backdrop, the climax of the scene reverts to the imagery of glass. When the governess finally succumbs to temptation and asks Flora where Miss Jessel is, thus breaking the self-imposed silence she has kept till now, she reports the child's reaction to this delivery of the name in these terms: "The quick smitten glare with which the child's face received it fairly likened my breach of the silence to the smash of a pane of glass" (71). This is precisely the image we have been led to expect by earlier mirror/window ambiguities. By "smashing the glass" with the utterance of the name, the governess is doing essentially what she did when she ran outside, around the window, to look for Peter Quint. The figurative shattering of the glass announces, she hopes, the end of all ambiguity. When she breaks the glass, it no longer will matter whether this glass was a mirror or a window; now she will see not through a glass darkly but face to face. All of this is to be accomplished through the long-delayed, cathartic naming of a name, just as in the yet later scene with Miles his "supreme surrender of the name" of Quint will precipitate the story's ultimate catastrophe.

The utterance of Miss Jessel's name seems at first to meet with success. The governess' speech produces Miss Jessel herself, who appears on the opposite shore, and the governess experiences "a thrill of joy at having brought on a proof" (71). But after another moment she must recognize that Flora and Mrs. Grose are giving no sign of seeing the ghost; even more upsetting, Flora is now returning the governess' gaze: "To see her . . . not even feign to glance in the direction of the prodigy I announced, but only, instead of that, to turn at *me* an expression of hard still gravity" (71). Flora's look "appeared to read and accuse and judge me" (71). This shift of attention from Miss Jessel back to the narrator occupies the remainder of the scene, until Flora finally calls out to Mrs. Grose. " 'Take me away, take me away—

oh take me away from *her*!' 'From *me*?' I panted. 'From you—from you!'
she cried'' (73).

This scene, then, ends on the same note of ambiguity as the earlier ones,
with the governess tugging the evidence in one direction while the structure
of events seems to call for the opposite interpretation. The smashing of the
glass fails to deliver on its promise; the ambiguous mirror/window remains
intact to the end of the story. This mirror/window confusion has proved to
be a major source, or reflection, of the key ambiguity in the entire text, that
of the undecidability of inside and outside, subjective and objective, for the
narrator. Despite her efforts, the imagery of glass prevents the governess
from ever unequivocally affirming the objective existence of the ghosts.

Moreover, by continually bringing her back to herself and to her symbolic identification with the ghosts, the imagery reminds her of her active
role in the ghost story. It helps establish the irreducible autobiographical
component of her narrative. It keeps her from being the self-effacing narrator she often seeks to be or the "outside spectator," telling her tale "tolerably obviously," whom James originally conceived for his novella.

By a final turn of the screw, the same stroke that makes the governess'
narrative autobiographical makes that autobiography thoroughly problematic, if not impossible. If, as our study of the imagery has shown, the governess can never finally judge whether she is creating the ghosts or not, if
she never acknowledges but also never refutes her symbolic identification
with the ghosts, then she is disqualified from making the most fundamental
discrimination on which an act of autobiography is based, the discrimination between what belongs to the "I" and what belongs to the "other." Her
story has become trapped, by her own metaphors, in a hall of mirrors where
the self does not benignly merge with but simply becomes confused with the
outside world.

The autobiographical dimension of *The Turn of the Screw* and *The Sacred
Fount* entails this turn of the narrative in upon the narrator-observer. The
"I" can no longer claim to be a transparent or objective eye but has become
part of the problem to be explored. This is the basic trap for the governess
that operates in the scenes we have examined. The cumulative effect of these
scenes is finally to make her doubt herself and her own innocence, as she
does in the last chapter: "If he *were* innocent what then on earth was I?"

She continues, "Paralysed, while it lasted, by the mere brush of the question, I let him [Miles] go a little" (87). Her momentary paralysis is the sign of the aporia with which the tale will end; her dilemma is, as she says at the same time, bottomless. Yet this epistemological dilemma does not totally dictate the governess' ethical behavior. Her force of character and conviction in her own rightness will allow her to proceed in her design to save Miles. This pragmatic forcefulness, on the other hand, cannot offer an epistemological solution to the story. The story simply breaks off with Miles's death, and the governess is not any more capable than Douglas or the other frame characters of offering a satisfactory explanation for what has occurred.

The same turn in upon the narrator—and the same resistance to that turn—can be seen in *The Sacred Fount*. Just as the governess does not want to admit her complicity or identification with the ghosts, so the Narrator wants to remain outside the sphere where the sacred fount operates, as a detached observer. He wants his scientific method (296) and his liberation from emotional interest in the people he is studying (192–93), but just as the governess' actions implicate her in the drama of the ghosts, so the Narrator's theorizing forces him to play a part in the sacred fount logic he is trying to expose. The earliest hints of his deeper involvement concern his attachment to May Server, which the Narrator himself betrays: "Had I myself suddenly fallen so much in love with Mrs. Server that the care for her reputation had become with me an obsession?" (60–61). The embarrassment the Narrator feels from this point forward is due to his increased involvement not only through the intellectual stake he has in his theory but through the intricate relations of jealousy and suspicion, affection and protection, that link him to other characters.[25]

This involvement culminates in the Narrator's being drawn into the economy of the sacred fount. Not only does he appear to pay emotionally for May Server (although this payment does not have the anticipated result of giving her strength), but he pays intellectually for the brilliant series of coups by which Mrs. Briss manages first to add to, then to undermine, his original theory. The first mention of this sacred fount relationship is made by Mrs.

25. For the most thorough treatment of the Narrator's complicity in the story, see Laurence Holland, *The Expense of Vision: Essays on The Craft of Henry James* (Princeton, 1964), 183–226.

Briss herself in Chapter 5: "You've *made* me sublime. You found me dense. You've affected me quite as much as Mrs. Server has affected Mr. Long" (81). The full implication of his being compared to the depleted May Server does not dawn on the Narrator yet—just as the governess resisted the implications of her assuming the position of Peter Quint. By Chapter 12, however, the signs that Mrs. Briss is taking strength from the Narrator have become unmistakable even to him: "It was a success, on her part, that, though I couldn't as yet fully measure it, there could be no doubt of whatever, any more than of my somehow paying for it" (240). His payment turns out to be not only intellectual but emotional and physical as well—that is, he pays as both May Server and Guy Brissenden have paid—when, on the last page, he suddenly feels the weight of his actual age for the first time (318).

These signs of his sacrifice are inconclusive and not to be trusted any more than the other pieces of evidence he finds to support his theory. At the same time, though, they are no *less* trustworthy than any other evidence, and so they jeopardize his claim to absolute detachment. As the Narrator confesses, rather late in the day, to Ford Obert: "I took my detachment too soon for granted. I haven't been detached. I'm not, hang me! detached now" (209).

Another way this loss of detachment is expressed is through the attention given to looks or glances. Exactly as the governess found her position damaged when Flora's gaze was trained on her rather than on the ghosts, so the Narrator is upset when his role as pure observer is taken from him and he finds himself being watched by others. " 'Oh, I've watched you,' said Ford Obert as if he had then perhaps after all the advantage of me" (219). Much earlier than this, the redoubtable Mrs. Briss has given the Narrator a similar scare: "So I all the more resent your making a scene on the extraordinary ground that I've observed as well as yourself. Perhaps what you don't like is that my observation may be turned on *you*. I confess it is" (76). With others beginning to observe him, the Narrator can no longer maintain that the only problem for analysis lies outside himself. Just as James referred (in the Preface to *The Turn of the Screw*) to the governess' own mystery, the Narrator must concede that he himself conceals a puzzle: "I daresay that, for that matter, my cogitations—for I must have bristled with them—would have made me as stiff a puzzle to interpretative minds as I had suffered other phenomena to become to my own'' (92).

All the evidence so far has shown how both of the narrators, far from being neutral observers, have become part of the subject matter of their narratives; they belong to the puzzle, not the solution. For this reason, they cannot be explained solely in terms of James's technical handling of narrative perspective; they are neither simply reliable nor unreliable narrators. On the other hand, they are not totally self-absorbed or autobiographical authors, either. The ''double privilege of subject and object'' bestowed on these narrators has caused that vacillation between two centers of interest, inside and outside, that we have had in view since the beginning. The resulting form is a hybrid that mixes autobiography with something else, whether ghost story, detective story, or romance. The ambivalence of these narrators toward their own texts is not unlike that of James in his autobiography, though they may be said to approach the same problem from the opposite side. James adopted the public form of autobiography and then confused the issue by writing of his father and his brother and of the impossibility of writing a life of himself alone. The two fictional narrators try to avoid the appearance of autobiography by concentrating on an objective story and overlooking their own role in it, but the story itself turns upon them and draws them in.

What is, finally, the puzzle or the mystery about these narrators that prevents them from unequivocally writing either about themselves or about something else? To answer this we must return to the question of the imagination and to two themes closely related to it: figurative language and madness.

The vacillation between two subjects, as just mentioned, affects what James calls the authority of the text or of its presumed author. We saw that the governess has an authority that is divided against itself. It might be called authority without mastery, since the governess is irretrievably cut off from the master.[26] This division within the principle of authority, which in James's terms separated record from explanation, brings about other separations as well. It divides the imagination from the simple perception of reality—or

26. On the undermining of narrative authority in *The Turn of the Screw*, see Felman, "Turning the Screw of Interpretation," 127–31.

intelligence from stupidity—and madness from sanity. Each of these op- positions is essential to the telling of the story. The narrator must be able to distinguish the first term from the second in order to have control over the narrative and its meaning. What happens in both stories, however, is that the hyperdevelopment of the imagination leads to an upsetting of its normal (positive) value relative to perception; this reversal, in turn, disturbs the normal or expected relation between the figurative and the literal, the intel- ligent and the stupid, the insane and the sane.

This disturbance does not occur with the sanction or even the total cog- nizance of the narrators. Instead, they try, first of all, to distinguish firmly between imagination and simple perception (in their view, between intel- ligence and stupidity) while cornering the market on imagination for them- selves. The Narrator sees his imagination as the gift that sets him apart from the rest of the company at Newmarch: "I remember feeling seriously warned, while dinner lasted, not to yield further to my idle habit of reading into mere human things an interest so much deeper than mere human things were in general prepared to supply. This especial hour, at Newmarch, had always a splendour that asked little of interpretation, that even carried itself, with an amiable arrogance, as indifferent to what the imagination could do for it. I think the imagination, in those halls of art and fortune, was almost inevit- ably accounted a poor matter" (156). The Narrator clearly sees the imagi- nation as a positive value, in fact as the originator of all value, the power that confers meaning on human situations. The imagination reads into events their full meaning; it adds a supplement of meaning.

The same association of the imagination with reading into occurs in *The Turn of the Screw*. The entire opposition between the governess and Mrs. Grose is expressed by the fact that the former is eminently a reader, while the latter is illiterate (10). Elsewhere, the governess is found reading into events quite as much as the Narrator. As she says after an early conversation with Mrs. Grose, "By the time the morrow's sun was high I had restlessly read into the facts before us almost all the meaning they were to receive from subsequent and more cruel occurrences" (27–28). The imagination creates meaning; for this reason it is a natural, even a necessary, attribute of the storyteller, and also of the reader, as we recall from James's Preface, where he admitted that the values of *The Turn of the Screw* would remain blanks

until the reader should ''proceed to read into them more or less fantastic figures.'' I shall return to these figures shortly.

This valuation, where the imagination is related to its absence as intelligence is to stupidity, is put into question by the encumbrances that the imagination imposes on the narrators in both works. In *The Turn of the Screw*,
Mrs. Grose's blindness to the ghosts, which is at first for the governess an
index of the older woman's stupidity, turns out to be her exemption from
the horrors of the situation (72). Although the governess may intend irony
when she calls Mrs. Grose ''a magnificent monument to the blessing of a
want of imagination'' (45), this blessing is a real one under the circumstances. The governess' gift is after all an ''infernal imagination'' (50) that
puts her in touch with the evil of the ghosts. Mrs. Grose may be immune
from imaginative flights, but she is also immune from contact with wicked-
ness. The governess' plight reminds us of her description of her position as
a trap to her imagination (14).

The Narrator of *The Sacred Fount* becomes trapped in the same way. By
Chapter 9, he is questioning the faith and pride we have earlier seen him
place in his unique imaginative gift: ''My personal privilege, on the basis
of the full consciousness, had become, on the spot, in the turn of an eye,
more than questionable, and I was really quite scared at the chance of having to face . . . another recognition. What did this alarm imply but the complete reversal of my estimate of the value of perception?'' (183). *Perception*
here is a synonym for the imagination, and what the Narrator is now discovering is that to have put Gilbert Long and Mrs. Briss ''on'' to his insights
is perhaps to have done them a disservice: ''To be without [imagination]
was the most consistent, the most successful, because the most amiable, form
of selfishness, and why should people so admirably equipped for remaining
so . . . be made to begin to vibrate, to crack and split, from within? Wasn't
it enough for *me* to pay, vicariously, the tax on being absurd?'' (184). To
pay this tax is to enter by implication into the economy of the sacred fount,
and it is the Narrator's imagination that has inconveniently placed him there.
Like the governess, he finds that the content of his imagination is largely
negative; as Lady John describes it, it is an ''imagination of atrocity'' (173).

The last part of the novel traces the Narrator's growing realization that
his destructive imagination has taken hold of him and is undermining his

position. He is no longer certain that it brings him light: "Light or darkness, my imagination rides me." The only release for him is "to quench . . . the flame of the fancy" that plagues him (276–77). But it is too late. His imagination has escaped his control so completely that it has gone over to the other side and is working for Mrs. Briss against him, so that "the case for her was really in almost any aspect she could now make it wear to my imagination. My wealth of that faculty, never so stimulated, was thus, in a manner, her strength; by which I mean the impossibility of my indifference to the mere immense suggestiveness of our circumstances" (240). His imagination, by stimulating his curiosity, leaves him vulnerable to his adversaries. They are paradoxically made secure by their inability to see as much as he does.

The value attached to the imagination in the two narratives, then, goes through the same change it underwent in the Preface to *The Turn of the Screw*, where, from being the source of the tale's merit, it became a trap for the narrator and the reader alike. The governess and the Narrator become prey to their hyperdeveloped imaginations. In the passage on the imagination in *Notes of a Son and Brother*, James was to refer to the possessor of imagination as "its subject or victim" (*NSB*, 369). In a letter of 1896 to A. C. Benson, James, sounding much like the Narrator of *The Sacred Fount*, had written: "I have the imagination of disaster—and see life as ferocious and sinister."[27] For the two fictional narrators, imagination can no longer be related to simple perception as acuity is to stupidity, because the imagination now appears prone to errors far more serious than any that beset the normal, empirical way of perceiving reality.

If the cognitive value of the imagination has been called into question, so too will be the cognitive value of the language the imagination employs. We now touch upon the opposition between literal and figurative language. In James's autobiography he defined the imagination as the figurative faculty, the faculty which, when it is applied to the past, adds embroidery to what was objectively real (*SBO*, 123; *NSB*, 481). The relation between figurative and literal language, then, is directly aligned with the relation between the

27. Henry James, *Letters to A. C. Benson and Auguste Monod*, ed. E. F. Benson (London, n.d.), 35.

imagination and reality. Just as the imagination is supposed to provide a supplement of meaning to reality, figurative language should provide a supplement—in the form of polysemy, or at least rich ambiguity—to literal language. A narrative saturated by the imagination, then, will not be susceptible to a literal interpretation. "The story *won't* tell," as Douglas tells his audience in the preface to the governess' manuscript, "not in any literal vulgar way" (3). The literal way *is* the vulgar way in such a case. But since we have already dealt at length with one chain of imagistic language in *The Turn of the Screw*, let us look at *The Sacred Fount* to see how the relation between the literal and the figurative is worked out in a narrative dominated by the imagination.

As we should expect, the Narrator's imaginative activity is described in the vocabulary that for James signifies the realm of the figurative, the vocabulary of embroidery, of figures in the carpet and loose threads. When the Narrator gloomily contemplates escaping from Newmarch, he says, "I should be in small haste to come back, for I should leave behind me my tangled theory, no loose thread of which need I ever again pick up, in no stray mesh of which need my foot again trip" (201). Later, when Mrs. Brissenden balks at following his lead in their conversation, he challenges her, "You haven't, with the force of your revulsion, I hope, literally lost our thread" (258). The curious use of *literally* here suggests the Narrator's habit of mistaking his figures for reality.[28] Both passages also suggest how tenuous are the threads of the Narrator's theory, how easily they can get lost and how easily they can trip up the theorist. Mrs. Briss sums up the Narrator's potential for error when she explains why people in general decline to share their secrets with him: "People have such a notion of what you embroider on things that they're rather afraid to commit themselves or to lead you on" (298).

The very nature of the embroidery of figurative language is to lead on— to lead the speaker further away from the literal term into a series of substitutes for it. The literal term is rarely used in *The Sacred Fount*. Even the novel's title is already a metaphor, and it is no doubt illegitimate to try to reduce it to a single, literal referent—such as sex, as Edmund Wilson pro-

28. On this habit of the Narrator, see Samuels, *The Ambiguity of Henry James*, 30–32.

THE PERILS OF THE "I"

posed.[29] Rather than leading back to a literal referent, such a metaphor engenders new figures, each of which is in turn provisional and leads further away from any original signified.

Thus, for example, the theory of the sacred fount comes to be called the Narrator's crystal palace (205) and later his house of cards (310–12). Symptomatically, these are metaphors that point to their own temporary, fragile nature and call for their own destruction. Like the golden bowl, the symbolic object standing for the various social conventions operating in the novel of that name, the Narrator's crystal palace can always be shattered, as the Narrator expressly invites Ford Obert to do: "How many panes will you reward me for amiably sitting up with you by smashing?" (205). The smashing of these panes reminds us too, of course, of the "smash of a pane of glass" that betokened the beginning of the end for the governess. The Narrator's crystal palace suffers even more damage in the hands of Mrs. Briss, who reminds the Narrator of the proverb: "Oh, those who live in glass houses—." But by this point (Chapter 14) the Narrator is ready to announce the dismantling of his theory himself: " 'I've spoken of it [the "quite sublime structure" of his theory] in my conceivable regret,' I conceded, 'as already a mere heap of disfigured fragments' " (311). The monumental figure of speech has thus become "disfigured." This does not, however, indicate a return to literality but only an admission of the dead end to which the theory has led.[30]

In the Narrator's own consciousness of the situation, it is true, this admission is more guarded. It is typical of his egotism that he continues to take extreme pride in his figures of speech even while Mrs. Briss is demolishing them. When she complains that his speech isn't simple enough, he replies, "I daresay, to do you justice, the interpretation of my tropes and figures *isn't*

29. Edmund Wilson, "The Ambiguity of Henry James," in Willen (ed.), *A Casebook on "The Turn of the Screw,"* 125. Against this reduction of the problem to sex, see Felman, "Turning the Screw of Interpretation," 102–13; Samuels, *The Ambiguity of Henry James*, 30–32.

30. Susanne Kappeler has recently tried to separate the fate of the Narrator from the fate of his theory, arguing (by a sacred fount logic) that his personal defeat is the price he must pay for the perfection of his intellectual construction. She appears, however, to overlook the substantial evidence showing that his theory is demolished just as soundly as he is by Mrs. Briss. See Kappeler, *Writing and Reading in Henry James* (New York, 1980), 139–41.

ever perfectly simple'' (284). Elsewhere the same pride appears: ''I took pleasure at the moment in my metaphor'' (260). Even to the end, he sees his figures of speech as the instrument of his triumph over his adversaries. Mrs. Briss, he remarks, ''had remained silent, as if really in the presence of the magnificence of my metaphor'' (312).

This bloated pride the Narrator feels in his language reaches its peak at the very moment he is losing the battle. The note of megalomania that begins to swell in the last pages of *The Sacred Fount* leads us to our third set of opposed terms—madness and sanity—for it is the Narrator's total, unreasoned commitment to his figurative language that eventually points to the possibility of his madness.

In both *The Turn of the Screw* and *The Sacred Fount*, the structure of madness and sanity resembles the structure of imagination and reality. Both narrators see the issue as a polarity; just as they tried to appropriate imagination for themselves and to view the other characters as unimaginative or even stupid, so they tend to divide their world into two camps, the crazy and the sane. This polarization is perhaps best seen in *The Turn of the Screw*, where the issue of the governess' possible insanity is raised at an earlier point than is that of the Narrator. In Chapter 6, after describing herself as a screen protecting the children from evil, the governess continues: ''The more I saw the less they would. I began to watch them in a stifled suspense, a disguised tension, that might well, had it continued too long, have turned into something like madness. What saved me, as I see now, was that it turned into another matter altogether.'' The ''other matter'' is of course the ghosts, so that their existence becomes the alternative to—the other of—her insanity. The same opposition underlies the climactic scene at the lake, when the governess sees Miss Jessel: ''She was there, so I was justified; she was there, so I was neither cruel nor mad'' (71).

Oddly enough, however, the existence of the ghosts is not necessary as a hypothesis to prove the governess' sanity. According to her bipolar reasoning, as long as she can locate insanity in someone else, she is freed from suspicion herself. For the governess, the proposition ''ghosts are visiting the children'' can be replaced by the proposition ''the children are insane.''[31] It is not always easy, however, for the governess to ascribe mad-

31. *Cf.* Felman, ''Turning the Screw of Interpretation,'' 194.

ness to others, as an exchange she has with Mrs. Grose in Chapter 12 illustrates. Mrs. Grose has suggested that the governess avert a catastrophe by writing to the master and asking for his help. The governess responds: " 'By writing to him that his house is poisoned and his little nephew and niece mad?' 'But if they *are*, Miss?' 'And if I am myself, you mean?' " (49–50). The governess tries to suggest that Miles and Flora are insane, but when Mrs. Grose seems (quite unexpectedly) to agree, the governess' tendency to read hidden meaning into Mrs. Grose's words betrays her, and she illogically hears an imputation against her own sanity (by implication granting the children the place of normality). The same structure of rigid alternatives informs her last, anxious cry of self-doubt, "If he *were* innocent what then on earth was I?" This question is, in her own words, "confounding and bottomless"— bottomless because the polarity according to which sanity and insanity are assigned does not remain stable but is always susceptible to reversal. Although the governess tries to stake out for herself the place of the sane, she cannot do so; the possibility of her insanity is raised so often through the narrative that the structure she seeks to establish is subverted and turns against her. The value of her sanity is in the end just as precarious as the value of her imagination.

The problem of sanity will also become bottomless for the Narrator in *The Sacred Fount*, though not so early as for the governess. Perhaps because his behavior is relatively innocuous, the possibility of his being mad does not come up before the final scene with Mrs. Briss, when he begins to take his "flight into luminous ether" and to display the same unsettling face that the governess so often displayed to Mrs. Grose: "I must have looked queer to my friend as I grinned to myself" (255). Whereas the governess raises the question of her own madness, the Narrator only receives this notion from outside, when Mrs. Briss tells him, "I think you're crazy" (278). The concluding phase of their dialogue is conducted in the light of this remark, and the dialogue form proves well suited to the same opposition of madness and sanity that we saw at work in *The Turn of the Screw*. When the Narrator asks Mrs. Briss if she has agreed to meet him precisely in order to "let me know I'm demented?" she replies, "To let you know I'm *not*" (280).

It is Mrs. Briss, then, and not the Narrator, who emulates the governess by forcefully establishing the polarity and preempting the position of sanity.

She also displays her superior power of logic (or persuasion) by manipulating another polarity, that of intelligence and stupidity. The Narrator's theory was based from the beginning on the premise that Gilbert Long had changed from stupid to bright. The final, virtually lethal blow Mrs. Briss delivers to the Narrator's system is her denial of this change. By denying Long's intelligence, she is of course impugning the Narrator's as well, while herself claiming to possess a greater insight. At this point the Narrator might very well have echoed the governess' question: "If Long *were* stupid what then on earth was I?" Instead, he prefers to think that Long's density is mistaken or faked, a "fictive ineptitude" (294), just as the governess preferred to think that the children always saw more than they confessed. But by this point the Narrator's ruses have little effect. Mrs. Briss has succeeded so well in isolating him and undermining his position that one of his last responses is simply to embrace his identification with the insane by comparing himself to "the exclusive king with his Wagner opera" (296).[32]

The final point is not that both narrators are certified insane—if they were, the ambiguities of their narratives would be transcended—but that their insanity remains a possibility up to the very end of their respective texts, and this possibility produces an aporia that precludes all final judgment. Just as the governess was paralyzed by the thought of Miles's innocence, the Narrator says of Mrs. Briss's attack, "practically it paralysed me" (296). The Narrator's paralysis is more definitive than the governess'. As he says in response to Mrs. Briss, "Then I go utterly to pieces! . . . I'm smashed" (297). On the final page, her closing word to him—"you *are* crazy, and I bid you goodnight!"—is described as "the word that put me altogether nowhere" (319).

This condition of being nowhere or in a bottomless place, the final consequence of first-person narration in these works, can be compared to the state of the omniscient, self-conscious narrator whom James described in his essay on Trollope: "It is only as an historian that he has the smallest *locus standi*. As a narrator of fictitious events he is nowhere" (*FN*, 248). Once again we see how the first-person narrator and the intrusive authorial

---

32. Jean Franz Blackall has conclusively shown that James intends an allusion to the mad King Ludwig of Bavaria. See Blackall, *Jamesian Ambiguity and "The Sacred Fount,"* Chap. 4.

narrator collapse for James into the same deluded figure and succumb to the same self-defeating logic. Like the Trollopean narrator, James's two first-person narrators have called attention to the possible fictionality of their own creation. Furthermore, they have implicated the real author who stands behind them, especially by putting into question the truth of the imagination, which is as much his instrument for the perception of reality as it is theirs.

What *The Turn of the Screw* and *The Sacred Fount* have also shown (as the essay on Trollope did not) is that the final penalty paid for their self-ironic position is the possibility, though not the certainty, of madness. The distinction between madness and sanity has become undecidable as a direct consequence of the blurring of those other crucial distinctions: between imagination and perception, figurative and literal language. All these confusions, finally, can be traced back to the major confusion that for James is inherent in the very nature of first-person narration in fiction, what he called in the Preface to *The Ambassadors* "the double privilege of subject and object" (*AN*, 321). By destroying the epistemological dualism on which mimetic realism is based, this double privilege also destroys the possibility of verifiable knowledge or meaning in the novel. By blurring the difference between subject and object, self and nonself, it also prevents the narrative from cohering in a readable autobiography of the first-person narrator. Ironically, the apparently most autobiographical of forms precludes the possibility of a successful self-revelation and allows only a fluidity in which the borders between self and world, imagination and reality, have been lost.

6

THE TALES
The Master and His Models

BECAUSE OF their subject matter, James's tales of artists and critics are usually taken to be his most autobiographical fictional works. Ora Segal, for one, has written that "those stories are . . . his most personal—indeed, most autobiographical—and may be viewed as dramatizations of his own problems and his own situation. Far from being, as James claimed in his Preface to *The Lesson of the Master*, 'portraits without models' for whom he was unable to give 'chapter and verse,' they are, in many crucial respects, self-portraits."[1] There is room, without contradicting the basic thesis of this statement, to refine it, to ask in exactly what sense, and for exactly what reasons, these stories are autobiographical. Subject matter alone—the fact that these are tales of sensitive authors—is not a sufficient reason to define them as self-portraits, for James sometimes writes stories about authors who in their situation or personality have little in common with himself: Mark Ambient of "The Author of Beltraffio," for example, or Henry St. George of "The Lesson of the Master." Moreover, other tales that do not have authors or even artists as their protagonists—including, most notably, "The Beast in the Jungle" (1903) and "The Jolly Corner" (1908)—are arguably at least as autobiographical as those that do.

1. Ora Segal, *The Lucid Reflector* (New Haven, 1969), 109.

These last examples suggest that where autobiography is at issue the category of James's literary tales needs to be studied in conjunction with the somewhat different (if overlapping) series of stories that James himself identified as his tales of "poor sensitive gentlemen" (*AN*, 246). This phrase, which refers most immediately to Stransom of "The Altar of the Dead," also defines characters like John Marcher of "The Beast in the Jungle" and Spencer Brydon of "The Jolly Corner," who, though not artists by vocation, are of an imaginative and sensitive cast that allows them to feel the embarrassments of their fortune and to articulate them acutely. In James's world, it is possible to lead an aesthetic life without being a practicing artist. *Aesthetics* originally has to do with perception, and as we have seen elsewhere, James refuses to draw a sharp line between active and passive modes of existence. Even his own autobiography, though it depicted the prelude to an artistic career, showed the young James as an aesthetic being only in the broadest sense of being receptive, appropriative, toward the phenomena around him. Moreover, as we shall soon see, James believed it was impossible to represent the artist *as* artist; in a work of fiction, the artist is first of all a man among men.

Yet the tales of artists do form a recognizable group within James's shorter works of fiction, and it is worth beginning by isolating them, because James's comments on these stories evoke certain autobiographical concerns from a unique angle. In dealing with these stories (and, shortly, with those of the "poor sensitive gentlemen"), I shall be interested not in uncovering the literal autobiographical content of the stories but in pursuing the literary questions of technique and representation that surround the question of autobiography for James. These questions belong in part to the matrix of technical alternatives that constitute the terms in which James thought out the problems of self-representation in fiction: the choice of first- or third-person narration, the difference between longer and shorter works, the opposition between realism and romance. These questions acquire a new dimension when they appear in the context of James's tales about authors and artists, for now, problems that appeared primarily technical are elevated to the status of themes, since these stories take the artist and his mode of life as their subject matter. Problems of narrative distance, for example, that underlie technical decisions like the choice of a narrative voice are recast in these stories as problems of the distance between the artist as creator and as man or the distance between his private and public selves. The opposition of romance and realism here takes the form of the opposition between the ideal imagined or created world of the artist and the real, all-too-human and uncomprehending world that makes up the general environment for him and his works. At the same time, of course, narrative distance remains a technical problem that James must solve for each story. Hence the stories are profoundly self-reflective; they represent the imaginative life of the author in a form that seems to yield a *theory* of art or of the aesthetic mode of existence. And it is through this theory, embodied in a fictional situation, that James is expressing his own sense of himself as an author.

How a fictional story can bear a reference to its author, or to anyone else, is one of the questions that dominates James's Prefaces to the literary tales. He raises the question of referentiality first in connection with ''The Aspern Papers'' (*AN*, 166–67), but returns to it at more length in the Preface to ''The Lesson of the Master'' and the other literary tales in Volume XV of the New York Edition. He begins this discussion with a confession: ''Whereas any anecdote about life pure and simple, as it were, proceeds almost as a matter of course from some good jog of fond fancy's elbow, some pencilled note on somebody else's case, so the material for any picture of personal states so specifically complicated as those of my hapless friends in the present volume will have been drawn preponderantly from the depths of the designer's own mind'' (*AN*, 221). James distinguishes, here and elsewhere, between the anecdote, which takes its material from outside (''somebody else's case''), and the picture, which comes from inside (''the depths of the designer's own mind'').[2] In the latter kind of story, ''the states represented, the embarrassments and predicaments studied, the tragedies and comedies recorded, can be intelligently fathered but on his [the author's] own intimate experience'' (*AN*, 221).

This distinction would appear clear-cut, but the metaphor of fathering, upon examination, complicates it. If the author's intimate experience plays a role in the generation of the story, it yet does not coincide with the story;

2. See for example *AN*, 139, and Henry James, ''The Story-teller at Large: Mr. Henry Harland,'' in Leon Edel (ed.), *The American Essays of Henry James* (New York, 1956), 190–91.

according to the metaphor, it is mother to the story. The fiction therefore is not simply a picture of the life of its author. Indeed, James recalls an accusation one reader made against him that his celebrated and intelligent fictional authors, his "supersubtle fry," could not possibly correspond to any real persons. He was charged with "painting pictures without models" (*AN*, 223) or, as the Preface to "The Aspen Papers" put it, creating characters without "some past or present producible counterfoil" (*AN*, 167).

Far from declaring himself to be the model for his literary portraits, James responds to the accusation by explaining that fictional stories should not, and perhaps cannot, have a referential basis in an actual case. He develops two arguments to prove his point. The first is the argument that art must supplement life when life fails to create artists who are both supremely intelligent and acclaimed by the public. In such cases, James reasons, "so much the worse for that life"; art must "*create* the record" that does not exist in historical reality (*AN*, 222). The mode of these literary fictions becomes ironic, where *irony* means precisely this discrepancy, or supplemental relation, between fiction and reality: "But this is exactly what we mean by operative irony. It implies and projects the possible other case, the case rich and edifying where the actuality is pretentious and vain" (*AN*, 222). Seemingly ignoring the autobiographical value of these tales for himself, James attributes their artistic merit to their pure ideality, their independence from any existing referent. The contribution of such fictions, he now states, lies in their "civic use of the imagination" (*AN*, 223). This key phrase, taken together with the earlier metaphor of the fathering of the tales, explains their exact relation to James's autobiography. The ultimate source of the fictional stories is the author's intimate experience, but the fiction is created only when the imagination of the author (the father) converts that experience into a story that has civic—that is, public and objective—validity. The imagination, in other words, mediates between what is private in James's case and what is universal, and therefore communicable, in it.

James's second argument about referentiality corroborates this universalist tendency. It arises in connection with "The Coxon Fund," which James admits is based on the life of Coleridge, or rather on "the S. T. Coleridge *type*" (*AN*, 229). (Similarly, in the Preface to "The Private Life" he will disclose that Robert Browning was the model for that story—*AN*, 252.)

Coleridge's experience, then, serves as the specific source for "The Coxon Fund" just as James's experience serves as the general source for all his pictures of the literary life. Once again, however, having given away his source, James shifts the burden of his argument in the opposite direction, toward the conclusion that no transplanting of a model from life into art is possible. Transplanting is mechanical, whereas the conversion performed in a fully wrought work of art would be thinkable only "in chemical, almost in mystical terms." It is a process of "rare alchemy," in which the artist submits reality to "the crucible of his imagination" (*AN*, 230).

This romantic distinction between the chemical (or organic) and the mechanical can be translated as the difference between fictional representation and referentiality. What James rejects as mechanical is only the factual model, the "producible counterfoil." He is still willing to admit that his characters may have a relation to an existing type or, as he puts it with reference to "The Lesson of the Master," that his fiction represents "in *essence* an observed reality" (*AN*, 223). The talk of alchemy, however, protects the work against the accusation of an immediate referential function (including an autobiographical referent). It is fitting, and it bears evidence to the consistency of James's terminology, that the *crucible* of the imagination is the same term that would appear in his letter of 1911 to H. G. Wells, in which he protested against Wells's indulgence in the "accurst autobiographical form" in the novel. There, he urged that only "the great stewpot or crucible of the imagination" can guarantee the artistic "detachment" that excludes autobiographical exposure.[3]

What the Preface gives with one hand, then, in admitting that the literary stories find their source in "the depths of the designer's own mind" or in his "hidden stores" (*AN*, 225), it takes away with the other, in denying that fictional characters can be based on living models. What James has done, in sum, is not to deny the autobiographical dimension of his fiction but to refine it considerably. Even if he is drawing upon his own store of imaginative experience, he is not simply transplanting that experience into fictional form. Like any outside model he might draw upon—Coleridge or

3. Henry James to H. G. Wells, March 3, 1911, in Percy Lubbock (ed.), *Letters of Henry James* (2 vols.; New York, 1920), II, 181–82.

Browning, for example—he must go through a sea change, an alchemical operation, before becoming the stuff of fiction. To paraphrase what James says about his use of Coleridge, the artists in his tales conform not to James but to a James *type*, a recognizable mode of aesthetic sensibility and experience. Whether James's specific character traits are retained in these characters thus becomes irrelevant. The autobiographical impulse in the stories does not aim at a portrait whose referent is James but only at a representation of the general condition of being a Jamesian artist.

This condition as it is represented in the tales is by no means ideal or governed solely by the requirements of the imagination. In these tales—unlike James's autobiography, where the young boy's imagination was largely in command—the artists are represented as immersed in a world that resists their imagination and neglects or misunderstands their works. The gap between the author's imaginative vision and its reception in the empirical world becomes a source of irony. James described this irony in his Preface to *The Tragic Muse*, where he debated the problem of representing the artist as a protagonist in fiction. His central point was that "any representation of the artist *in triumph* must be flat in proportion as it really sticks to its subject—it can only smuggle in variety and relief. . . . The privilege of the hero—that is of the martyr or of the interesting and appealing and comparatively floundering *person*—places him in quite a different category, belongs to him only as to the artist deluded, diverted, frustrated or vanquished; when the 'amateur' in him gains, for our admiration or compassion or whatever, all that the expert has to do without" (*AN*, 96–97). As pure subject, creator of his own fictive world, the artist cannot be made into the object of another fictive world. Only insofar as he fails as an artist or exists as a "floundering *person*" like other people can he be portrayed. The reasoning here is close to that of the preceding Preface, where James had insisted on the necessity of fools in fiction (*AN*, 66–67). The artist can be represented only to the degree in which he too is the fool of his art.

The potential for irony in this situation is apparent, and James spells it out again in the Preface to *The Lesson of the Master* volume. He explains his grouping of these stories (besides the title story and "The Coxon Fund," they include "The Death of the Lion," "The Next Time," and "The Figure in the Carpet") as follows: "These pieces have this in common that they deal all with the literary life, gathering their motive, in each case, from some noted adventure, some felt embarrassment, some extreme predicament, of the artist enamoured of perfection, ridden by his idea or paying for his sincerity'' (*AN*, 220–21). This embarrassment and predicament can be read as belonging to the fictive authors or to James equally. Their experience reinforces his own: "My attested predilection for poor sensitive gentlemen almost embarrasses me as I march!" (*AN*, 246). Just as his fictive artists are divided between their drive for perfection and the predicaments their experience offers, so James is divided between his roles as the man whose intimate experience furnished the material for the tales and the author whose imagination projected that material into fiction. James's "civic use of the imagination" points to his attempt to mediate between the romance of the artist living by his imagination and creating an ideal self and the realism of the artist as "floundering *person*," caught in the net of his relations to the world.

In the fictions themselves, however, the author's fate is not successfully mediated or reconciled with the world. The gap between the ideal and the real remains, and the mode of the tales is ironic rather than romantic. The split between James's two roles is carried over into the fiction, where it appears as a theory about the incompatibility of the artist and his environment or of his imaginative and empirical selves.

Sometimes this split gets projected in other directions, too. In several of the tales James juxtaposes two contrasting artistic cases. The resulting "precious element of contrast and antithesis," as the Preface to "The Private Life" describes it (*AN*, 251), has the effect of defeating the absoluteness of either case by making each take its particular value or meaning only in relation to the other. The specific relation in which the two examples stand, or the specific irony that arises from that relation, can of course vary in different stories. In "The Real Thing" (1892), the contrast is between the Monarchs, the "real thing" in life but the wrong thing in art (as it seems), and the two young working-class people, Miss Churm and Oronte, who have no standing in society but have a great value as models for the narrator's art.[4] In "The Next Time" (1895), the popular novelist Mrs. Highmore, who

4. Of course many critics would modify or reject this straightforward interpretation put forth by the narrator himself. For a recent example, see Richard Hocks, *Henry James and Pragmatistic Thought* (Chapel Hill, 1974), 120–34.

fails in her attempt to write a book that would be both subtle and unpopular, is contrasted with Ray Limbert, the gifted author who repeatedly fails to suppress his genius and write a simple potboiler. In "The Private Life" (1892), the two opposite cases are those of the painter Lord Mellifont, a powerful presence in public who has no private life at all, and the writer Clare Vawdrey, a nullity in society who turns out to exist only as the private self who writes the books.

The boldly parallel construction of these stories ranks them among James's most schematic, even allegorical.[5] They seem merely to illustrate a general idea or to offer a parable, as the narrator of "The Next Time" puts it.[6] Once again, this reveals how James converts his autobiographical preoccupations into a universal drama. This effect is perhaps most noteworthy in the instance of "The Next Time," because one half of this story clearly reflects an episode from James's own career. Twice in his notebook entries for this tale, James recalls to himself his own abortive attempts, some twenty years earlier, to write below his ordinary standard for the readers of the New York Tribune (*NB*, 180, 200–201). The experience is alchemically transformed when it is put alongside an opposite case and thereby loses its absolute, referential value and takes on a purely ironic and differential value within the narrative.

But James does not always rely on the juxtaposition of two separate cases to express his ideas about the artist's problematic relation to the world. More basically, it is the narrative situation in the tales that expresses James's complex autobiographical relation to his fiction as well as his theory of the artist's split and "deluded" self. For this reason, the narrative technique in these tales is never merely technical. Although the narrative situation is of course closely bound up with the theme in all James's works, in the literary tales the narrative situation acquires a unique importance. In a sense it becomes the theme, since the distance between the artist and the other char-

5. On the abstract or allegorical nature of some of James's short-story subjects, see Hildegard Domaniecki, *Zum Problem literarischer Ökonomie: Henry James's Erzählungen zwischen Markt und Kunst* (Stuttgart, 1974), 156–65.

6. Leon Edel (ed.), *The Complete Tales of Henry James* (12 vols.; London, 1961–64), IX, 186. All references to the tales in the text of this chapter are to this edition. After the first reference to each story, I omit the volume number.

acters who constitute his world is crucial to the aesthetic theory the stories embody. Hence, the narrative distance both between James, as author, and his fictive protagonists and among the various characters in the fiction becomes paramount.

These tales of artists, consistent with James's belief that first-person narration is permissible in short fiction, show an indifference to the "person" of the narrator; some are written in the first, and others in the third person. What needs to be explained, then, is why James did not deem first-person narration a threat to the impersonality or objectivity of these stories, even though their subject matter, as he freely admits, points ultimately to his own experience.

If we look specifically at those literary tales written in the first person, one answer becomes apparent. Nowhere in these stories does James give the reader an immediate view of that "embarrassed" author with whom James would seem most naturally to identify himself. The acknowledged master, or Jamesian artist, never tells his own story. Instead, the first-person narrator is always the younger critic or aspiring author who stands at a distance, usually an admiring distance, from the master. This situation most clearly defines "The Author of Beltraffio," "The Private Life," "The Death of the Lion," and "The Figure in the Carpet." (It also defines "The Aspern Papers" if we elect to see the master artist in Jeffrey Aspern.) The seeming immediacy or subjectivity of the first-person form is thus tempered and rendered acceptable by the fact that the narrator is never—at least ostensibly— telling his own story. What most essentially characterizes almost all of the literary tales, in fact, is not the person in which they are told but the precise distance that obtains between the master and some other, less masterly, consciousness. "The Real Thing," which contains no master but only the narrator and his even less masterly adviser and publishers, forms an exception to this rule. Yet it may be the unique narrative situation in this story that has occasioned the difficulties in interpreting it.

The division between the consciousnesses defines the mode of the literary tales and also suggests one important similarity between them and the tales of "poor sensitive gentlemen." In the literary stories the relation is most typically between an intelligent but limited younger man and an accomplished author who is endowed, in the eyes of the young man, with a more penetrating and wider consciousness or even with a specific mystery or secret. For this reason, "The Lesson of the Master" and "The Figure in the Carpet" are the most central and typical of these stories. In the tales of sensitive gentlemen, this relationship is of course embodied in different characters, but the basic structure of a division between a lesser and a greater consciousness remains central, even while taking on some curious twists. In "The Altar of the Dead" (1895), the focalized consciousness of Stransom is dominated by the ghostly consciousness of his dead fiancée, Mary Antrim, who, even though departed, still seems alive for him; his life "was still ruled by a pale ghost, it was still ordered by a sovereign presence" (IX, 231). In "The Jolly Corner," Spencer Brydon's intelligence is obsessed and baffled by the idea of a ghost, or alter ego, which seems to hold the secret to his life. Finally, in "The Beast in the Jungle," John Marcher grows more and more convinced that his friend May Bartram is in possession of the secret key to his fate, which has always eluded him.

This doubling of consciousness has an effect similar to that of the doubling of plot in the three tales mentioned earlier: it complicates and partially disguises the autobiographical content of the tales, rather in the same way as Joyce, in *Ulysses*, would refine the autobiographical tendency of *A Portrait of the Artist as a Young Man* by doubling Stephen Dedalus with Leopold Bloom.[7] Even in those of James's third-person, focalized stories that seem most intensely and directly autobiographical—"The Beast in the Jungle" and "The Jolly Corner"—the central character does not possess his own identity; his real identity always appears as something distinct from him, something that might happen to him as an event from outside. Thus, the doubling of the hero of such tales in an alter ego or ghost of himself creates approximately the same structure as we found in those literary tales where the young critic, technically the center of consciousness, has his attention riveted by the older master whose secret he is trying to penetrate. The resulting narrative, told through the young man's point of view (and sometimes in his voice) may of course turn out to be his story as much as the

7. For a good discussion of Joyce's autobiographical involvement in *Ulysses*, see S. L. Goldberg, *The Classical Temper* (London, 1961), 66–99. For a psychological interpretation of the double in James, which links this figure to the experience of shame, see Manfred Mackenzie, *Communities of Love and Honor in Henry James* (Cambridge, Mass., 1976), 45–70.

master's, but if it does, it is usually through the same ironic turn of the narrative back upon the narrator that we saw in *The Turn of the Screw* and *The Sacred Fount*. The ambivalence as to whether the young man is telling his story or that of someone else is, again, structurally comparable to the ambivalence James expressed in his autobiography as to whether he was recounting his own life or that of his brother William.

These late stories may be among James's strictest exercises in point of view, then, but this should not obscure the fact that almost all of them actually operate with two centers of consciousness, one of which is brought into the foreground by the narrative technique and the second of which, through its very opacity and its distance from the protagonist or narrator, exercises a fascination over him and becomes central to the story. The latter center is what James, referring specifically to the role of May Bartram in "The Beast in the Jungle," calls the tale's "second consciousness" (*NB*, 311). The split between the two consciousnesses, one of them revealed through the narrative act and the other largely concealed, creates a question as to where the true center of the story lies. In "The Figure in the Carpet," for example, is the center the nameless narrator or Hugh Vereker? There is at least a possibility that the story's technical center of consciousness does not coincide with its thematic center.[8]

In fact, if we study the psychology of the character who acts as reflector, we find almost invariably that he experiences his own consciousness as being on the periphery or in the dark in relation to another, more luminous, consciousness. He feels that he lives in ignorance while true authority, mastery of knowledge resides elsewhere, in what Stransom of "The Altar of the Dead" calls "the Others" (IX, 233). These characters suffer something of the same anxiety as the young Henry James of *A Small Boy and Others*, obsessed by the mystery represented by the consciousness of other people and wanting to be other. In many of the protagonists of the late tales, this obsession ends by draining all value from the self's own experience and assigning it to the second consciousness. The protagonist's life becomes a mere "negative adventure," as James says of John Marcher's life in "The Beast in the

8. On the shift of the thematic center from the ostensible subject to the reflecting or narrating figure in other tales, see Wayne Booth, *The Rhetoric of Fiction* (Chicago, 1961), 340–64; Ora Segal, *The Lucid Reflector*, esp. 114.

Jungle'' (*AN*, 247) (or as Henry James was tempted to estimate his own life in comparison to the adventures of his brother William, in the *Notes of a Son and Brother*). Meanwhile the other consciousness, in its inaccessibility, tends more and more to be revered or even deified, as the religious imagery in many tales from ''The Aspern Papers'' to ''The Altar of the Dead'' suggests.

The distance between the central character and this other, deified person (or persons) can be defined in terms of the ''metaphysical desire'' that René Girard has proposed for the study of the novel.[9] Starting from the sense of his own lack of plenitude, the individual attributes a godlike plenitude to someone else, who then either becomes the object of his desire or mediates the desire he feels for other people or objects. This general pattern can be seen running through most of the tales of literary life, and it also links them to the tales of the ''poor sensitive gentlemen'' (and to the tales of some sensitive ladies—the protagonists of *The Turn of the Screw* and *In the Cage*, for instance). These tales all establish the same general structure and then work a surprising number of variations on it, some of which may be hard to recognize when the second consciousness appears as a dead person, a ghost, or an alter ego of the hero.

To establish an order among the variations offered by the diverse stories, we may begin by using Girard's distinction between external and internal mediators. The external mediator is the deified model who exists in a different realm from the hero, so that no direct contact or competition between them is possible. The internal mediator is the one who occupies the hero's own world and can therefore become, in addition to being the mediator of desire, an immediate rival for an object of desire.[10]

James's tales excel in the invention of different situations of external mediation. The most radical motivation for an external relation occurs in those cases where the idol is already dead, as are Aspern in ''The Aspern Papers,'' Ashton Doyne in ''The Real Right Thing'' (1899), and John Delavoy in his eponymous story (1898). Other motivations than death can keep the mediator external, too. In *The Turn of the Screw* it is the transparent

9. René Girard, *Deceit, Desire, and the Novel*, trans. Yvonne Freccero (Baltimore, 1965).
10. *Ibid.*, 9.

strategem, described as the ''main condition'' of the governess's employment, that she, or anyone else for that matter, may never appeal to the master, who thereby effectively absents himself from the story. A similarly obvious strategem is the series of complications and travels that remove Hugh Vereker from the reach of the narrator in ''The Figure in the Carpet.'' Vereker's eventual death is only the last in a series of displacements that render him inaccessible. In all these cases, the distance at which the master is placed—even the ultimate distance of death—enhances his prestige and heightens the fascinated desire he arouses in the admiring but mystified hero.

As long as the ''master'' is dead, it is possible for the young admirer to worship him from afar and still to lead his own life, even to fulfill it through a romantic attachment. One way for the younger man to combine his pursuits is to become romantically involved with someone who joins him in the worship of his ''god.'' This situation leads to the uncharacteristically ''happy'' endings of two of the literary tales, ''The Death of the Lion'' (1894) and ''John Delavoy.'' In the first of these, the author Neil Paraday conveniently sinks toward death while the narrator makes the acquaintance of his girl, and the love affair between the two is practically founded on their agreement to treat Paraday as if he were already dead and reachable only through the negative path of his works. In ''John Delavoy,'' the fact that the narrator's coworshiper, and eventual wife, is the sister of the dead author leads to the inference that the narrator's two interests are really one, that he uses the brother to get at the sister and the sister to get at the brother. But there are less happy versions of this triangle as well. In ''The Next Time,'' the narrator has once been the rival of the author, Ray Limbert, for the hand of the woman who has become the latter's wife. More treacherously still, Stransom of ''The Altar of the Dead'' enlists the participation of a young woman in his worship of the dead only to find that the one she really worships, Acton Hague, is the enemy whom he has excluded from his circle of sacred memories. The two worshipers have been praying to different idols, and this difference drives a wedge between them.

In all these stories, the stress has been laid on the mediator or idol as someone external to the world of the hero, but the distance of the mediator is always relative, and his external position can shift to one that is more or less internal. This shift can occur, oddly, even when he is dead. Such is one way of interpreting what we have just seen in "The Altar of the Dead": Acton Hague, once Stransom's closest friend, has come back from beyond the grave, as it were, to rob Stransom of the young woman who might otherwise have become his. Something similar occurs in "The Aspern Papers," where the triangle is made up of Aspern, the narrator who professes to worship Aspern (he calls himself one of the ministers guarding the temple of the poet), and Tita (as the double of her aunt Juliana, Aspern's mistress). But Aspern, though dead, belongs to a "*visitable* past" (*AN*, 164), and in the narrator's fantasy Aspern indeed revisits him, taunting him at a climactic moment over the ineptness of his romantic dealings with Tita: "It was embarrassing, and I bent my head over Jeffrey Aspern's portrait. What an odd expression was on his face. 'Get out of it as you can, my dear fellow!'" (VI, 374).

The one tale, however, that is actually about the process whereby an external mediator becomes an internal one is "The Lesson of the Master." Here the triangle—made up of the master Henry St. George, the young author Paul Overt, and the delightful Miss Fancourt—at first seems likely to evolve in the same direction as the triangle of "The Next Time," with the two young people brought together by a common admiration for the senior author, who would obligingly retreat as Neil Paraday did. The problem is of course that Henry St. George declines to retreat. After he begins as a relatively external master who offers disinterested advice from an Olympian height, his "lesson" becomes increasingly ambiguous, he becomes the "fallible master" and finishes as the direct—and successful—rival to Paul Overt. The external mediator has become internal with a vengeance.

If we follow to its logical conclusion this process of the internalization of the mediator, we come to those latest and most important of the tales of "poor sensitive gentlemen," "The Beast in the Jungle" and "The Jolly Corner." The deep psychological probing in these stories, with their plunge into the ghostly or fantastic, may not at first sight seem to have much in common with the urbane and ironic tone of the literary tales. But actually the ghostly or fantastic dimension of these stories creates the same structure of opposing consciousness we have traced in the literary tales; only what was there most typically represented as a relation between disciple and master here becomes a relation between the conscious ego and its dark alter ego or lurking fate. Certain stories can even be seen as transitional between the two series, incorporating elements of both. "The Private Life," for example, is a parable of art, which portrays the standard relationship between the young narrator and the established master (or masters) but also borrows from the fantastic by postulating the doppelgänger of Clare Vawdrey and that of Lord Mellifont in order to illustrate the typical thematic tension between the demands of life and art. (Another literary tale, "The Real Right Thing," also makes a discreet use of the fantastic, comparable to that of "The Jolly Corner.") "The Altar of the Dead" offers another transitional form. Its use of religious imagery and its hero's posture of reverence before the dead are halfway between the situation in literary tales like "The Aspern Papers" or "John Delavoy" and the quasi-religious awe that both John Marcher and Spencer Brydon feel before the projected versions of their own selves. The dead are, in the one case, revered authors, in another, former friends and lovers, in the third, mysterious versions of one's self; but all of them become what Mary Antrim becomes for Stransom, a "sovereign presence" dominating the hero's consciousness.

If we approach them, then, from the perspective offered by the literary tales, what distinguishes "The Beast in the Jungle" and "The Jolly Corner" is the degree to which the second consciousness has been internalized. No longer lodged in an outside master, the sovereign consciousness now belongs to another version of the protagonist's own self. Yet it is still distinctly other. For John Marcher, the "beast in the jungle" is something that will spring upon him unexpectedly; for Spencer Brydon, the ghost of his American self is something that must be doggedly tracked down. Put differently, if we consider these two tales in their own right as psychological studies of the protagonists (and not simply as a later development of the literary tales), then what is striking is not that they internalize a second consciousness but that they project the hero's own self, or a part of it, onto an alter ego. This projection appears to be in the mode of romance, since it operates in the guise of a ghost in "The Jolly Corner" and in that of an elaborate conceit that finally becomes a "hallucination" in "The Beast in the Jungle," but here, for once, these elements of romance do not lead to the threat of subjectivity. Paradoxically, they protect these tales from being excessively subjective or merely psychological. The doubling of the protagonists in these stories serves the same purpose as the third-person, focalized mode in which they are told:

it protects them from being immediate exercises in autobiography. The projections provide an objectified image of the hero, an image that transcends his own single consciousness and becomes an object of perception for him as well as for the women characters and the impersonal narrator.

The fact that these tales of "poor sensitive gentlemen" (including "The Altar of the Dead") are all told by the impersonal narrator, whereas the literary tales are told either in the first or the third person, is a consequence of their new degree of internalization. The literary tales could be told by a fictive narrator as long as the master's consciousness was maintained, but in the other series of stories, where the hero's own consciousness has become the mystery and the thematic center, a first-person narrative could not successfully have represented the projection or the otherness of that consciousness to itself. This is precisely what went amiss in *The Turn of the Screw*, where the governess, like Spencer Brydon, sees ghosts but is unable to acknowledge the sense in which she has projected herself into them and therefore can never wholly convince us of their objective existence.

We can now see that the distinction with which we began, between stories that come from "somebody else's case" and those that grow out of "the designer's own mind," is not so absolute as it appeared. Possibly James can uphold the distinction as it regards the source or germ of his stories. In their finished form, however, even those stories that are in some sense autobiographical are presented through "somebody else's case," somebody else, that is, than the character who would seem to be identified with James. Indeed, James's autobiographical impulse can reveal itself in fiction *only* in this way, by showing a character radically divided from himself. If James is to recover himself through his fiction, he can do so only by acknowledging a self that is already split. Such a split would characterize James's autobiography, most notably in the relation between him and his brother William. It also characterizes the short tales, two of which I shall examine in more detail. One of these, "The Figure in the Carpet," comes from the series of literary tales and is told in the first person. The other, "The Beast in the Jungle," is a story of a "sensitive gentleman" and is told in the third person. In both, James's identification with the central character is complicated by the division of characters in the stories; it is also made problematic by the fact that the central character remains all too ''embarrassed'' and deluded concerning the locus of his own selfhood.

''The Figure in the Carpet'' can be taken as the epitome of the literary tales, so fully does it rehearse the characteristic themes and devices of these stories: the portrayal of the literary master Hugh Vereker, ''all aloft in his indifference'' (IX, 303), the use of the point of view of the aspiring critic (here, the anonymous narrator), the image of a life devoted to the absolute demands of art, and the peculiar mixture in the plot of a purely artistic question with a love story. Moreover, this story surpasses practically all the other stories of artists in its elaboration of the typical, triangular relationship of desire and mastery. Here in fact the customary triangle of characters is expanded into a foursome, made up of the narrator, Vereker, the rival critic George Corvick, and the young author Gwendolen Erme.

If one of these characters would seem to be a projection of James himself, it must of course be Hugh Vereker, the master. In working out the character of Vereker in his notebooks, James immediately conceived of him as a novelist: ''I should premise that I think I see [the author's] books necessarily to be NOVELS; it is in fact essentially as a novelist that he *se présente à ma pensée*'' (*NB*, 220). Specifically, James's sympathy for Vereker—if not identification with him—is implied in the theme of the author's possession of a ''latent intention'' in his works that is misunderstood or ignored by his readers. In notebook entries and the Preface, James appears unwaveringly to locate the main theme of his tale in this drama of the author's intentions. In the Preface, James traces the tale back to ''the charming idea of some artist whose most characteristic intention, or cluster of intentions, should have taken all vainly for granted the public, or at the worst the not unthinkable private, exercise of penetration'' (*AN*, 228).

Centered thus on the theme of authorial intention, ''The Figure in the Carpet'' becomes the metacritical tale par excellence among all of James's tales. It reflects that central pursuit in the Prefaces to measure the relation between James's own subjective intention and its objective embodiment in the finished work. ''The Figure in the Carpet'' is a fictional acting out and testing of this idea. Hugh Vereker's position in the short story is similar to that of James in his Prefaces (though not identical with it, as we shall see). The Preface and the notebook entries, since they comment on James's own intentions in writing the story, can be read as a *mise-en-abîme* of what takes place in the fiction itself.

This complex situation shows how much reason James has to identify with his fictional author, Vereker. But this identification, as always in the literary tales, is qualified by the ironic mode of the story. In the Preface, James twice uses the term *ironic* to describe this tale; the second of these uses in particular recalls that "operative irony" he defined as the mode of the literary tales in general: "The mere quality and play of an ironic consciousness in the designer [*i.e.*, Vereker] left wholly alone, amid a chattering unperceiving world, with the thing he has most wanted to do, with the design more or less realised—some effectual glimpse of that might by itself, for instance, reward one's experiment" (*AN*, 228–29). This irony would result from the consciousness of the gap between the ideal and the real, that is, between Vereker's intentions in their pure state and the ability of his readers to perceive them in his works. The intentions are only "more or less realised"; a page earlier, James has spoken of Vereker's "undiscovered, not to say undiscoverable, secret" (*AN*, 228). These phrases represent a new complication in the theme of the story. They suggest that the dramatic tension does not simply lie between an all-knowing master and a set of unperceiving critics (though the Preface does appear, in part, to support this interpretation) but that the "figure in the carpet" may itself be a mystification, the product of "too fond an imagination," as the narrator at one point suggests (292). Nothing is more striking in the tale, of course, than the fact that Vereker's figure is never revealed to the reader. And the narrator is there, for one, to raise the possibility that the figure does not exist.

The narrator's role, in this sense, compromises that of Vereker. Part of the ironic quality of the story comes from the distance between these two characters, each of whom could claim to be at its center. If James's primary identification seemed to be with Vereker, that identification is deflected to the extent that James's narrator and center of consciousness is the young critic, while Vereker, after the first four sections, recedes more and more toward the periphery of the action where he is reachable only through indirect reports and telegrams. In the Preface, James hesitates as to whether the tale is "Vereker's drama indeed—or I should perhaps rather say that of the aspiring young analyst whose report we read" (*AN*, 229). Moreover, in the notebooks he had already identified himself with his narrator—not with Vereker—through his characteristic use of the "I": "*Mettons* that he [Vereker] mentions, after all, the fact of the thing to only one person—to *me*, say, who narrate, in my proper identity, the little episode. Say *I'm* a critic" (*NB*, 220).[11]

If the narrator is the technical center of the story, however, Vereker, with his secret, remains at its thematic center, and the relations not only between these two but among all of the principal characters rapidly organize themselves into the situation of mediated desire typical of other tales. Mediation, indeed, already appears as a keynote in the opening pages: the publication for which the narrator writes his critical reviews is called *The Middle*, and the country house where he first meets Vereker is called Bridges. All the bridges in the story lead to Vereker, the center of desire or the god, to approach whose work is "to approach the altar" (293) or to attempt to "unveil the idol" (304). His name itself is a promise of the truth, *veritas*, which the others hope to confront "face to face" (309). Gwendolen Erme actually uses the formula of epiphany from the *Aeneid* (Book I, line 405), relating the unveiling of Venus to Aeneas, "Vera incessu patuit dea," to describe the revelation of Vereker's secret to Corvick.[12] The relations between the narrator, George Corvick, and Gwendolen Erme are determined by the relation in which they stand to Vereker's mystery and, consequently, are dominated by jealousy and rivalry. The possession of Vereker's secret becomes the main justification for living. "It's my life!" says Gwendolen after Corvick's death (307). Even the narrator's attempt to dismiss the whole affair with mockery (as in Section 4) is only a temporary reaction, an "unhappy rebound" (292) by which he tries to protect his feelings, hurt when he is excluded from his master's secret. Later he must "confess abjectly" that the search is still "the obsession of which I'm forever conscious" (306). At the end of the story,

11. Ora Segal's use of a similar quotation from *NB*, 201, as proof that "in these literary tales the observer's voice is indistinguishable from James's own" (*The Lucid Reflector*, 110), loses some of its force if we remember that James made frequent use of such an "I" in reference to tales other than the literary ones.

12. For a critic who sees in a constellation of such *V* figures as Vera, Vereker, Venus, and others something like the figure in the story's carpet, see Peter W. Lock, " 'The Figure in the Carpet': The Text as Riddle and Force," *Nineteenth-Century Fiction*, XXXVI (1981), 157–75.

he sees both himself and Drayton Deane (Gwendolen's second husband) as "victims of unappeased desire" (315).

The new twist that "The Figure in the Carpet" adds to this recognizable situation of mediation lies in its multiplication of characters and its new distribution of functions among them. The narrator and George Corvick, for example, embody two versions of the ambitious young critic—a doubling unique in James's literary tales. If we compare this story to the somewhat similar "Lesson of the Master," we see that Corvick is in fact the new element, a highly problematic one. To begin, he is clearly the narrator's alter ego, competing with him (successfully) both for Vereker's figure and for the hand of Gwendolen. Yet later, when he outpaces the narrator in the quest for Vereker's secret, Corvick begins to take on the traits of the master, to become a mirror image of Vereker himself. This mirror relation is notably suggested, first, by Corvick's name, which in its cluster of consonants is a scrambled version of Vereker's own name, and second, by the narrator's image of Corvick and Vereker as two chess players facing each other across a board (292). From the narrator's perspective, indeed, Corvick becomes as enigmatic as the master, especially after he claims to have found the latter's secret and to have been pressed to his bosom as a reward (299). Corvick's physical remoteness (he sends telegrams from Bombay and Italy) imitates that of the master, just as his sudden death, before he has had time to publish his discovery, anticipates the master's.

In Corvick, then, James has combined the functions of rival and master in a single character who mediates between the narrator and Vereker. But "The Figure in the Carpet" also contains, alongside Corvick, the real master, Vereker. Compared, once again, to "The Lesson of the Master," this story has split the two roles that belonged there to Henry St. George—Paul Overt's master but also his rival for the girl—between two people. The placing of both of these in the same story, then, represents a proliferation of characters in excess of those the other literary tales offer. This proliferation—the final stage, as it were, of James's toying with the structure of triangular desire—contains the most complex possibilities for the identification or projection of the author into his characters. James's "I" belongs to the narrator; the narrator is doubled by George Corvick; and Corvick stands in a specular relation to Vereker, the James-like master. All of these characters are necessary to James's portrait of the artist. Vereker and the narrator stand at opposite poles from each other, representing mastery and embarrassment, the artistic imagination in control and the anonymity of empty, desiring consciousness. Corvick assumes the role of the mediator, doubling both the narrator and the novelist, as we have seen, and bringing the authorial secret within grasp of the critical mind.

Yet there is grave question whether this mediation is successful within the story. We still need to face the irony inherent in the fact that Vereker's secret intention is never revealed. Corvick's supposed discovery—whether it must be taken at face value or not—can afford no satisfaction to the reader.[13] Instead of a solution, the reader gets only a series of figures of speech, beginning with the figure in the carpet itself and leading through all the other metaphors that the narrator and Vereker substitute for a literal statement (especially in Sections 3 and 4 of the story). It is at least admissible, then, to read this story as suggesting that Vereker's statement has indeed been lost, not just because he suffers from imperceptive critics but because the intention itself is only a figure of speech, not something objectively present in his work.[14]

To maintain this reading, it is not necessary to accuse Vereker of being a liar, as the narrator is once tempted to do (286). It is necessary only to recognize the gap that separates Vereker as author of his works, with his various intentions, from Vereker as reader of his works. James demonstrated his consciousness of this gap in his notebooks and the Prefaces. In the Preface to *The Wings of the Dove* he even formulated a law according to which the author's intention, or ''prime object,'' must invariably misfire, so that to become master of what he finally does create, he must submit to being

13. For one argument denying that Corvick ever discovers the ''figure,'' see Kirshna Baldev Vaid, *Technique in the Tales of Henry James* (Cambridge, Mass., 1964), 79–89.

14. Many critics have questioned whether the figure is something that can be discovered in Vereker's works. See R. P. Blackmur, ''In the Country of the Blue,'' in F. W. Dupee (ed.), *The Question of Henry James* (New York, 1945), 191–211; *cf.* Tzvetan Todorov, ''The Tales of Henry James,'' in David Robey (ed.), *Structuralism: An Introduction* (Oxford, 1973), 73–103. In *The Act of Reading* (Baltimore, 1978), Wolfgang Iser reads the story as a kind of allegory that shows that meaning can be grasped only as a process, not an object. Finally, on the unreadability of the tropes in the story, see J. Hillis Miller, ''The Figure in the Carpet,'' *Poetics Today*, I (Spring, 1980), 107–18.

the dupe of what he ideally would have created (*AN*, 296–97). Is it not possible that Vereker is as much subject to this law as James is?

If we want a practical example of the law of authorial fallibility, as James calls it, we need look no further than to his designs for "The Figure in the Carpet" itself. The notebook entries mention at least one intention that was not to be fulfilled in the completed tale. This intention had to do, ironically, with the way in which James was to represent the communication of Vereker's intention to Corvick. At the end of his scenario for the story, James adds: "Two little things, in relation to this, occur to me. One is the importance of my [*i.e.*, the narrator's] being *sure* the disclosure has been made to the wife by her 1st husband. The other is the importance of *his* having been sure he had got hold of the right thing. The only way for this would be to have made him submit his idea to the Author himself" (*NB*, 223). This is as clear a statement as one might wish of James's intention, but it is a misleading guide to the published story. There, although Corvick and later Gwendolen do of course claim to possess the secret, James has multiplied the circumstances that put their claim into question. Corvick announces his discovery by telegram; he dies before revealing its content, and the article he is writing at the time of his death offers no clues; he has a strong motive to tell Gwendolen he has the secret (whether he has it or not) to persuade her to marry him; Gwendolen, in turn, may have motives of resentment or jealousy that lead her to tantalize the narrator with her possession of the secret; if she does possess it, she never reveals it to her second husband, Drayton Deane; finally, of course, Vereker dies without having vouched for Corvick's discovery. Taken together, these details are far more than "the extraordinary series of accidents" the narrator sees in them (315). They represent a definite shift from, or at least a blurring of, James's original intention of making the narrator (and the reader) sure that Vereker's intention has been recovered. The Preface, with its much more cautious and devious commentary, appears to acknowledge that the story has grown problematic: "The reader is, on the evidence, left to conclude" (*AN*, 229).

As a reflection on the theme of authorial intention, then, "The Figure in the Carpet" has taken on a new twist. James intended to write a story that vindicated the notion of an author's "general intention" and the possibility of its being communicated to his readers. Instead, James's own intention was lost to the extent that he wrote a highly ambiguous story that puts into question not only the communication of Vereker's secret intention but its very existence.[15] If this story, like the literary tales in general, was drawn from "the depths of the designer's own mind," it is yet a paradoxical, negative form of self-expression, which, like many of the Prefaces, demonstrates not the continuity between the designer and his work but the discontinuity. The pivotal character in the story is no doubt the would-be mediator Corvick, who holds out the promise of a reconciliation between the author and the world of his readers but who cannot realize this promise in the concrete world represented in the story. The failure of mediation signifies the growing estrangement of all the characters to the very end of the story, when Vereker and Corvick are dead and the narrator is left alone with "the obsession of which I'm forever conscious" (306). There can be no reconciliation among these different consciousnesses, and James can be identified with none of them singly; rather he has objectified his complex position as furnisher of the "intimate experience," author of the self-reflective story, and critic of his own tales, in the general situation of the fiction.

"The Beast in the Jungle" offers a rough structural parallel to "The Figure in the Carpet." Each story depicts a quest organized around a mystery whose exact nature is not known, so that it can only be designated obliquely, through a metaphor that provides the title for the tale.[16] Whereas "The Figure in the Carpet" develops a relatively large number of characters defined by their varying relations to the secret, "The Beast in the Jungle" concentrates attention on its main character, John Marcher, and only secondarily on his companion, May Bartram. This concentration reflects the fact that, for Marcher, the quest has become internalized: the mystery is no longer "out there"—for instance, in the works of a Hugh Vereker—but is inside himself. Other extraordinary men "had indeed been wondrous for others, while he was but wondrous for himself" (XI, 397). Marcher's obsession with his own character and fate carries the threat of egotism, as he repeat-

15. For a strict definition of the "ambiguous" mode of "The Figure in the Carpet," see Shlomith Rimmon, *The Concept of Ambiguity—the Example of James* (Chicago, 1977), 95–115.

16. *Cf.* Todorov ("The Tales of Henry James"), who sees many of James's tales as organized around "the search for an absent cause."

edly but inadequately acknowledges, or even the threat of solipsism. This danger may explain why James does not choose to tell Marcher's story as an autobiographical one by giving him the privilege of the first person. The risk of fluidity would have been overwhelming. James protects his own distance—as he did not need to do in creating the narrator of "The Figure in the Carpet," who was not telling his own story—by presenting Marcher through a focalized, third-person narrative.

Marcher is a salient example in James's work of a rigid center of consciousness," close to Strether of *The Ambassadors*, which James had completed about a year before composing "The Beast in the Jungle" in 1902. But Marcher also illustrates the general rule that a Jamesian reflector, no matter how faithfully adhered to, is never responsible for everything in the text. James always maintains his own authority at a distance from his reflector—and very clearly so in "The Beast in the Jungle," where the demonstration of the final limits to Marcher's consciousness is so crucial to the theme. Even in the case of Strether, James made it clear that an absolute limitation of the narrative to the content of the hero's consciousness would entail an awkward constraint on the expression of his subject matter: "The thing was to be so much this worthy's intimate adventure that even the projection of his consciousness upon it from beginning to end without intermission or deviation would probably leave a part of its value for him, and *a fortiori* for ourselves, unexpressed" (*AN*, 317). Deviations from strict point of view are even more imperative in "The Beast in the Jungle," where Marcher's story is, in itself, a "negative adventure" (*AN*, 247). It can receive its full positive value only when Marcher's consciousness is supplemented by that of the impersonal author and, indirectly, by that of May Bartram as well.

Even in the opening paragraph, without technically departing from Marcher's angle of vision, James lays the stress on what his protagonist does not know, on how the entire outside world appears strange and inexplicable to him. Here is his perception of the other weekend guests at the country house: "There were persons to be observed, singly or in doubles, bending toward objects in out-of-the-way corners with their hands on their knees and their heads nodding quite as with the emphasis of an excited sense of smell. When they were two they either mingled their sounds of ecstasy or melted into silences of even deeper import'' (351). The language is both sexual and animalistic in a vaguely distasteful way. Immediately after, Marcher thinks of ''a dog sniffing a cupboard,'' but the sexual connotation apparently never rises to the level of his consciousness. This inability to seize the real implications of the images in which his thought is expressed or to find the literal term for what he is thinking foreshadows the elaborate and misleading metaphor of the beast in which he will envelop and conceal the idea of his own fate. His failure to grasp the sexual dimension of his own perceptions of course also anticipates the failure of his relation with May Bartram. Marcher's dim sense of something important going on from which he is excluded can be compared to the same sense in the narrator of ''The Figure in the Carpet'' or in other Jamesian characters like the governess in *The Turn of the Screw* or Maisie in *What Maisie Knew*. Still in the first paragraph, James describes Marcher's sense of society as being divided between ''those who knew too much'' and ''those who knew nothing'' (152). It is already clear to which group he belongs.

This portrayal of the limits of Marcher's understanding is deepened during his first encounter with May. That she remembers distinctly every detail of their first meeting while he remembers it scarcely at all is an embarrassment for Marcher, who takes such pride in his lucid attention to his own fate. It is even more embarrassing that he has ''lost the consciousness'' of having imparted to May the secret of his unique fate (358). This ''missing link'' (353) in Marcher's memory of his own past is also expressed through a series of metaphors of geological or archaeological layers. Their earlier meeting is ''too deeply buried'' to be revived, but later May's memory of the meeting becomes itself the ''buried treasure'' that saves the situation (355, 363). As if to confirm these archaeological images, the encounter had actually occurred at the site of an excavation at Pompeii, where the two of them had been present at ''an important find'' (354).

These metaphors of archaic depths strongly suggest that James is exploiting the sense of an unconscious, and certainly this story, like ''The Jolly Corner,'' invites an interpretation that would treat much of the narrative language as arising from Marcher's, if not James's, unconscious. But the story nowhere explicitly raises the notion of an unconscious. Instead, James has used an alternative way of getting around the limits of Marcher's consciousness: he develops what the notebook entry for the tale calls a second consciousness in the person of May Bartram (*NB*, 311). May functions, as it were, in place of Marcher's unconscious, but she is in herself supremely conscious, much more so than he. She offers a new variation on that role I have suggested to be an essential one in many of the literary tales as well as the tales of "poor sensitive gentlemen"—the second consciousness who appears to the narrator or reflector, always at a certain distance, as the master or as a privileged figure who holds the key to a fundamental, secret knowledge.

This is not, however, the role May occupies at the outset; in fact her function in the story is singularly complex, largely because the triangular relation evident in other tales is here embodied in just two characters. Marcher's own role, as we have begun to see, is double. As the searcher after a mystery, he corresponds to the narrator in "The Figure in the Carpet." But insofar as it is his own destiny that forms the mystery, he is alienated from himself; the secret half of himself seems masterful, like Vereker and his literary secret, and it exercises a fascination, as Vereker's works do. May Bartram's relation to Marcher's mystery is also ambiguous. In part she is a fellow seeker with Marcher, just as Corvick is with the narrator in "The Figure." In his egotism, Marcher is even inclined to see her as a "mere confidant" (364), and at the beginning her main function may indeed seem to be that of a Jamesian *ficelle*. But May develops into more than "the reader's friend" (James's term for his *ficelle* character, Maria Gostrey, in *The Ambassadors—AN*, 322). Her proper role, as Marcher sees too late, would have been as an object of his desire. Instead of becoming Marcher's lover or wife, however, she acquires another, unexpected role, becoming the mediator and interpreter between Marcher and the mystery of the beast. This new function first becomes apparent in Chapter 3, when Marcher becomes aware that her knowledge has now outstripped his own: "It had come up for him then that she 'knew' something and that what she knew was bad—too bad to tell him" (375). Having presumably divined the truth of his fate, she becomes like Corvick after his presumed discovery of Vereker's secret. From this time on, her authority (384) in Marcher's eyes and her distance from him increase. Her fatal illness, which is announced at the same time as her superior knowledge and which immediately threatens to remove her from

Marcher's grasp, enhances the importance she now attains for him. No longer merely human, she becomes a sibyl (389), cryptically relating the message of an unknown god or, even more strikingly, an "impenetrable sphinx" (380), putting to Marcher—as Oedipus—the riddle of his own nature.[17]

This mythical and religious characterization of May's function culminates in her death. In dying and so leaving Marcher without imparting her knowledge, she becomes not so much like Corvick as like Vereker himelf. Impending death already confers a certain divinity on her, as her last conversations with Marcher show. In submitting to her sibylline knowledge, he makes a sacrifice of the intellect: "I believe you; but I can't pretend I understand" (391). He concludes that he cannot question the wisdom of her ways, even if he feels she is toying with him: "She had deceived him to save him—to put him off with something in which he should be able to rest" (388). The religious aura that surrounds May once she is dead provides a clear link between this tale and "The Altar of the Dead," which James placed next to it in the New York Edition with the intention of setting "like with like" (*AN*, 245). Even more than Stransom, Marcher after May's death is afflicted by what could be called in Hegelian terms an "unhappy consciousness," the sense of being a finite consciousness longing after, but cut off from, the source of the absolute. After a futile trip to Asia, which again teaches him the irrelevance of external "scenes of romantic interest" to his own inner mystery, he finds himself drawn to May's grave, as if "from the circumference to the centre of his desert" (396–97). The dead May has become so much his center that his identity now depends upon her recognition of it: "The creature beneath the sod *knew* of his rare experience. . . . It was as if, being nothing anywhere else for anyone, nothing even for himself, he were just everything here" (397–98). The meditation on May's grave leads to the following remarkable image of the relationships in the novella:

He seemed to wander through the old years with his hand in the arm of a companion who was, in the most extraordinary manner, his other, his younger self; and to wander, which was more extraordinary yet, round and round a

17. For an interpretation of Marcher's search for meaning in terms of the sacred and the profane, see Rachel Salmon, "Naming and Knowing in Henry James's 'The Beast in the Jungle': The Hermeneutics of a Sacred Text," *Orbis Litterarum*, XXXVI (1981), 302–22.

third presence—not wandering she, but stationary, still, whose eyes, turning
with his revolution, never ceased to follow him, and whose seat was his point,
so to speak, of orientation. Thus in short he settled to live—feeding on the
sense that he once *had* lived, and dependent on it not only for a support but
for an identity. (398)

Although we need to distinguish the part of Marcher's self-deception in this
passage, it does provide us with a new formulation of the triangular structure. May, in her final apotheosis, has become the center of Marcher's identity, displacing even the mystery of his fate. Marcher also accurately sees
himself as two separate persons, alienated from each other, like Spencer
Brydon's two selves in ''The Jolly Corner.'' But Marcher is wrong in seeing
the image of his younger self as a proof that ''he once *had* lived''; this is his
chronic error of believing that his fate is something outside of or behind him,
while in fact he is still at this very moment fulfilling it, in being ''the man
of his time, *the* man, to whom nothing on earth was to have happened'' (401).
His identity is thus even more radically divided than he recognizes.
Throughout his life he has invested his sense of a real self—the ''real truth''
about himself—in the idea of ''the beast in the jungle''; he has then lost
touch with his own mystery and delivered it over to a second person, May,
who grows so closely identified with that mystery that she becomes the center of his own being. May finally saves Marcher from a self-consuming egotism, or solipsism, even before he realizes her importance at the very end
of the tale. His story never rises to the level of genuine autobiography, not
only because there is no story to tell, his life being ''a great negative adventure,'' but also because he possesses no independent consciousness. His
consciousness is framed not only by that of the impersonal, Jamesian narrator who looks down at Marcher from an ironic height, but also by that of
May, the second consciousness within the tale, who contains his consciousness and keeps it from becoming fluid but who is also the index to Marcher's
failure to attain an autonomous sense of identity.

Paradoxically, John Marcher is not, ultimately, so much the center of
consciousness of the tale as he is its *lack* of a center of consciousness. What
he is not aware of comes to overshadow what he is aware of. Marcher's tragedy is not so much that nothing ever happens to him—this is only the dis-

appointment of that romantic yearning for outward adventure that the tale shows to be inauthentic—but rather that, for all his self-absorption, he is totally unconscious of his real fate while it is occurring. After May's death, he begins to glimpse, and to regret, his failure of consciousness: "It wasn't that he wanted, he argued for fairness, that anything that had happened to him should happen over again; it was only that he shouldn't, as an anticlimax, have been taken sleeping so sound as not to be able to win back by an effort of thought the lost stuff of consciousness. He declared to himself at moments that he would either win it back or have done with consciousness forever" (395). Marcher's misfortune is that he cannot become conscious, after the fact, of things of which he was unconscious at the time they happened. The only alternative is indeed for him to "have done with consciousness forever," and this is what occurs at the end of the story. Marcher has his revelation, but it is a peculiarly negative one, like his adventure in general, and it is followed by that darkening of his sight (again, an echo of the story of Oedipus) that, if it is not yet death, certainly stands for the extinction of consciousness.

Marcher's final loss of consciousness, the fitting punishment for his life-long failure to be aware of his own fate, suggests how far he is from James, who was "one of the people on whom nothing is lost" (FN, 13). Richard Hocks has pointed out that, despite superficial resemblances between the two characters, Marcher's closed and abstracted attitude toward experience makes him the opposite of Lambert Strether.[18] Thus, even though the focalized narration James uses with both Marcher and Strether is roughly the same, his autobiographical investment in the two cases is different. Even if in his Preface he claims that his series of "poor sensitive gentlemen," including Marcher, almost embarrasses him, "The Beast in the Jungle" shows him as author drawing progressively away from his character until, at the moment when Marcher loses consciousness, author and character are totally detached from each other. If there is a character in the tale who participates in James's vision, it is not Marcher but May. James's authorial view comes close to coinciding not with the supposed center of consciousness but with the tale's second consciousness.

18. Hocks, *Henry James and Pragmatistic Thought*, 181–82.

James's distance from Marcher is also underscored in his comments about this story. Whereas with "The Figure in the Carpet" we found a mystifying shift of emphasis from the notebook entries to the published tale and then to the Preface, "The Beast in the Jungle" offers a record of remarkable consistency. In the Preface, James remarks that the essence of the story was already present in the earliest notebook entry (made on August 27, 1901) as an "accomplished fact" (*AN*, 246), and indeed he admits he cannot remember a time when the germ of the story was not already present to him. This story, in other words, is one of those that spring from "the depth of the designer's own mind," just as the beast in the jungle springs on Marcher.

James's obsession with this story is apparently such that in the Preface he can only repeat his tale, rather than criticize it. Instead of discussing technical problems of composition, as he does in most of the essays, here he is content to give an emphatic restatement of the story's theme. Twice in the brief Preface he worries that the theme may not "stand out sharp" enough for the reader—as if, paradoxically, its obviousness for the author were a measure of its obscurity for his audience. At the conclusion of his paraphrase, describing Marcher's defeat he writes: "My picture leaves him overwhelmed—at last he has understood; though in thus disengaging my treated theme for the reader's benefit I seem to acknowledge that this more detached witness may not successfully have done so" (*AN*, 247–48).[19] Therefore the Preface merely repeats the point of the story, and James practically quotes the story's climax in describing Marcher's fortune as "precisely to have been the man in the world to whom nothing whatever was to happen" (*AN*, 247).

If we recall again James's confessed embarrassment over his "poor sensitive gentlemen," we may see in this unusually literal-minded Preface his final attempt to distance himself from his protagonist. Marcher, in fact, is a virtually unique example of a Jamesian protagonist whom his author cannot appreciate. The Preface is a careful condemnation of Marcher in which James insists on the point I made above, that Marcher's deafness to experience

19. In his commentary on this passage, Hocks curiously interprets the "more detached witness" to be Marcher, which is clearly impossible since Marcher has just been dealt with in the first half of the sentence, while the reader becomes the obvious antecedent of witness. See Hocks, *Henry James and Pragmatistic Thought*, 245 n.

represents the very opposite quality from the one James's more affirmative protagonists are meant to cultivate: "Therefore as each item of experience comes, with its possibilities into view, he can but dismiss it under this sterilising habit of the failure to find it good enough and thence to appropriate it" (AN, 246–47). The failure to appropriate experience is the final sign of the distance separating Marcher from his creator.

Thus the result of both stories we have examined is similar. Starting out with an idea coming from the depth of his own mind and experience, James has yet created fictions that have none of the outward forms of autobiography, not even in the case of the first-person "Figure in the Carpet." James first asserts his detachment by alienating himself in the figure of a protagonist who is far from enjoying the full consciousness of the author himself. Then—and here is the oblique operation that stamps the procedure as peculiarly Jamesian—he subjects that figure to a further alienation by locating the seat of his identity outside of himself, in Vereker's literary works or in the mysterious beast. This self-alienation on the part of the fictive protagonist is reminiscent of the way in which James in his autobiography was able to define his self only through the mediation of his primary other, William James. But whereas James acknowledged and dealt with the relation with his brother, both fictional protagonists finally fail in their relations and end up totally isolated. Whereas George Corvick barters his knowledge of Vereker's secret into a marriage with Gwendolen Erme, the narrator dismisses his chance to marry Gwendolen after Corvick's death, just as Marcher persistently neglects the opportunity to take May Bartram as his partner.

In the tales, then, James's own identity is doubly mediated, first through the narrator or reflector, then through *his* other. By a process of double negation, James may appear to enter the fiction through this last figure, the other of his other, or the second consciousness embodied in Hugh Vereker or May Bartram. These are, after all, the masterly characters who are assumed to hold the key to the protagonists' identity. Yet James does not really identify with them, either. Vereker and May Bartram can never fully exist as subjects; their role is purely objective in that they are known only through their words and gestures, that is, as they appear to the narrators. In these stories, then, James has avoided the immediate dangers of autobiography by splitting "the double privilege of subject and object" between different characters. The protagonists, who ostensibly enjoy subjectivity and whose "intimate experience" is chronicled, have their consciousness directed toward an object that holds the secret to their sense of self.

At the same time, James's own roles have been divided among the various characters. The stories are autobiographical in the sense that they are grounded in James's intimate experience, but that experience becomes a general one in the fiction, shared among the characters in their various positions. James's mastery consists of taking on the fictive roles of both the master (Vereker or May Bartram) and the "floundering *person*" (the narrator or John Marcher). This duality of roles corresponds to James's double role as author of autobiographical fiction: that is, as the man whose intimate experience is mother to the fiction and as the creative author who fathers the fiction from his own material. This process is not, as it was for T. S. Eliot, an escape from personality, even though Eliot's distinction in "Tradition and the Individual Talent" between the man that suffers and the mind that creates may well owe much to James's example. Rather than escaping from his personality, James projects it in the form of a fictive situation that universalizes it as the expression of an aesthetic dilemma, perhaps of an aesthetic theory. But this theory, despite its claim to universality, remains recognizably Jamesian, an expression of the problems peculiar to his own aesthetic temperament and stance as an author.

7

THE AMBASSADORS
Avoiding the Abyss

*T*HE AMBASSADORS (1903) constitutes a summa or résumé of the problems raised by the element of autobiography in fiction for James. Critics through the decades have assumed, as they have for *The Sacred Fount*, a degree of autobiographical identification between James and his protagonist Lambert Strether. Strether's centrality as reflector, along with facts such as his age, the vicarious quality of his experience, and his move from America to Europe, make *The Ambassadors* appear at least potentially autobiographical in a way that the other late novels, *The Wings of the Dove* and *The Golden Bowl*, are not. Christof Wegelin has written that Strether is "the one among all of James's important characters one is most tempted to identify with his author," and Oscar Cargill, "I am inclined to think that James identified himself with Strether in the latter's dilemma more closely than he identified himself with any other character in his fiction."[1] James himself, moreover, hinted at an identification with his protagonist in a letter

1. Christof Wegelin, *The Image of Europe in Henry James* (Dallas, 1958), 88; Oscar Cargill, *The Novels of Henry James* (New York, 1961), 335 n. More recently, Richard A. Hocks has argued for the identification of Strether with James, as the embodiment of the perfect pragmatist. Hocks, *Henry James and Pragmatistic Thought* (Chapel Hill, 1974), 152–81. See also Susan M. Greenstein, "*The Ambassadors*: The Man of Imagination Encaged and Provided For," *Studies in the Novel*, IX (1977), 137–53.

he wrote to Jocelyn Persse concerning the recently published *Ambassadors*: "Don't try to thank me for it—but if you are able successfully to struggle with it, try to like the poor old hero, in whom you will perhaps find a vague resemblance (though not facial!) to yours always."[2] This resemblance may explain why James always found Strether such a likable character. In the scenario of the novel he wrote for his publisher, he noted: "In fact I'm afraid I shall represent everyone, rather monotonously, as liking Strether (which is a bad note for his intensity of identity, though we must risk it)" (*NB*, 226). His sense of closeness to Strether also betrays itself in the fact that it is in his Preface to this novel that he delivers his major statement on first-person narration or "autobiography," in which he implies that he had considered allowing Strether to have "the subjective 'say'" in the novel (*AN*, 320–21).

This Preface reveals at the same time how many-sided was the question of autobiographical narration for James and how reluctant he was to commit himself to its implications of self-reference. Not only did James eventually choose not to allow Strether to tell his own story, but he also declined to treat first-person narrative overtly as a question of referentiality. Rather, the Preface treats autobiography in the context of sheerly technical questions and refuses to determine which question has priority: that of the author's personal stance in relation to his fictional characters or that of the author's rhetorical grasp of his materials with the intention of achieving certain literary effects. By suspending the question of first-person narration at the boundary line between a referential and a formal definition of the fictional text, James retreats from that identification with its hero that *The Ambassadors* has suggested to many of its critics. Moreover, the technique of the novel itself establishes a parallel between Strether and the author, only to qualify this parallel in the end. James must finally separate himself from Strether, rather in the way that he distanced himself from John Marcher in "The Beast in the Jungle," and more successfully than he was able to do with the first-person narrator of *The Sacred Fount*.

Strether presents certain obvious similarities with these and other protag-

2. Henry James to Jocelyn Persse, October 26, 1903, in Henry James, *Letters*, ed. Leon Edel (4 vols.; Cambridge, Mass., 1974–84), IV, 286.

onists from the same period in James's fiction. He shares traits with both the literary figures and the "poor sensitive gentlemen" of the short stories. Like the former, Strether is in "a felt predicament or a false position" (AN, 313), which is revealed in his famous "Live all you can" speech to Little Bilham in Gloriani's garden.[3] (The literary tales had been predicated on "some felt embarrassment, some extreme predicament" of the protagonists—AN, 221.) Strether is not strictly an author but he has a literary sensibility; he was to be "*fine*, clever, literary almost" (NB, 226), and he is of course the editor of a periodical. Like the "poor sensitive gentlemen," Strether has a powerful sensibility and an imagination that are directed not into works of art but into his own experience. Strether sometimes resembles John Marcher, in particular, by the passive curiosity he brings to the problem of his own fate. "There were instants at which he could ask whether . . . the fate after all decreed for him hadn't been only to *be* kept. Kept for something, in that event, that he didn't pretend, didn't possibly dare as yet to divine" (I, 86). Strether's detached, almost objectified, view of his own destiny produces in him a "double consciousness" (I, 5) like that of Marcher or of Spencer Brydon in "The Jolly Corner." Though Strether will never develop a theory of a beast in the jungle or a ghostly alter ego to express this view of himself, he does have a vision of "the pale figure of his real youth," which he will pursue through much of the novel (I, 83–84). Moreover, this projection of another version of himself will call for the mediation of a guide to lead him through the maze of his experience (I, 11 and 120). This guide, Maria Gostrey, whom James designated as a *ficelle* (AN, 322), plays a role parallel to that of May Bartram, Marcher's confidant.[4] Like May, she will be used by the hero as a guide and in the end will be overlooked as a possible lover.

The Ambassadors also presents analogies—perhaps more disturbing ones—with *The Sacred Fount*, published in the same year in which most of *The Ambassadors* was written (1901). As other critics have remarked, *The Ambassadors* repeats—through Chad and Madame de Vionnet espe-

3. *The Ambassadors* (2 vols.; New York, 1909), I, 217. This, the New York Edition, will be cited parenthetically in the text of this chapter.

4. On the role of Maria Gostrey as *ficelle*, see Sister M. Corona Sharp, *The Confidant in Henry James* (Notre Dame, 1963), 150–80, and for a comparison of Maria with May Bartram, 51–57.

cially—the theme of the sacred fount, one lover's loss as the other's gain, and the corollary theme of a person's total transformation—here, Chad's— through this process.[5] Like the Narrator of *The Sacred Fount*, Strether functions as an acute observer who through his imagination penetrates the meaning of the transformations and the other phenomena he encounters. Both of them remain largely passive and vicarious in their attitude, and both are notably reluctant to acknowledge a more active role for themselves or to have attention directed at their own case. Yet these evident similarities finally lead to the precautions James had to take in order to keep *The Ambassadors* from becoming a second *Sacred Fount* and to keep Strether from suffering the fate of the Narrator. The most important of these precautions was in fact to change from first-person, or "autobiographical," narration to focalized narration. As we shall see, this change allows James in part to sacrifice Strether at the end of the novel, but in a way that is less devastating for the hero and less threatening for the author.

To see how James succeeds, we can begin by examining the claims he makes in his Preface to the novel, which, as I have suggested, balances a recognition of the subjectivity potentially contained in Strether's story with a rehearsal of the conditions making for objectivity of treatment. Part of James's strategy in this essay is to make the avoidance of autobiography appear to be a purely technical decision. James's emphasis throughout falls on the objectivity, even impersonality, of his act of composition. The germ of the story came not from introspection (as with the literary tales) but from an anecdote concerning James's lifelong friend, W. D. Howells. Once the germ was planted, the composition proceeded naturally, as though without James's participation: the steps "continued to fall together, as by the neat action of their own weight and form, even while their commentator scratched his head about them; he easily sees now that they were always well in advance of him" (*AN*, 315). The passage from intention to execution was flawless, offering "no moment of subjective intermittence" such as would plague the writing of *The Wings of the Dove* (*AN*, 309). Since origin and result are at

5. See for example Oscar Cargill, *The Novels of Henry James*, 305–306; Bernard Richards, "*The Ambassadors* and *The Sacred Fount*: The Artist Manqué," in John Goode (ed.), *The Air of Reality: New Essays on Henry James* (London, 1972), 219–43; Laurence Holland, *The Expense of Vision: Essays on the Craft of Henry James* (Princeton, 1964), 223, 231.

one ("Nothing can exceed the closeness with which the whole fits again into its germ"–*AN*, 308), James is now free to concentrate on the work itself and the technical interest it represents, even more exclusively than he does in the other Prefaces. The content of the novel—Strether's story and Strether's consciousness—now interests him less than the objective questions of the novel's form: "There is the story of one's hero, and then, thanks to the intimate connexion of things, the story of one's story itself. I blush to confess it, but if one's a dramatist one's a dramatist, and the latter imbroglio is liable on occasion to strike me as really the more objective of the two" (*AN*, 313). The Preface becomes a veritable paean to the "refinements and ecstasies of method" (*AN*, 324).

Yet the Preface is not quite so consistent as I have just described it. Both implicitly and explicitly, it suggests that *The Ambassadors* posed problems that are more than technical and that Strether himself, and his relation to James, cannot be disposed of in perfectly objective terms. James declares, for instance, that the "major propriety" he obeyed in the novel was the rule of respecting Strether's point of view absolutely, of making the whole narrative into "the projection of his consciousness" (*AN*, 317). Thus Strether becomes, to use the term of the following Preface, "the impersonal author's deputy or delegate" (*AN*, 327). This phrase, besides doubling the theme of deputation that appears in the title and the text of *The Ambassadors* (a point I shall return to) reminds us of the peculiarly intimate relation between Strether and James. The language of the Preface hints at this intimacy in other ways. too. An entire vocabulary describing the author's composition of the work is applied to Strether's activity as well, suggesting that the hero doubles the creative process of the author. The author must control the "*process*" whereby the germ is converted to the stuff of art; likewise the content of the novel is simply Strether's "process of vision" (*AN*, 312, 308). The author's task is to "project imaginatively," while the whole book is also "the projection of [Strether's] consciousness" (*AN*, 324, 317). James had to make "precious discriminations" to determine the form of his work, just as Strether's note is "the note of discrimination" and his drama, "the drama of discrimination" (*AN*, 321, 316).

Such terms imply at least a formal parallel, if not an identification, between James and his fictional hero. This obvious threat of the author's identification with his hero calls forth a countermovement, an act that will protect James by keeping Strether distinct from him, a prisoner, as it were, of the fictional text. To this end the Preface employs the image of encaging. In contrast to a first-person narrator, "Strether, on the other hand, encaged and provided for as 'the Ambassadors' encages and provides, has to keep in view proprieties much stiffer and more salutary than any our straight and credulous gape are likely to bring home to him, has exhibitional conditions to meet, in a word, that forbid the terrible *fluidity* of self-revelation" (*AN*, 321). The familiar imagery of tightness versus fluidity operates here in a way uncomfortable for Strether. He is encaged and subject to the "stiffer proprieties" of James's focalized narrative so that he cannot escape the fictional bounds of the text and be confused with his author. In practical terms Strether's encagement is concerned with at least two things—point of view and temporal relations.

As the Preface tells us, James's crucial choice was that of a focalized third-person narrative over a first-person narrative. The form he chose has the double advantage of providing as thorough an inside view of Strether as possible even while framing Strether's consciousness in a more comprehensive, objective narrative, but it is an inherently ambiguous form, close to the dual voice of Flaubertian *style indirect libre*.[6] Ian Watt, in his stylistic analysis of *The Ambassadors*, has shown how the indirect report of Strether's thought often leads to confusion as to whose reflections we are reading, the character's or the narrator's. Yet James rarely, or never, fuses his narrative language with that of his characters, as Flaubert does through his *style indirect libre*. As Watt points out, James's entire method depends on maintaining a distance between narrator and character, even if this distance is hard to measure in certain passages. Watt calls this a "split narrative point of view" and remarks, "We and the narrator are inside Strether's mind, and yet we are also outside it, knowing more about Strether than he knows about himself. This is the classic posture of irony."[7] Irony and sympathy are the two poles of our possible attitudes toward the protagonist, and most of the

6. See Roy Pascal, *The Dual Voice* (Manchester, 1977).
7. Ian Watt, "The First Paragraph of *The Ambassadors*: An Explication," in James, *The Ambassadors*, ed. S. P. Rosenbaum (New York, 1964), 465–84, 480.

HENRY JAMES AND THE DARKEST ABYSS OF ROMANCE

latitude in actual interpretations of this novel could probably be defined along the range between these poles.

Strether's encagement and his relation to the author also affect the temporality of the narrative. Since practically the entire novel is filtered through Strether's consciousness, the time of the narration tends to follow the time of the material narrated, but Strether's point of view is not limited to the single moment of time reached by the narrative. It also includes passages of memory, during which Strether reflects back on his experience. Parts of the story are thus doubly filtered, first through Strether's consciousness and then through his memory of the primary experience. Readers of the novel will recognize the complicated temporal stance that this situation engenders. Often the doubly filtered narration is motivated by the sudden occurrence of an event whose full significance requires time to be digested, such as Chad's surprise appearance in front of Strether and Maria at the theater in Book 3. Immediately after the sentence recording the surprise—"They were in presence of Chad himself"—the narrative leaps ahead to an indeterminate future time: "Our friend was to go over it afterwards again and again" (I, 135). The rest of this chapter and the beginning of the next, when Strether and Chad sit down in a café, alternate between such prolepsis and a pluperfect retrospect, pluperfect because now the preterite tense of the novel as a whole is compounded by the past tense of Strether's act of memory occurring within fictional time.[8] In this situation even direct dialogue cannot establish a firm sense of a scenic present moment but is imbedded in the forward and backward movement of the text: " 'Do I strike you as being improved?' Strether was to recall that Chad had at this point inquired" (I, 148). Thus the narrative sequence of events is replaced by the time frame of Strether's acts of recollection; this method liberates Strether, at least temporarily, from the diachrony of the story and makes the outward events of the novel reverberate in what seem to be almost the atemporal depths of his consciousness.

The result might appear to be a kind of fluidity; events in the novel would

8. For a more detailed description of temporality in the novel, see Pierre Vitoux, "Le Récit dans *The Ambassadors*," *Poétique*, VI (1975), 460–78. Others who have commented on this phenomenon include Holland, *The Expense of Vision*, 230; Franz Stanzel, *Narrative Situations in the Novel*, trans. James P. Pusack (Bloomington, Ind., 1971), esp. 105–14.

not belong merely to their time and place but would lead a second life in the capacious, subjective reservoir of Strether's memory. In this sense Strether's consciousness threatens to exceed the boundaries of the fiction and to merge with the consciousness of the author, in other words, to produce the fluidity of a mingling of these two identities. It is as though Strether might unmask himself at the end of the novel as a first-person narrator after all, rather as Dr. Rieux does at the end of Albert Camus' *La Peste.* This, however, is precisely what James does not allow to happen. Although Strether's act of memory often seems to have an indefinite duration, its time frame remains that of the fictional story and never merges with that of the author. The relation between these two might be called an asymptotic one: the curve of Strether's memory span can approach James's temporality by an infinitesimal margin but can never coincide with it. This asymptote is what James has achieved by encaging Strether and denying him the privilege of first-person speech.

Even if Strether's memory is not sufficient, then, to identify him with James's position as author, one of his other closely related faculties—his imagination—does threaten to do so. For Strether, like James and like the first-person narrators of *The Turn of the Screw* and *The Sacred Fount,* is a "man of imagination" (*AN,* 313). In Chapter 1, I have already pointed out how the Preface to the novel establishes Strether as the major predecessor to the total man of imagination, James himself. As we saw, however, Strether is only a relative or comparative case of the imaginative type. Although he possesses "imagination galore," imagination is not his "prime faculty"; yet even in moderation, his imagination threatens to "wreck" him (*AN,* 310). James's assurance that Strether has not been wrecked seems gratuitous, since James is defending Strether against a danger that only he has discovered and named as such. This very defensiveness does indicate an important component in the author's attitude toward his protagonist, however, and it may also suggest that there is a sense—which James is reluctant to admit—in which Strether *is* ruined by his imagination.

At first, however, Strether's imagination acts constructively rather than destructively. His combined memory and fancy (II, 276) help create the drama of *The Ambassadors* by creating the sense of Europe and of Paris in particular. "Poor Strether had . . . to recognise the truth that wherever one stopped in Paris the imagination reacted before one could stop it" (I, 96). A well-known passage from "The Art of Fiction" describes what Strether does upon his arrival in Europe, in the opening books of the novel: "When the mind is imaginative . . . it takes to itself the faintest hints of life, it converts the very pulses of the air into revelations" (*FN*, 12). To be imaginative as Strether is does not mean to substitute vicarious or fictive experience for the real thing but to create the real thing by perceiving it in its fullest realization. This is the faculty that enables Strether to realize the full dimensions of Chad's alteration, as the Pococks cannot. In fact, in a typically Jamesian complication of active and passive roles, Strether is said to bring about Chad's transformation almost as much as Madame de Vionnet had done: "Strether had the sense that *he* had made him [Chad] too; his high appreciation had, as it were, consecrated her work" (II, 284).

Even as late as Book 11 both Maria Gostrey and Chad are paying tribute to Strether's "treasures of imagination" (II, 224, 244). Maria contrasts Strether's abundance of this faculty to the deficiency exhibited by the two Newsomes, mother and son. Strether's imagination, she implies, must compensate for Chad's lack of one. Strether must also compensate for Mrs. Newsome, whose ambassador he is, by the generosity of his imagination, since "she imagined stupidly. . . . she imagined meanly" (II, 225). But the generosity of Strether's imagination—certainly one of the traits that made him likable to James—can go too far. Indeed, the liberal terms in which he pictures Chad's transformation turn out to be excessive, and he must finally acknowledge of his young friend that "he was none the less only Chad" (II, 284). Moreover, Maria's praise for his imagination comes at an ironic moment, just preceding Strether's retreat into the Lambinet-like French countryside where his imagination sets him up for his greatest fall in the novel, a fall which will almost wreck him.

The problem for James, then, is how to give license to his hero's imagination, and to his own imagination through his hero's, without participating in whatever ruin befalls Strether as a result of his imaginative activity. It is a problem he perceived as well in Flaubert's masterpiece, *Madame Bovary*, with which James was concerning himself around the same time he was writing *The Ambassadors*. In his article "Gustave Flaubert," published in 1902 and later collected in *Notes on Novelists*, James is interested in Flaubert's partial identification with his heroine, an identification explained by her imagination and by the French novelist's literary personality, divided according to James into "two quite distinct compartments, a sense of the real and a sense of the romantic" (*FN*, 132). What compounds the connection between *Madame Bovary* and *The Ambassadors* is James's confession that he cannot speak of *Madame Bovary* without speaking of his own relation to it, and that relation strangely resembles Strether's relation to the French literature that has served as his imaginative bond to Paris during his years in America. James recalls when, as a young boy in his parents' Parisian apartment, he picked up the periodical in which Flaubert's novel was appearing: "The cover of the old *Revue de Paris* was yellow, if I mistake not, like that of the new, and *Madame Bovary: Moeurs de Province*, on the inside of it, was already, on the spot, as a title, mysteriously arresting, inscrutably charged." Strether likewise recalls the "lemon-coloured volumes" he had bought on his first trip to Paris, which now symbolize the unfulfilled promises of his youth: "They were still somewhere at home, the dozen [volumes]—stale and soiled and never sent to the binder; but what had become of the sharp initiation they represented?" (I, 86–87). Strether and James both share this trait with Emma Bovary, that they allow certain books, endowed with a romantic aura, to mediate their conception of reality—reality meaning, for all three of them, Paris. Emma never gets to Paris, of course, while Strether does, but the intense, if impressionistic, quality of their respective imaginations is almost the same. Here is Emma: "Paris, more vague than the ocean, glimmered before Emma's eyes with a silvery glow. . . . The world of ambassadors moved over polished floors in drawing-rooms lined with mirrors, round oval tables covered with velvet and gold-fringed cloths. . . . Then came the society of the duchesses; all were pale, all got up at four o'clock."[9] Strether, at Gloriani's reception, is like an Emma who has confronted the real Paris and now faces disillusionment: "He was to ask himself soon afterwards, that evening, what *really* had happened—conscious as he could after all remain that for a gentleman taken, and taken the first time, into the 'great world,' the world of ambassadors and duchesses, the items made a meagre total. It was nothing new to him, however, as we

9. Gustave Flaubert, *Madame Bovary*, ed. and trans. Paul de Man (New York, 1965), 42.

know, that a man might have—at all events such a man as he—an amount
of experience out of any proportion to his adventures'' (II, 227).

This excess of experience over adventures is precisely what marks both
Emma and Strether as imaginative, indeed romantic characters. And it is
here that, according to James, Flaubert took a not very calculated risk. James
suggests that Flaubert compensated for his banal material by endowing his
heroine with a romantic imagination that could ''distill the rich and the rare,''
and he adds: ''He of course knew more or less what he was doing for his
book in making Emma Bovary a victim of the imaginative habit, but he must
have been far from designing or measuring the total effect which renders the
work so general, so complete an expression of himself'' (*FN*, 134). Flaubert's quasi identification with his heroine (''Madame Bovary, c'est moi'')
makes his portrait of her partly autobiographical. Emma being ''an embodiment of helpless romanticism,'' James argues, ''Flaubert himself but narrowly escaped being such an embodiment after all, and he is thus able to
express the romantic mind with extraordinary truth'' (*FN*, 134).

James might have been speaking of himself. Like Flaubert, he too is in
part a man of romantic imagination, and he uses Strether's imagination to
express the richness of a subject matter that might otherwise appear banal.
(In the Preface he voices the fear that a plot revolving around an aging man's
moral temptation in Paris would betray a ''*trivial* association, one of the
vulgarest in the world''—*AN*, 316). But whereas Flaubert only ''more or
less'' knew the extent to which he was compromising himself through his
characterization of Emma, the far more self-conscious and cautious James
is not willing to take the same risk. If his hero should turn out to be, like
Emma, a ''victim of the imaginative habit,'' James does not want to victim-
ize himself. The solution he finds in *The Ambassadors* is much the same one
Flaubert discovered fortuitously. Emma ''makes of the business an inordi-
nate failure, a failure which in its turn makes for Flaubert the most pointed,
the most *told* of anecdotes'' (*FN*, 132). Emma's subjective loss, then, is
Flaubert's objective gain. James would later sum all this up in the Preface
to *The American*, where once again the theme of the opposition of the romantic and the real automatically brought Flaubert's masterpiece to his mind:
''It would be impossible to have a more romantic temper than Flaubert's
Madame Bovary, and yet nothing less resembles a romance than the record

of her adventures'' (*AN*, 33). If we set aside obvious differences of character, the same could be said of Strether, and of *The Ambassadors*. Through its focalized method of narration—partly anticipated by *Madame Bovary*— *The Ambassadors* uses Strether's imagination to ''distil the rich and the rare'' of its theme, but it must also ultimately separate itself from Strether's sense of reality, so as to avoid falling into the genre of romance.

To see how the novel finally asserts its difference from Strether's imagination, we need to consider not only the main character's relation to the author but also his position within the fictional story. We saw above that Strether's role as central reflector makes him James's deputy, as though a perfect correspondence exists between the protagonist and the author; the analogy with *Madame Bovary* also suggests that one side of James, at least, identifies with Strether. But Strether's role as central consciousness becomes more complicated if we study his relations to the other characters in the novel. The novel presents not a system of relations among independent consciousnesses but a system in which characters represent, double, or otherwise symbolically support one another. As in James's literary tales, the identity of any one character, even the central one, must be seen as a function of the kinds of relations that bind him to other characters. Strether belongs to a network of characters who function as foils, *ficelles*, or ''ambassadors'' for one another. Strether's own centrality, as well as his correspondence to James, accordingly becomes problematic.

The title of the novel already indicates that Strether appears not in his own capacity but as one in a series of substitutable representatives of another agent. This agent is specifically Mrs. Newsome, though sometimes it is designated by extension as ''Woollett.'' Later in the novel, Woollett is represented by the Pococks, Sarah, Jim, and Mamie (II, 71, 75–76). Strether must now be replaced because he has failed to represent the interests and the intentions of Woollett, as embodied in Mrs. Newsome, faithfully. Strether must serve two masters at once, as it were: he represents James as well as Mrs. Newsome, and only by misrepresenting the latter's intentions can he loyally serve the author by achieving the dramatic tension and irony on which the novel is based. The degree of Strether's deviation from his ''deputed duty'' (*NB*, 387) is measured by his distance from his friend, Waymarsh, whom James identified as a foil (*NB*, 377) and who might also be called Strether's double, representing an alternative reaction to the conflicting claims of Europe and New England.

Strether is not the only character to represent another in the novel, or to be doubled by another in turn. Little Bilham, whom Strether meets before meeting Chad, is defined as "Chad's intimate and deputy" (I, 113)—a doubling that mimics the reflector's role as "the impersonal author's concrete deputy or delegate." Marie de Vionnet and Maria Gostrey (herself a *ficelle* rather than a personage in her own right, according to James), schoolmates with the same first name and both potential mates for Strether, double each other. Even the young and innocent Jeanne de Vionnet is matched up with an American rival for the attentions of Chad in the person of Mamie Pocock. Thus, virtually every character in the book, including Strether, represents someone else or serves as a foil, *ficelle*, or deputy. What appear in the mimetic realism of the novel as autonomous intersubjective relations can also be read—to use the terms of the Preface—as the result of "delightful dissimulation." What James says of Maria Gostrey's relation to Strether contains some truth for practically all the relations: it is "a relation that has nothing to do with the matter (the matter of my subject) but has everything to do with the manner (the manner of my presentation of the same)" (*AN*, 325). One might, without irreverence, pose a question concerning Strether in similar terms: is he essentially not the matter of the novel but only a kind of glorified *ficelle*, an ambassador of James and Mrs. Newsome or a foil for Waymarsh as Waymarsh is a foil for him?

When the question is put so bluntly, even the Preface—despite its urge to reduce all questions to technical ones—seems to falter. After all, the Preface identifies Strether's speech to Little Bilham in Gloriani's garden as the thematic core of the novel, and it describes this scene in terms of Strether's own situation: "Will there yet perhaps be time for reparations?" Moreover, elsewhere in the Preface James states the purpose of the novel to be "the demonstration of this [*i.e.*, Strether's] process of vision" (*AN*, 308). This last phrase, however, already suggests the complexity of Strether's relation to the main theme and plot of the novel. The novel borrows his point of view, but his "process of vision" is not primarily reflexive. For all his analytic lucidity, Strether is not primarily given to self-contemplation. Hence, to show his vision or imagination at work means largely to show the outside material it works on, just as for James to write his autobiography as "the history of the growth of one's imagination" meant to concentrate on the world that his imagination helped create around him, not on the imagination itself. Like the young James of the autobiography, Strether tends to be reduced precisely to the function of a reflector or an eye, a fine medium through which the story can be transmitted.

To Strether's own sense, he indeed belongs chiefly to the manner of the telling, while the story he transmits belongs primarily to Chad. As Laurence Holland has pointed out, Chad's story is central to the novel even though the limitation of the narrative to Strether's consciousness seems to consign Chad to the background and to leave his true character in doubt.[10] James admits that the presentation of Chad posed a problem to which he found no adequate solution; consequently, "Chad's whole figure and presence" suffers from "a direct presentability diminished and compromised—despoiled, that is, of its *proportional* advantage" (*AN*, 325). What we see throughout is Chad-as-seen-by-Strether, which means that the "process of vision" represented in the novel concerns a subject and an object, an observer and an observed, taken together as a relation. Like Marlow and Jim in *Lord Jim*, Strether and Chad exist primarily in an epistemological relation to each other, where the older man's task is to observe and interpret the younger man's adventure: Jim's moral choices, Chad's transformation of character. This epistemological relation is not, however, the only one that binds the two characters. Holland shows that there is also an analogy between Strether's and Chad's situations, since both are torn between the moral and financial demands of Woollett and the aesthetic attraction of Paris and both become entangled in an affair of honor and possible treachery with a mistress or a would-be mistress.[11] Finally, the relation is also a symbolic one, involving a partial exchange of identity, since Strether clearly sees in Chad that "pale figure of his [own] real youth" that greets him upon his return to Europe (I, 83–84).

All of these kinds of relations, especially the epistemological and symbolic ones, explain why Strether not only accepts but embraces a subordi-

10. Holland, *The Expense of Vision*, 231.
11. *Ibid.*, 234–48.

nate role—the role of mere ambassador or of transparent eye—in relation to Chad. Exactly like the young James of the autobiography, he believes that he personally provides only a "poor show" for others (II, 50); like the narrator of *The Sacred Fount*, he prefers to remain on the sidelines while formulating theories of behavior that concern only other people. Even as late as Book 9 we are told that, when employing the term *hero*, "Strether was incapable of meaning anyone but Chad" (II, 151), and still later, "it was in truth essentially by bringing down his personal life to a function all subsidiary to the young man's own that he held together" (II, 231). In one of the dramatic metaphors that run through the novel, Strether describes himself as a mere spectator of Chad's play: "we poor people who watch the play from the pit," he says to Chad (II, 233). From this perspective, Strether's much criticized declaration to Maria Gostrey at the end of the novel, that his logic has been "not, out of the whole affair, to have got anything for myself" (II, 326), becomes more understandable. His statement derives in part, no doubt, from a lingering Woollett-like sense of ethical renunciation but also from his fond belief that he was never a full participant in the plot anyway. Strether would like to treat not only Maria but himself too as a mere *ficelle*.

Yet, despite his reluctance, Strether does get drawn closer to the center of the drama, and he feels this himself, especially after Book 7, with the announcement of the arrival of the Pococks as the new ambassadors. Ironically, it is at the moment when his original role as ambassador has been terminated—Strether feels that it is "the preposterous end of his mission" (II, 70)—that his own case becomes more interesting. Strether's "conversion" (II, 41) to the cause of Madame de Vionnet begins to take on equal importance to the question of Chad's transformation. "He had before this had many moments of wondering if he himself weren't changed even as Chad was changed" (II, 79). Though Strether is not yet certain what his own change entails, it promises to make him more interesting, a better show, than previously. Faced with the Pococks, Strether suddenly becomes aware that he is part of the "performance of 'Europe' " being staged for their benefit; later he confides to Chad that the Pococks apparently crossed the ocean just as much to see him as to see Chad and Madame de Vionnet (II, 105). After seeing Sarah Pocock, Strether admits to Madame de Vionnet that he feels suspense not only over what will happen to Chad but "about my own case too!" (II, 113). By the time of Chad's dinner party in Book 10, Miss Barrace is able to tell Strether with only slight hyperbole: "We know you as the hero of the drama, and we're gathered to see what you'll do." Strether, however, speaking of himself in the third person, demurs: "He's scared at his heroism—he shrinks from his part" (II, 179).

It is not only Miss Barrace who embarrasses Strether when she directs attention to his case. Like many of James's first-person narrators, Strether is not at ease with introspection or with investigating his "relation to [his] own nature" (*AN*, 174). When he is forced to do so, especially in front of other people, he echoes the attitude, and even the language, of the narrators of *The Sacred Fount* and *The Turn of the Screw*. "I'm extremely wonderful just now. I dare say in fact I'm quite fantastic, and I shouldn't be at all surprised if I were mad," he tells Maria Gostrey shortly before the Pococks' arrival (II, 40). (Later he will say to Chad: "I'm true but I'm incredible. I'm fantastic and ridiculous—I don't explain myself even *to* myself"—II, 238.) The allusion to fantasticality and madness gives us an unusual glimpse into Strether's "relation to his own nature" and reminds us how close he is, on one side, to the problematics of *The Sacred Fount*. If Strether stops short of the serious threat of madness that afflicts the narrator of the earlier work, it is largely because he has been denied "the double privilege of subject and object," that is, the first-person form of address. Contrary to what we might expect, James's "point of view" technique in *The Ambassadors* does not especially promote Strether's self-consciousness in the form of the outbreaks just quoted (which appear, in any case, in dialogue); instead, it makes him literally a reflector of people and events outside himself. The reflector is technically at the center of the book, but he is not necessarily its hero. The resulting ambiguity in Strether's position can be felt both in his own attitude concerning himself and in the form of the novel. It is an ambiguity that remains unresolved to the end of the novel, just as James's autobiography never entirely resolved the paradox inherent in filial or fraternal autobiography.

Strether's ambivalence concerning his own role is prefigured by an early scene in the novel that suggests a metaphor for his situation in general. Strether, still in London, is taken to the theater for the first time by Maria Gostrey. Awash in his new impressions, Strether reacts to the play in a curious manner: ''It was an evening, it was a world of types, and this was a connexion above all in which the figures and faces in the stalls were interchangeable with those on the stage'' (I, 53). This easy exchange between stage and house, actors and audience, is a good image for Strether's own shifting relation to the other characters, especially Chad, later in the novel. We have already seen the confusion as to whether Strether is hero or spectator of the novel's drama. More generally, the theater and the metaphors that derive from it will offer a complete imaginative analogy for Strether's experience. Theater becomes the appropriate and inevitable source of imagery, not only because it suits the aestheticism and the obsession with surface appearances that characterize Paris in the novel but also because it provides the terms in which Strether's imagination tends to work. Strether not only reflects but also projects and constructs an image of himself and others as engaged in a dramatic or spectacular action. His imagination, already at work in the theater in London, will continue to color his experience and will lead directly to the novel's climax and denouement. Even while Strether cannot decide whether he is the hero of the story or not, his imagination will be deciding his fate for him. It will be setting him up for a collision with reality that puts into question James's assertion in the Preface that Strether's imagination has not wrecked him.

Strether's adventure throughout the novel takes place under the aegis of drama, art, and illusion in general. His initiation to London through the theater in Book 2 is repeated in Paris in Book 3 when Maria takes him to the *Comédie-Française* and Chad upsets the boundary between stage and audience once again by his theatrical entry into the box where Maria, Waymarsh, and Strether sit (I, 135). These early scenes will be counterbalanced by the famous scene late in the novel when Strether journeys to the countryside for a solitary idyll, which is destroyed by the intrusion of Chad and Madame de Vionnet (Book 11). Here, as we shall see shortly, Strether's imagination borrows its metaphors not so much from drama as from pictorial art and literature, but whether its source is drama, narrative fiction, or the other arts, this imagination is bound to recall for us the imagination of the young Henry James as it was depicted above all in *A Small Boy and Others*. The young Henry's world was saturated with the fictions of Thackeray and Dickens, with the melodramas of the New York and London stages; the autobiography stopped just at the moment when James was being forced to acknowledge the difference between the artistic metaphors of his imagination and sober reality. *The Ambassadors*, likewise, comes to its conclusion just after Strether has been subjected to a trial of his imagination that in large measure exposes the failure of that imagination. Moreover, just as, at the moment of the young Henry's disillusionment with London in *The Middle Years*, the autobiography broke off and the older, narrating James implicitly asserted his distance from the boy he had been, so at the end of *The Ambassadors* the demystification of Strether leads James to assert his superiority over his character by clearly calling attention to the childlike errors the latter has made.

James's separation of himself from Strether at the end of the novel is all the more striking because up until that point James has himself contributed to the creation of the dramatic and imaginative environment that surrounds Strether. Of course this environment is attributable in part, as we have seen, to Strether's own imagination; this process is especially well documented in the case of the "Lambinet" landscape in Book 11. It is less often remarked that the artistic, even fairy-tale, medium in which Strether is submerged much of the time is not entirely of his own making but is in part objectively determined as such; that is, it is created in these terms by James himself. For instance, it may be Strether's fault that the plays he attends early in the novel affect his views of his experience later, but it is hardly his fault that the first play he sees in London seems to point directly to the melodrama that grips Chad, and by extension Strether himself: "It befell that in the drama precisely there was a bad woman in a yellow frock who made a pleasant weak good-looking young man in perpetual evening dress do the most dreadful things" (I, 53). The play manages to be reminiscent of both *La Dame aux camélias* and *The Ambassadors* itself; it seems to coax Strether's own adventure into the realm of the fictional "lemon-coloured volumes."

Strether's Paris altogether, in fact, belongs more to the world of fiction than to the world of fact, and again it is James, not Strether, who is primarily responsible for this. In the Preface, as we have seen, James betrays embarrassment over the setting of the novel because his choice of Paris conformed to "one of the platitudes of the human comedy"; it confirmed "a *trivial* association, one of the vulgarest in the world" (*AN*, 316). Thus the author admits that he consciously placed Strether in the midst of a literary cliché, and it is hardly surprising that Strether then complies by transforming Paris into a "vast bright Babylon" (I, 89). Finally, James not only appealed to a literary convention for the setting of his novel but assigned a literary model to the protagonist himself. Lewis Lambert Strether is perhaps the only character in all of James to be named after a specific character from another literary work, the hero of Balzac's autobiographical novel, *Louis Lambert*, a novel Maria Gostrey calls "an awfully bad one" (I, 14). *The Ambassadors* thus asserts a parallel between Strether and Balzac's Swedenborgian hero, a man of imagination par excellence whose imagination *does* wreck him.[12] By naming Strether, James has already consigned him to the realm of intertextual allegory and has made him in a sense doubly fictional. Once again, the author seems to make it inevitable that Strether's imagination should confuse fiction and reality. Thus James's imagination, by creating the fictional world where Strether dwells and by marking it explicitly as fictional, is responsible for the fabrications of Strether's imagination, just as Flaubert was responsible for the imagination of his character, Emma. This makes it all the more unexpected—but perhaps all the more necessary too, from James's point of view—that James so brutally separates himself from Strether and pulls the ground from under his hero at the climax of the novel. This he does through Strether's trip to the countryside in Book 16.

This episode has already been placed under the sign of the imagination by Strether's conversations with Chad and Maria earlier in the same book. Both of them have paid tribute to Strether's imaginative faculty, which Maria calls monstrous (II, 224). When Strether decides to leave Paris for the day, he does so with the express intention of finding a landscape that will match the Lambinet painting he had once been too poor to purchase in Boston. He thus calls upon his imagination to redeem a past failure, just as the entire present trip to Europe is meant to compensate for his missed youth. The imagination rises to the challenge. Like Alice stepping through the looking glass, Strether passes into "the oblong gilt frame" of the painting and doesn't "overstep" it (II, 247, 252). He does not stop with this pictorial metaphor,

12. For one discussion of James's use of the Balzacian model, see Quentin Anderson, *The American Henry James* (New Brunswick, 1957), 213–14. See also Leon Edel, *Henry James: The Master* (Philadelphia, 1972), 70–71.

though. The surroundings remind him also of a Maupassant story and, most characteristically, of drama; he is struck by "a scene and a stage . . . the very air of the play" (II, 253). The imagination converts the scene into a metaphor that combines the present and the past: "It was all there in short— it was what he wanted; it was Tremont Street, it was France, it was Lambinet. Moreover he was freely walking about in it" (II, 247).

It is an ominous note that, for the first time in the novel, Strether's imagination meets absolutely no resistance; it has for once become his "prime faculty." The terms James used for *The Turn of the Screw* could apply to this scene, too. It is "an exercise of the imagination unassisted, unassociated—playing the game, making the score, in the phrase of our sporting day, off its own bat" (*AN*, 171). At least this expresses Strether's sense of the ease with which he circulates here in a world of his own making. That it is not James's own sense can be inferred from the narrator's unobtrusive comments, made even while Strether is moving deeper into his picture frame. "Romance could weave itself, for Strether's sense, out of elements mild enough" (II, 245) suggests the danger but also the pettiness of a romance scaled down to the modest requirements of Strether's imagination. Two pages later, when the narrator observes that Strether is beside "a river of which he didn't know, and didn't want to know, the name," he is underlining that will to ignorance in Strether that will make his imminent discovery of Chad and Madame de Vionnet such a shock for him.

Strether's imagination, while still in command, has the power to absorb everything it confronts: "Not a single one of his observations but somehow fell into a place in it; not a breath of the cooler evening that wasn't somehow a syllable of the text"—the text that is being written by the imagination itself. In this way even Chad and Madame de Vionnet, when they first appear as two figures in a boat, can be accommodated in Strether's fantasy, as if they "had been wanted in the picture" (II, 256). The very moment when Strether's imaginative picture is completed, however, is also the moment when it is exceeded, when the frame or border the imagination had carefully erected around the experience is violated. What has exceeded Strether's imagination is the fact of Chad and Madame de Vionnet's love affair, the fact of which now for the first time intrudes itself on the heretofore pure stage of the imagination. Strether's startling encounter with this fact has been prepared by certain signals dropped by James: when Strether got off the train, it was "as if to keep an appointment"; Strether's drama is said to be complete except for its catastrophe (II, 246, 253). These forebodings should not be taken as evidence that Strether has already had an unconscious premonition of what he now faces. If the scene takes on the uncanny quality of a "recognition" scene, as Ruth Bernard Yeazell has suggested, it is not because Strether's conscious knowledge is catching up with his unconscious but because his ignorance is being ironically confronted by James's knowledge as narrator and author.[13] The "intimacy" of Chad and Madame de Vionnet is James's fact, which he uses to prick the bubble of Strether's imagination. The growing gulf between narrator and character becomes apparent at this moment: "His theory, as we know, had bountifully been that the facts were specifically none of his business, and were, over and above, so far as one had to do with them, intrinsically beautiful; and this might have prepared him for anything, as well as rendered him proof against mystification. When he reached home that night, however, he knew he had been, at bottom, neither prepared nor proof" (II, 261–62).

Part of the irony practiced at Strether's expense is that the final truth is close to what was feared by Woollett and what was portended in the first play Strether saw in London, in which the young man's morals were corrupted by the woman in the yellow frock. The truth is more complex, but it is closer to this—the mode of melodrama and literary cliché that James has been playing upon all along—than it is to the beautiful facts Strether imagined. Strether's imaginative world is now exposed as having been imaginary, in the bad sense; it can be sustained only by make-believe, by "fiction and fable" (II, 265, 262). His imagination has failed him, not because he has imagined meanly, as Mrs. Newsome did, but because he has not imagined enough. Strether anticipates Maria Gostrey's surprise at his own shock and fears "her 'What on earth—that's what I want to know now—had you then supposed?' He recognized at last that he had really been trying all along to suppose nothing. Verily, verily, his labour had been lost" (II, 266). The last irony is that Strether, the man of imagination, has failed to imagine the

13. Ruth Bernard Yeazell, *Language and Knowledge in the Late Novels of Henry James* (Chicago, 1976), 21–25.

crucial fact in the novel, a fact Maria and most of the other characters had seen long before.

Despite James's assurances in the Preface, then, it is as if he has arranged the plot so that Strether's imagination does indeed wreck him. The novelist has at first created a fictional world that seems to meet the demands Strether imposes on it, a world of spectacle, image, and artifice. He has made Strether a character who is both likable and acute, endowed with a monstrous imagination and intelligence. Then, just when he leads Strether into a charmed area where his imagination appears to be "in *supreme* command," he removes his *locus standi* by revealing to the reader, and simultaneously to Strether himself, that the latter's version of fictional reality is not the same as James's. The degree to which James has left Strether exposed here can be appreciated if we consider how he might have handled the plot otherwise: by leaving the affair between Chad and Madame de Vionnet only adumbrated, for instance, or by allowing Strether to anticipate it and discover it in a more active way. As it stands, Strether's humiliation at the end of Book 11 is comparable to the embarrassment of the Narrator near the end of *The Sacred Fount* when Mrs. Brissenden demolishes his "perfect palace of thought." Speaking with Maria in Book 12, Strether looks back at his imaginative period prior to the river episode in terms reminiscent of the Narrator: "I had phases. I had flights" (II, 302).

After this analogy between the two protagonists' defeat, however, we must return to the source of their difference, James's decision to forbid Strether the privilege of autobiography. By encaging Strether, James makes sure that the victim of the imagination is the fictional character and not the author, as had been threatened in *The Sacred Fount*. As we have seen, the episode of Strether's disillusion is told from a point of view that gradually reveals itself to be double, as James carefully and even sternly asserts his own distance from Strether's mistake. For all his likableness, Strether must be sacrificed to the "stiffer proprieties" of James's form. The various leave-takings of the final book express different aspects of his defeat. He leaves a Maria whom he has disappointed and even frustrated, a Chad who seems ready to forsake his mistress for a career in advertising, and finally a Madame Vionnet who is "afraid for [her] life" (II, 285). The celebrated open ending of *The Ambassadors* has, however, left room for those critics who want to judge

Strether's obvious failure in his ambassadorial mission as being compensated for or redeemed by a personal gain in inward growth or vision. The view that Strether's final renunciation is a fully warranted affirmative gesture is represented by Frederick Crews: "Neither Woollett's abstemious Puritanism nor Paris' amoral secularism can account for the sense of Life that Strether has achieved through the expansion of his social and moral awareness."[14] James seems to lend support to this interpretation when, in his scenario for the novel, he remarks that Strether "has come out the other side" of where he formerly was, so that to commit himself to Maria Gostrey now—not to mention to Mrs. Newsome—would be to take a step backward (NB, 415).

It must be admitted, however, that Strether's inner rewards are only speculative, while his outward embarrassment and loss are painfully tangible. When he pays his last visit to Madame de Vionnet, we see Strether himself striving to compensate for his present embarrassment and future abnegation by committing to memory the special historical flavor of the apartment: "He should soon be going to where such things were not, and it would be a small mercy for memory, for fancy, to have, in that stress, a loaf on the shelf" (II, 275–76). Is it really possible to conclude from this, with Richard Poirier, that Strether's "variety of impressions" will "sustain" him in his future life?[15] The "loaf on the shelf" seems a banal compensation indeed.

James has conspired with Strether's imagination to punish him, indeed, to come closer to wrecking him than the author of the Preface was willing to admit. Strether may have "come out the other side," but the self-con-

14. Frederick Crews, *The Tragedy of Manners* (New Haven, 1957), 55. See also Daniel Mark Fogel, *Henry James and the Structure of the Romantic Imagination* (Baton Rouge, 1981), 14–48.

15. Richard Poirier, *A World Elsewhere* (1966; rpr. New York, 1973), 139. Two critics who are closer to my own sense of the criticism of Strether made toward the end of the novel are Sally Sears, *The Negative Imagination: Form and Perspective in the Novels of Henry James* (Ithaca, 1968), 101–51; and Philip M. Weinstein, *Henry James and the Requirements of the Imagination* (Cambridge, Mass., 1971), 121–64. Both, however, see Strether's main problem as James's problem too: the choice of a passive over an active life and the failure to imagine a credible version of the latter. Weinstein, oddly, after making this critique of Strether, concludes nonetheless that he has "matured" at the novel's end and has "redeemed" his "blank decades" (163).

sciousness he has attained by the end is not totally reassuring. The exposure of the falsity of his imagination in Book 11 has been handled severely; his imagination is compared to the immature faculty of a child: "He almost blushed, in the dark, for the way he had dressed the possibility in vagueness, as a little girl might have dressed her doll" (II, 266). Though he had earlier believed he had outgrown Maria's tutelage and could "toddle alone" (II, 48), in the end he is obliged to see both Maria and himself as "Babes in the Woods" in comparison to Chad and Madame de Vionnet (II, 293). Strether's return to second childhood puts the seal on his encagement and separates him forever from the position of the author, whose growing irony toward Strether in the final two books we have now seen, just as the young Henry James belonged to the period of childhood represented in the autobiography and could not rejoin the point of view of the adult author. This separation ensures that Strether's ruin will not be James's. *The Ambassadors* thus avoids a repetition of the fate of *The Sacred Fount*; in fact, it redeems its predecessor and replaces it, as it were, in the New York Edition where it becomes "the best, 'all round,' of my productions" (*AN*, 309). Despite the similarity between Strether and the Narrator of *The Sacred Fount*, the ending of the later novel reverses and undoes that of the earlier. The Narrator, accused of madness and deprived of his theory, had been put "altogether nowhere." Strether, likewise stripped of his theory concerning Chad and Madame de Vionnet, and reduced to a state of childlike docility, is nevertheless still! somewhere: "Then there we are!" (II, 327). Strether may not know exactly where he is, but James does.

CONCLUSION

WITH STRETHER we come full circle in the study of James's representation of himself in his work. It was in the Preface to *The Ambassadors* that James publicly stated his objection to the use of the first person in the novel, and his avoidance of the first person in his creation of Strether was clearly related to his judgment that this novel was "the best, 'all round,' of [his] productions." In Strether, too, he created the partial man of imagination who was the closest approximation to himself, the man of imagination who became the subject of the autobiography. Strether both is and is not James; he is close enough to the author to make it imperative that the latter separate himself as clearly as possible not only through the use of the third person but also through the critique of Strether that, as we have seen, grows in force towards the end of the novel. In his naïve faith in his own imagination, in his isolation from certain aspects of reality, and in his confusion of the forms of art with those of life, Strether prefigures the young James of *A Small Boy and Others* and the other volumes of autobiography. It is therefore significant that Strether comes to grief precisely because of the quality and the extent of his imagination. He has too little imagination to conceive the central fact in the relationship between Chad and Madame de Vionnet. He is, after all, only a "comparative case" of the imaginative mind, as the Preface put it, and the novel carefully defines him as the editor of an intellectual journal, not as an artist. On the other hand, he has too much imagination for his actual role. He is not an artist but only an ambassador; so he cannot channel his imaginative energy into a work of art but expends it on speculation, for instance, about the miraculous transformation that he judges Chad to have undergone.

In the limitations of his imagination, Strether is like the narrators of *The Turn of the Screw* and *The Sacred Fount*, just as he is like the young James we glimpse at the end of the autobiography. All these works offer similar portrayals of the imaginative life, of its triumphs in the production of a world full of artistic meaning and of its failures when it confronts another world outside of its imaginative orbit. But the vast differences among these works are a function of the different attitudes the author assumes in each case towards the imagination he depicts. In *The Turn of the Screw* and *The Sacred Fount*, he participates in it; his indiscriminate use of the "I" makes it impossible to distinguish his own creative activity from that of his narrators, and the result, especially in *The Sacred Fount*, can be confused with an unflattering parody of the Jamesian artist. In *The Ambassadors*, by consistently remaining the "impersonal author," he saves himself from Strether's embarrassments and is able to perform an objective critique of a tendency in his own imaginative constitution even while composing an appreciative portrait of what is intelligent and commendable in that character. In his autobiography, James allows himself that "double privilege of subject and object" that he denied Strether and so many others of his centers of consciousness, but in this case the double consciousness proves manageable because the subject and the object—that is, James the autobiographer and James the young man—are kept distinct, even to the point that it is only concerning himself as other that James can write. As we saw, however, in writing the autobiography, James also sought to protect the sanctity of the imaginative world in which the young boy lived, and this desire imposed a constraint on the material and the time span that the autobiography could treat. At ease only with the childhood years, during which the world responded fully to the construction he put upon it, James was forced to interrupt his narrative at the point when the world began to grow problematic. In this sense, the ending of the autobiography resembles the ending of *The Sacred Fount*, which occurs abruptly as the narrator's theory unravels, or even the ending of *The Ambassadors*, after Strether's discovery of the true relationship between the two lovers.

In its referential status and its use of the first person, then, James's autobiography sets itself off from his fiction, but in its portrayal of the imaginative perception of life, it manifests a profound continuity with the novels that precede it. Moreover, despite its use of the "I," the autobiography shows the same reticence towards writing about the self that the fiction, with its customary avoidance of the "I," also showed. Just as James sought, as author, to remain utterly distinct from his fictional characters even if he was expressing himself (as he said of Maupassant) willy-nilly in every line of his text, so, in the autobiography, he does not directly portray the literary artist he has become but only the small boy whose experience served as the implicit foundation for the mature James's work. The autobiography resists becoming explicitly self-reflective in the same way the fiction had done. The eschewing of the "I" in the novels is related to their virtual banishment of autobiographical content and also to the autobiography's avoidance of an explicit portrait of the artist.

James's aversion to assuming the "I" in his fictional works is unquestionably the most striking symptom of his complex attitude towards the author's self-expression. His judgment concerning the author's proper place in his fiction is, in a sense, too personal to be explained fully as a stage in the history of the ideal of impersonality as it appears in the work of authors like Flaubert, Mallarmé, and T. S. Eliot, even though all of these could be fruitfully compared to James on this point. Although I have not chosen here to stress the psychological sources of James's reticence towards the use of the first person, it is obvious that his attempt to make the avoidance of the autobiographical form a practically universal principle of novel writing is an example of what Rémy de Gourmont meant when he said (in a phrase that T. S. Eliot liked to quote) that the critic does nothing but "ériger en lois ses impressions personnelles." It would be absurd, then, to make this particular aspect of James's theory of fiction into a general dogma that would hold good for the work of other authors, periods, or genres of fiction. Yet part of my goal here has been to show that in the context of the fiction of Henry James, at least, the question of person does serve as a consistent ordering principle that dictates other formal and generic characteristics of

James's works. James's thinking about the modes of the author's appearance in his work also fits coherently into the history of fiction both before and after his work, even if his injunctions cannot be made into a canon by which other novelists' work can be judged. James's place in a historical scheme, however, must appear paradoxical, or perhaps it can be explained only by a dialectic in which its value is reversible depending upon whether one views it in relation to what precedes James or to what follows him.

In his criticism of contemporary and near-contemporary Victorian and Edwardian novelists, from Trollope to H. G. Wells and Conrad, we already saw James's own view of the primary difference between his art and theirs. Although the omniscient narrator is usually considered to be the norm for Victorian fiction, the first-person narrator, often rivaling the omniscient author in many of his prerogatives, was just as important a form.[1] The similarity between these two modes of narration is precisely what James revealed when he attacked both of them for violating the objectivity of fiction by diverting attention from the mimetic to the diegetic level of the work and exposing the artifices of the author. The real point, however, of James's critique of what he saw as the lax forms of Victorian fiction was not simply to preach for "the disappearance of the author," as it would be called by Joseph Warren Beach and others after him. James believed he was clearing the way for a reaffirmation of the author, a recovery of his authority on a surer basis than before. Instead of withdrawing from his work, James saw his technique as allowing him to "get down into the arena" with his characters (AN, 328). The result, James's practice of what Laurence Holland calls the novel of intimacy, thus brought about a more intense version of the author's commitment to his characters and of his self-expression through them. Even while James lamented Conrad's method of giving the author away in Chance, his own development of the novel had done much to render Conrad's practice possible. Conrad's example shows how the lesson of the master could be learned and then applied in ways the master would never have admitted into his own work.

In his essay on Maupassant, James acknowledged that a work of fiction

1. On the Victorian narrator as a "general consciousness" halfway between a godlike omniscience and an individual subjectivity, see J. Hillis Miller, *The Form of Victorian Fiction* (Notre Dame, 1968), 53–89.

is always in some sense autobiographical for its author, even if he simultaneously encouraged the effort "to convey the impression of something that is not one's self" (*FN*, 205). For many of James's successors in the novel, it is as though the first half of this statement became self-evident while the second half was forgotten. The modern novel, the one that began to develop around the time James was writing his autobiography, takes for granted, in many of its most important examples, that the most appropriate subject of fiction, and perhaps the only possible one, is the author himself—hence the tremendous autobiographical impulse and intention behind much of the best and most characteristic work of such diverse authors as D. H. Lawrence (to whose *Sons and Lovers* James devoted some disparaging words in "The New Novel"–*FN*, 261, 270), Virginia Woolf, Joyce, and on the Continent, Thomas Mann (whose *Buddenbrooks* actually appeared in print before *The Ambassadors*), Gide, and Proust.

The difference between these authors' autobiographical investment in their works and James's is not specifically or primarily formal. Of the authors just named, only Proust wrote his major work in the first-person form (after setting aside a long first version of his novel, *Jean Santeuil*, written in the third person).[2] At least two of them, Joyce and Mann, were indebted to the same impersonal aesthetic that James had first discovered in Flaubert and his French disciples. Yet all of these authors wrote fictional works that reflect a much more explicit autobiographical content, regardless of the divergences of their forms, than James ever allowed in his work. In close alliance with the new autobiographical impulse is the fact that one of the characteristic forms of the modern novel now became the *Künstlerroman*, the self-absorbed work that takes as its hero the artist himself and as its ultimate subject matter, its own production. (From the authors just mentioned, examples would include *The Portrait of the Artist as a Young Man*, "Death in Venice," *Les Faux-Monnayeurs*, and *A la recherche du temps perdu*.) Once again, James can be seen to have prefigured this tendency with his own two *Künstlerromane*, *Roderick Hudson* (1876) and *The Tragic Muse* (1890), as

2. On the transition from *Jean Santeuil* to *A la recherche du temps perdu*, see for instance Germaine Brée, *Marcel Proust and Deliverance from Time*, trans. C. J. Richards and A. D. Truitt (2nd ed.; New Brunswick, 1969), 8; Gérard Genette, *Narrative Discourse*, trans. Jane E. Lewin (Ithaca, 1980), 247–52.

well as with the shorter tales of artists and authors. These tales (and the same would hold for the two novels) were far from being representations of James's own career as a man or an artist, however; their theoretical, sometimes allegorical mode converted their autobiographical tendency into something relatively abstract.[3] There is a qualitative difference between James's portraits of artists and those of the following generation, which come directly out of the author's personal experience with only a minimal effort to conceal this fact.

Thus James's attitude towards the author's presence in his work provides a way to define his crucial transitional role between the Victorian and the modern novel. His position is paradoxical (or, within a plotting of historical phases, dialectical) because it signifies both an apparent disappearance of the author from his previous omniscient, authoritative role and a new placement of the author as the source and, ultimately, subject matter, of everything in the fiction. James's rejection of the outward *signs* of authorial presence accompanies the implicit recognition that such signs are no longer needed or desirable when the author has penetrated his material and stamped it with the quality of his artistic imagination. Yet what sets James off from the modernists who follow him is that he stops short of the explicit representation of himself as an artist in his fiction and that he insists that the autobiographical tendency of the work is something to be "taken for granted," not revealed or displayed in the work. "We take for granted by the general law of fiction a primary author, take him so much for granted that we forget him in proportion as he works upon us, and that he works upon us most in fact by making us forget him" (*FN*, 281).

To see the consistency, if also the ambivalence, of James's position is to see how completely it transcends whatever subjective and half-conscious motives it may have sprung from in James's psyche. His theory of the author's proper place in his work thus fulfills his own stated condition for the rules that govern art: that it be an "objective, projected result" and not merely part of the "floundering cause" of life (*FN*, 101). James's attitude towards the "I" thus proves itself to be not only one of the keys to his own art but also a key to an important moment in the history of modern fiction.

3. See William R. Goetz, "The Allegory of Representation in *The Tragic Muse*," *Journal of Narrative Technique*, VIII (1978), 151–64.

INDEX